Salary Administration

SALARY ADMINISTRATION

Third Edition

G. McBEATH
and
D. N. RANDS

BUSINESS BOOKS LIMITED
London

First published 1964
Second impression 1965
Third impression 1966
Fourth impression 1968
Second edition 1969
Second impression 1970
Third impression 1973
Third edition 1976

The author has invented names for companies and people. These have no relation to real identities and any resemblance between the names he has used and those of real companies and individuals is purely coincidental

ISBN 0 220 66285 1

Printed in Great Britain by litho
by The Anchor Press Ltd
and bound by Wm Brendon & Son Ltd
both of Tiptree, Essex

Contents

Part 2 OPERATIONS

Preface

This book has its roots in *Salary Administration*, which I wrote with Nick Rands in 1964, and *Management Remuneration Policy* which I wrote four years later. It has grown from much innovation and experience over ten further years, and has responded to the changing pressures of inflation, participation and internationalism. I offer it as a comprehensive practical guide to Salary Administration—which also takes time to answer the 'Why?' behind the policies and practice.

GORDON McBEATH

Part 1

Introduction

Chapter 1

Salary Administration

Salary administration is about equitable salary relationships, which, in an age of participation with progressively greater disclosure of salaries, means getting these relationships—internally and externally—right for all to see.

Today there can be few companies of any size which have not developed some systematic approach to administering the salaries of their staff. The days of completely haphazard salaries, bearing little relationship to competitive rates for different jobs or to internal relationships and merit, these days have gone.

The present position is one in which managements need to keep on top of a game of many pressures, which are frequently in conflict, and to ensure that the end results satisfy all the varied individuals involved from the shop steward to the shareholder. In this process the Salary Administrator who is not informed of trade union matters, thinking about profitability, and trying to use some motivation theory may find himself out of his depth. It is unlikely that he could survive by concentrating on technical excellence in his field alone, without sensitive antennae reacting to such questions as the company's ability to pay, efficient manning and use of non-financial motivators, and the requirements of relevant trade unions.

Central to much of salary administration is the assessment of *market values*. These stem from the simple economics of supply and demand—in this case, for people with the skills and abilities to do particular jobs. At one time this was relatively simple when individual employees offered their services to various employers, each negotiating the best deal he could. Skills in short supply and high demand would command a high price, and the bulk of relatively low-skilled factory employees had little economic pressure and low pay. Organized labour today has altered this situation totally, and a major factor in salary administration is now the impact of various organized groups. The relative strength of these groups is a major factor in determining differentials, which have moved away from logical and from socially desirable patterns into situations which are sometimes difficult to justify and damaging to employee relationships.

The 'free' market

Salaries in a 'free' market situation are influenced by the basic economic laws of supply and demand.

In the market, the company would like to buy at minimum cost and the individual would like to sell his services at maximum cost. Their skills in buying and selling, the availability of alternatives, and the detailed 'content' of the package to be bought or sold, all influence price.

The environment, in terms of company policies, attitudes to people, philosophy of management, attitudes to pace and change, will tend to provide or deny job satisfaction. Most individuals seek satisfaction from their work as an overriding factor, so environment will influence the style of staffing more than remuneration standards.

The individual seeks time and opportunity to use his income to satisfy other needs.

Subject to the motivational factors discussed in Chapter 2, most professional managers hire their services to the highest bidder. In contrast, the 'bidder', or employer, is seeking the best ability at the lowest price. It is from this market situation that the strongest influence on management salaries emerges.

Remuneration in a 'free' market situation is increasingly being restricted to management staff. A 'free' market exists where the majority of appointments are made in free negotiation between employers and employees, where employers take the initiative in salary reviews which individual employees accept, attempt to alter personally, or reject (by resignation); and where this process takes place with minimal impact of negotiations covering other staff. It is true that long-term and older employees are less mobile, but they can increasingly 'vote with their feet' if the level of their remuneration is felt to be out of line with the market, for the market place has extremes which are recognized by those involved.

In common usage, the 'management salary structure' may embrace not only the posts of appointed managers of an organization, but often those posts in which future managers are likely to be employed during their development. There is some logic in a line drawn to take in posts occupied by the fresh graduate intake as the first level of the management structure. This grade might also include production foremen and senior clerical supervisors as 'the first level of management'.

Most employees have a very fair idea of their commercial worth or the market value of the services they can offer. Their views are based on studies of current advertised rates for similar jobs in the daily papers, and on their associates' performance and salary levels which are soon inevitably known to them. Where large inequalities exist between the rates paid to similar employees there will be considerable ill feeling, more so, probably, as a result of comparison between salaries within an organization than in comparison outside with other companies' pay.

The market value concept, which is fundamental to much of our thinking throughout this book, has rather less impact on the so-called 'public' sector of employment. Knowledge of scales of pay for different grades which may be only partially related to jobs appears to introduce an element of stodginess in salary thinking and an atmosphere where individual performance and merit is almost wholly disregarded and salary increments arrive as a birthday treat. But even in this situation jealousies of a more general kind occur between groups which tend to be associated: such as associated technical staff groups across the Civil Service, public service and nationalized undertakings.

Ideological thoughts on theoretical or moral values of work may be praiseworthy, but they are more a matter for national influence and legislation than for the individual Salary Administrator. These special factors do not exert a significant influence on market values in the free industrial situation. However, their influence is felt to some extent in the public sector.

In the public sector rates are also influenced by generous benefits, greater security and the lower work pressure which salary comparisons must take into account.

Conditions resulting from lack of salary administration exist mainly where the salary administration plan has been allowed to become out of date and ineffective. As we shall explain fully in the course of this book, equitable salary relationships depend on sound job classification, periodic salary surveys of competitive levels, employee appraisal and effective salary planning. These are the main elements of a salary administration plan and they are all essential and interrelated.

An approach to salary administration

Any organization which needs to update its salary administration plan may feel uneasily that the devil it knows may be preferable! If it engaged a new Salary Administrator, what would be his impact on the organization and what might he do for them; or to them?

Let us take such an organization, a hypothetical one without an effective salary plan, and consider what modern salary administration procedures and concepts have to offer. In considering the situation, in fact, let us look at it from the viewpoint of the person appointed to carry out the study.

First of all, he would certainly examine the existing company position. The lack of available data would possibly cause him some surprise, but he would begin by making a study of the company's organization to obtain a clear picture of its make-up. If organization charts are available, well and good, but he is likely to have to draw up his own, showing the relationships between senior posts and subsequently the organization under the head of each company unit. (Figure 1.1 shows a typical sketch organization chart which may be prepared for this purpose.)

Strength figures covering the numbers of staff and hourly-rated employees in each department should be noted on these organization charts to help in assessing the size of the various units as well as the magnitude of the overall study. They also give a guide as to how long the task of bringing order out of chaos will take, as the length of time a job evaluation study takes can usually be assessed according to the number of people to be covered.

The Salary Administrator visits the various organizations to get close to the problems. His discussions with senior and middle-level managers begin to suggest the probable nature of past in-

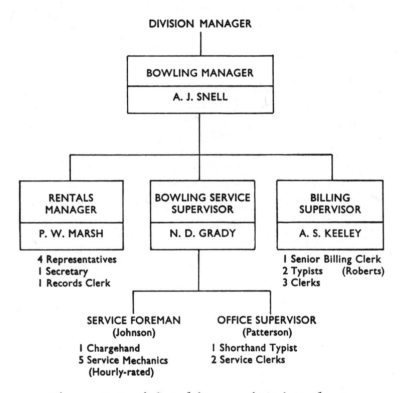

DIVISION MANAGER

BOWLING MANAGER

A. J. SNELL

RENTALS MANAGER	BOWLING SERVICE SUPERVISOR	BILLING SUPERVISOR
P. W. MARSH	N. D. GRADY	A. S. KEELEY

4 Representatives
1 Secretary
1 Records Clerk

1 Senior Billing Clerk
2 Typists　(Roberts)
3 Clerks

SERVICE FOREMAN
(Johnson)

1 Chargehand
5 Service Mechanics
(Hourly-rated)

OFFICE SUPERVISOR
(Patterson)

1 Shorthand Typist
2 Service Clerks

Figure 1.1　'Sketch' organisation chart

fluences on salary matters and the form of the most urgent needs.

Making spot checks of jobs and salary levels, he quickly finds that job titles in use are confusing in variety and largely meaningless, that individual salaries are grouped together in job title groups, or that age or service play an important part in the pattern. Merit increases are granted from time to time, of course, but individual merit has little to do with them. And such salary ranges as exist are related to job titles with unfortunate results.

Staff turnover is apparently high but no one knows much about it. The same spot checks confirm the high level, and sample termination interviews begin to show the story of low pay and the loss of good-calibre employees.

The Salary Administrator reports to management on the problems as he sees them and the methods he proposes to use to solve them.

If the job titles are meaningless, he has to bypass them and obtain meaningful job information. A grading structure will be necessary and the most suitable form is recommended : the salary structure will be based on salary surveys and a careful analysis of the competitive picture. This exercise will be used as a basis for subsequent analysis of the actual salary position, in relation to the new structure, and will enable him to plan and budget for future salary progress, and also staffing standards, organization, and so on.

In addition to the top management, the whole middle structure must be advised of the short- and long-term proposals to improve the situation, be persuaded to participate in the exercise, and be convinced of its value to them and their staff. The Salary Administrator who thinks he can omit this stage is not only of no use on salary administration but in personnel management as a whole. He is not developing a private hobby but is advising and helping line management to achieve what they need to administer salaries for their own staff, and is thus contributing in no small way to the company's progress and profitability.

At this stage, some organizations begin to form committees. However, even the most meeting-conscious organization can be dissuaded from this approach provided guarantees of complete management participation on a less formal basis are made. This means that the results can be achieved faster, and without most of the noise and fury to which job evaluation and salary committees seem particularly prone.

How salary administration can be strengthened

To launch the study, the Salary Administrator prepares a brief-ing talk to put over to the many groups of managers and super-visors—a talk explaining the purpose, method, and anticipated result of the study, say on the following lines :

> What salary administration is . . .
> The company position . . .
> The elements of the Salary Administration Plan . . .
> How the company will create these elements of the Plan . . .
> What part managers will play . . .
> The end results . . .
> The future . . .

Around these jotted headlines he chooses his own words to fit the people and atmosphere at each session.

He also prepares a package of material for hand out and for independent distribution, a package which must be fairly con-cise but includes a brief write-up of the exercise (see Fig. 1.2), and examples of documents of the various stages.

Now come the most difficult decisions which will have to be made. What methods and procedures should be employed : points evaluation or job ranking; large management evaluation committees or salary administration specialists; what kind of salary structures; what policies and procedures will be acceptable ?

If the choice is yours, make your decisions in the light of the facts—is it to be a large or small study, quick or leisurely; has it to line up with certain top management stipulations ?

The Administrator should make a definite plan with a fore-cast time-table which he can sell completely to his top manage-ment, and here let us again say emphatically that unless one has their full support and is seen to have this support it is practically pointless to start introducing salary administration into an organization.

Let us assume that the major stages of determining methods (these are covered in later chapters) have been successfully surmounted, in which case the next stage is to put over the briefing talk. We suggest that this is tackled in two phases in

SALARY ADMINISTRATION

This Company is establishing a new Salary Administration Plan which will have the following primary purpose.

It will set out to ensure that each employee is paid a salary which meets the following requirements:

A. That the relative value to the Company of each job shall be taken into account.

B. That the relative level of performance potential and contribution of each staff employee shall be taken into account.

C. That the overall level of salaries paid shall be competitive in the labour market.

These objectives will be attained by use of systems which we shall establish as speedily as possible.

1. *Job evaluation*

All staff posts will be analysed and graded to establish the pattern of internal relationships.

Posts will be assigned to grades in the course of a job ranking study in which the job analyses will be used to ensure that common standards are evolved for each grade level across the whole Company, e.g. grade 'G' will have the same value in all departments and sections of the organization, and all posts graded 'G' will be considered of equal value for salary purposes, and distinct in value from posts in other grades.

Gradings will subsequently be reviewable at all times to keep grades in line with changes in responsibilities, and maintain equitable and common standards.

2. *Salary ranges*

Each grade will have an assigned salary range, and the individual ranges will fit into an overall salary range structure extending over the whole grading structure.

A typical structure might have salary ranges which have maxima 50 per cent above minima, and where the step up from the minimum of one grade to that of the next would be 20 per cent. Precise figures will be dependent on the number of grades we establish and the data from the salary survey we shall undertake.

Subsequent reviews of our salary ranges will be based on competitive movement, on which we shall keep a close watch.

3. *Salary adjustments*

We shall continue to carry out annual reviews of salaries, but the data available for guidance in these reviews will be much greater than was previously the case.

Individual changes in salary should be planned. The principles of salary planning will be covered in our coming training programme.

Figure 1.2   A company statement of salary administration aims

each company organization, the first essentially a local top
management meeting at which the company Chief Executive
discusses the study, after handing out material describing it,
and requests the co-operation of those present and, in effect,
the whole company.

A letter addressed to all participating employees, explaining
the study and signed by the Chief Executive should be sent out
through all managers (see Fig. 1.3).

To: All staff employees

From: Chief Executive

Subject: JOB ANALYSIS STUDY

We are embarking on an important study covering all staff posts in the Company.
as part of the overall organization review programme.

The purpose of this study is to provide a complete record of all staff post requirements as a basis for a number of services. It will provide a sound basis for the
selection, placement and training of staff. It will also help in planning career
progression and interdepartmental promotions, and in determining bases for
establishing equitable salary relationships between posts throughout the Company.

You are asked to assist in this study by completing the questionnaires which will
be handed to you by your supervisor or manager, and returning the form to him
within seven days of receiving it.

Signed...

Figure 1.3 A letter to staff

This action should be followed up immediately by 'briefing'
sessions attended by groups of department managers and supervisors throughout the company. At these briefing sessions
the talk provides the outline of what they should be told of the
present job and salary problems which exist in the organization,
what salary administration is, how it will solve these problems,
precisely how the study will be carried out and what their role
will be.

At the end of each operational level briefing session, material
such as job description and job specification forms or questionnaires, in sufficient quantities to cover each organization,

should be handed out together with examples of how the forms should be completed and any instructions necessary (see examples in Chapter 5).

The system is evolved later. Methods of numbering which can be used vary from a fairly involved decimalized system to simple systems which are suitable for small company application.

When the evaluation and classification side of the study has been completed with line managers and the Salary Administrator or Evaluator, each manager should be given his appropriate part of the overall company classification schedule. Their schedules should be accompanied by related regional salary scales, as well as a manual of the policies and procedures which tie together the salary plan. Further briefing sessions on methods of planning salaries and maintaining the classification up to date should be given throughout the company.

The approach discussed in this section is typical of the way a Salary Administrator might tackle these problems. Out of his efforts, with reasonable management interest and support, should come the structures, policies and procedures necessary to provide management with the tools they need to solve their old problems—of salary inequities, of haggling and bargaining with staff, of inadequate budget information and of loss of good staff through lack of salary planning.

Salary administration—development and maintenance

Creating salary administration is not like making a piece of furniture which, once made, is complete. It is perhaps more like growing a vine, for once it is initially established it will live and give fruit or die according to whether or not it is cared for properly.

As a living thing, it is constantly changing and growing, and this must be recognized. The job classification structure which is 'established for all time' with no thought of care or maintenance will wither away and become useless, for at least a tenth of the job gradings should be reviewed each year, and many will change as organizations and jobs evolve and alter, by planning, and around individuals.

In the early paragraphs of this chapter, we spoke of problems arising from structures which had become obsolete. One of the fundamental aspects of Salary Administration is upkeep; the recognition of constant change as a basic part of the function. Each change in job content or organization, in market salary levels, must be observed by the Salary Administrator and *every significant change must be acted upon. The system which does not provide for immediate positive action in all such cases of change is worse than useless and it would have been better for the company if it had never been created.*

The Salary Administrator's part in updating the Plan consists largely of encouraging line managers to ensure that everything is well, for it is at the operational level that job changes can be seen and not from some remote central point.

Regular visits to senior managers and to their department heads enable the Salary Administrator to keep them in touch with developments, perhaps to emphasize the changing picture of market salary levels which must be constantly watched, and to contrast this with the greater movement of job content and people which must also be watched. Sometimes, the non-co-operators find themselves in difficulty for various reasons and the Salary Administrator should counsel and try to bring them into line.

On his tours, he can also talk about salary reviews which are imminent or in progress, and give on-the-spot help on individual salary planning. This activity can, of course, go on year-wide and during the off-review periods, and detailed studies can highlight low pay for immediate correction.

The Salary Administrator is teacher, adviser, salesman. As he tours his company he applies something of each of these arts, plus his basic salary administration knowledge, to all the situations which arise. He keeps his function an alive and dynamic operation in which all management participate.

Salary budgetary control and manning standards

Appreciation and use of basic salary administration techniques have developed extremely fast over recent years. The old-fashioned attitudes of many companies have been wiped away and salary matters may now be discussed openly instead of in whispers behind locked doors.

There is general understanding of the basic techniques of job evaluation, salary structures and appraisal (at least managers understand their local practices), and acceptance of the contribution which these make to staff management. However, there is a tendency to 'systematize' for administrative convenience rather than to achieve more effective management. This tendency is not necessarily deliberate, but may arise from insufficient knowledge of the forces at work in any given situation. This frequently happens with the selection of grading methods and the design of salary structures where lack of knowledge of market pressures leads to over-rigid practice. Further, the sheer dynamism of a modern industrial situation generates a pace of change which, in itself, presents an administrative problem. And the administrator is faced with demands for facts on which budgets and controls may be based, for the financial control of the business.

We find ourselves today in a world which is increasingly conscious of finance. In business, the company which keeps its costs down has an advantage over competitors. But payment of low salaries as a contributing factor to low costs is nonsensical, for low salaries retain only low calibre employees. The answer relates evaluation of manning standards with proper payment levels for all types of staff required.

Salary administration begins with, and must constantly refer back to, the specific objectives of the organization and the division of work required to achieve these objectives as a basis for establishing manning requirements.

At the stage of justifying an initial investment, we should not accept an arbitrary allocation of, say, £100,000 for salaries. The work required will be done by specific people, who have clear market values. We need to know the *manning requirement* so that this can be costed.

In all existing operations, all work requirements can be costed properly only through defining the manpower needed. These data are relevant to salary budgeting in particular and to financial budgeting in general. That it is somewhat complicated by the actual mix of present employees makes it no different in principle from budgeting where we are concerned with utilization of machinery. But the complexity of the development of individual personnel and the need to relate their development closely to organizational requirements does add a variable, the influence of which we must examine closely.

We are, inevitably, striving for unattainable ideals. All situations have ideal manning requirements, but these have to be adapted to utilize available manpower to a varying extent, and both the requirement and the available manpower are evolutionary. Planning manpower utilization is akin to production sheduling and control problems in a multi- and cross-related situation.

We can examine this situation in value analysis terms. Value analysis is concerned with analysis of the design and component parts of a product to ensure that costs are kept as low as possible without loss of quality, and the analysis may lead to reduction in costs, alteration of processing, substitution of all materials, or re-design, and so on. This style of analysis can be applied to the utilization of personnel, taking into account ideal manning standards, available manpower and the differing market values of different categories.

In planning the utilization of people, we link the tasks to be done with the skills capable of carrying them out successfully. By this means, we are likely to staff a unit effectively from both cost and job satisfaction viewpoints.

But there are few work situations which do not have some history, some existing staff, and some resistance to change. The extent to which staff changes are initiated to achieve optimum manning may be one of the most difficult management decisions. Yet on such decisions may rest whether an operation is carried through inadequately by ineffective personnel at low cost where expensive specialist skills were required, or, alternatively, whether expensive help is being retained where the task has been reduced to clerical simplicity.

Value analysis concepts, applied to problems of personnel utilization, do have a real impact on employee motivation and the requirements from a salary policy.

A fairly detailed picture of the short-term future manpower requirements, and an inventory of the abilities and development potential of available staff is necessary to the planned optimum utilization of staff, especially managerial staff, in individual career development planning.

Salary planning is complementary with career planning. As the planned career line unfolds, so the employee's salary should continually reflect his worth, in terms of his contribution to his company and his evolving value in the free market. Analysis of these values and their extension into the future provide the basic factors for budgeting.

Remuneration and motivation

Remuneration is no longer recognized as the prime motivator for senior staff. An appreciation of the factors of motivation is important to every manager, and helps to set remuneration in perspective. For this reason, the first major chapter of this book is devoted to a summary of present thinking.

In brief, it is still vitally important that the level of pay for any executive should be appropriate for the role he plays; appropriate, that is, in relation to the market value of his services, for his effectiveness in his job, and for the environment in which he operates. If the pay level is out of line, the executive is likely to feel disgruntled and to allow his dissatisfaction to influence other factors. But pay will only be significant if it is out of line. It does not lead to positive motivation simply by being right, although an effective salary policy which responds strongly to individual achievement can provide this.

The positive motivators are factors like job satisfaction and being able to take credit for one's successes (or kicks for failures). If these are not present, or if the organization style restricts satisfaction, then it is unlikely that high salary will offset these to a lasting extent.

Opportunity to advance career (and salary in parallel) is a further major motivator. Wherever an individual has, or expects to acquire, the ability and know-how to advance his career, then opportunity to take the next step up is a positive spur.

In contrast, opportunity to earn a bonus by the achievement of specific targets does not have a great deal of incentive value. The professional manager who reckons that he is working at full stretch at all times because his job is satisfying does not feel that he has reserves to pull out to achieve these objectives, and may well know that success or failure to hit these targets is not wholly in his hands.

Man specification

Clearly, the proper setting of man specifications is critical, and especially so for executive posts. If a specification is set too high, the level of salary assessed may be too high also, and the man employed will find that the post provides him with insufficient satisfaction so that frustration builds up. If the specification is set too low, the job holder either fails or recognizes that he is underpaid if he succeeds.

Executive pay levels derive from man specifications, which must be based on the manning standard required for achievement of business objectives in the face of anticipated difficulties. There is no clear, simple pattern of pay for 'expert sales managers'; a complex pattern of factors and environment influences the pay and value for such people—and we must wade through this if we wish to get a meaningful and reasonably precise answer. We can identify the factors which influence values and ascertain those which are relevant for our evaluation of a particular post—but only through studied analysis.

There is no absolute set of relative job values within which each post has its place. Market values make up an infinitely variable series of patterns for the various job families, depending on the ranges of factors influenced by supply and demand and the degree of individual mobility within and between groups of jobs. Within each job family there are series of levels of work and we shall examine the factors which enable us to identify these levels.

Summary

A company salary structure which is made up of a series of structures covering each of the market groups, integrated on an arbitrary but logical basis and acceptable in the company environment, may produce the optimum framework for salary administration. Individual salaries are reviewed against it and its standards. Manpower budgets are costed on it. All salary controls are related to it.

The importance of the framework is clear. Its place within a company's salary philosophy and practice, which in turn contribute to a larger motivation pattern, must be understood by those who will use it. This book endeavours to present this concept as a practical guide to the creation and use of a framework of executive remuneration policy and practice.

Chapter 2

Salary and Motivation

Is salary a motivator?

The view that salary is the prime motivator is widely held. It is particularly necessary for the Salary Administrator to get salary into perspective and get his views across to his line managers. This is never more important than when dealing with the manager who says, 'Joe is leaving. He must be underpaid. Give him more money and he will stay.'

The *probability* is that Joe is already adequately paid and that his real reason for leaving is because he is not properly motivated. In other words, the manager is trying to buy off the effects of his own incompetence or inadequacy.

Motivation theory seems to have taken clear shape from the work and publications of Frederick Herzberg. Today we recognize that people are motivated by the opportunity to do satisfying work, to take credit for their achievements, and not by good company policies or even by good salaries—although these things need to be 'right' or they will de-motivate.

Salary, then, is not primarily a motivator but has the potential to have a negative effect. However, it can be used to motivate as a 'recognition' factor, to indicate recognition of a job well done in the form of a salary increase. It seems that even this has a short-term effect as a motivator, for the individual quickly adjusts to the new level and continued motivation by salary must be through a further increase. As Herzberg says, 'I had a good meal last night, but it doesn't stop me being hungry again today.' Apparently, salary increases are absorbed just as speedily.

Salary must be right—it is the Salary Administrator's job to make sure it is right—but motivation comes primarily from other factors. While applied motivational theory is outside the responsibility of most Salary Administrators, it has become necessary for him to know the basics as part of his defences!

During the sixties, leading researchers such as Herzberg, Gellerman and Lawler were indicating that with selective use of research findings from the preceding fifty years, it was possible to argue every position and 'prove' a point of view. By the end of that decade, there was some acceptance of the place of salary as a motivator, and also of the differing ways in which individuals may respond to motivators.

Salary—motivator or potential dissatisfier?

'As an affector of job attitudes, salary has more potency as a job dissatisfier than as a job 'satisfier.' So concluded Professor Herzberg from his studies. Investigating the apparent conflict in motivational research findings, he suggested that much of the confusion was due to there being two separate groups of factors. The first of these groups consisted of factors with the potential to motivate positively. The second group appeared to have the potential to demotivate or dissatisfy, and at best were 'alright'— they would not positively motivate. He placed salary in this second category, but added a number of comments linking salary to factors in the first list.

The factors he identified that can motivate positively include :

1   *Achievement*—the personal satisfaction of completing a job and seeing the results of your efforts.
2   *Recognition*—of a job well done : the personal accomplishment.
3   *Work itself*—the actual content of the job and the satisfaction from doing that work.
4   *Responsibility*—related to individual control over the work, and the authority to do what the individual considers necessary.
5   *Advancement*—the aspect of a job providing opportunity for actual change upwards (which links closely with recognition).

6   *Growth*—the opportunity in a job to acquire new skills which in turn increase the possibility of advancement.

The second group of factors, sometimes called 'hygiene' or 'good housekeeping' factors include :

1   *Company policy and administration*—if these are inadequate, the opportunities arising for frustration and de-motivation are clearly high, and demonstrate the nature of the 'hygiene' factors.

2   *Supervision*—this factor is concerned with the technical competence of supervision.

3   *Interpersonal relationships*—including relationship with supervision, and with subordinates and equals.

4   *Working conditions*—the physical environment and the facilities for doing the job.

5   *Salary*—Herzberg found that most strongly felt attitudes to salary were negative, such as unfulfilled expectations for salary increases, and related feelings about low payment.

6   *Security*—the evident signs of job security.

In summary, the second set of factors—the potential dissatisfiers—are environmental. Only when this 'environment' is right do the real motivators have a chance to be effective.

The factors that truly motivate are 'growth' factors, or those which give a sense of personal achievement through the nature of the work. The motivation stems from the individual's involvement in what he is accomplishing.

The fact that a salary is appropriate to the level of work and the level of performance, in relation to the market, is accepted as right and proper. By itself, it does not motivate. If salary is low, then dissatisfaction arises, which acts as a de-motivator and may be strong enough to override the major motivating factors.

Salary may become a motivator where it is a 'recognition' factor; for example, where an immediate salary increase or bonus reinforces the words of praise and thanks for a job well done. Then it is the bonus or increase which is the motivator, rather than the absolute level of remuneration. The duration of the accompanying feelings—the motivational effect—is generally short. I quoted Herzberg's comment that 'the fact that I have a good meal today doesn't stop me being hungry tomorrow'. He does not mean that we need continual salary increases, but rather that the motivators need to feed continuously on achievement, recognition, the work itself, and so on. Salary, used in this way as an aspect of recognition, can be one of the strongest of these if properly used.

Herzberg's work has its most valuable application in 'job enrichment', the redesign of work and jobs to increase the motivators in each job, which we shall consider at the end of this chapter.

'To some people money seems to represent social respectability; to others it may mean recognition for achievement; to still others it stands for worldliness, materialism and the "root of all evil".' This quote from Saul Gellerman summarizes the problem at the stage beyond Herzberg. While we have placed salary in general perspective, the view of it is individual.

The more important pay is to an individual, the more power it has to motivate behaviour. It follows that actions to increase the importance of pay to a group of employees would increase the opportunity to motivate them by financial means.

As people feel their performance is improving, they expect recognition in the form of higher salary. If this is forthcoming quickly, they are satisfied and motivated. This situation is helped if their manager has the authority to act quickly on salary adjustments, for he is then free to respond to performance improvements with the most effective form of recognition. Other motivators, such as growth in the form of promotion, tend to be far less frequent, with the opportunity and contact being outside the full control of the immediate manager.

If financial recognition is to be related closely to performance, it is important that the measures of performance should be as clear as possible, and capable of measurement by the employee as well as the manager. Where there is also free and open discussion of performance standards and achievement, the opportunity for motivation through salary is taken to its full extent.

Where jobs have limited independence, or are difficult to measure, the opportunities for linking performance and salary are equally limited. Some very large organizations have very diffuse lines of responsibility to the point where 'no one can really be blamed' for what may go wrong. Any measure of personal achievement is likely to be almost meaningless, and salary has no value as a motivator.

In summary, each individual can be expected to make an assessment of his job situation, to evaluate what he thinks is expected of him, how it may be measured, and the probable form and extent of rewards for achievement. Progressively, he evaluates his own achievements and the rewards received against those standards and continually revises them. The extent to which he is motivated will depend on the correlation. Clearly measurable performance achievement, rewarded by expected salary increases, will provide most frustration. Where 'reward' does not appear to be related to achievement, he will not be motivated to do better —but if he is paid well, he may be 'satisfied' with the job and draw motivation from other factors.

Two other views of the organization of work and motivation are worth brief coverage here; the organization alternatives offered by Douglas McGregor known as 'theory X and theory Y'; and the link between the 'urge to achieve' and motivation.

Theory X and Theory Y

Traditional organization structures based on 'theory X' make assumptions which appear to limit full utilization of human potential. The main assumption is that the average human being has an inherent dislike of work and will avoid it if he can. The organizational approach reflects a belief that management must counteract this human tendency to avoid work, and leads to emphasis on productivity measurement and a 'fair day's work for a fair day's pay'. It is assumed that people must be controlled, directed and threatened to get them to achieve required objectives, as promise of rewards alone will not be a strong enough inducement, It is assumed, too, that the average human prefers to be directed, wishes to avoid responsibility and seek security. Many managers are prepared to accept this concept in its entirety, and many organizations are based upon its assumptions.

Professor Douglas McGregor suggests that 'theory X' is an acceptance of mediocrity and presents 'theory Y' as a much more attractive alternative.

His starting-point is that 'the expenditure of physical and mental effort in work is as natural as play or rest'. The average

B

human does not dislike work which may be a source of considerable satisfaction to him.

Control and threat of punishment are not the only means for directing effort to achievement of objectives. The individual will take the initiative himself to achieve results where he feels committed. In fact, the satisfaction he gains will be related to the commitment he feels, and from his involvement.

Avoidance of responsibility and emphasis on security are generally reactions to experience. The average human learns to accept and even to seek responsibility in the right environment. The intellectual capacities of the average human are only partly used in most industrial activities.

The application of these assumptions to managerial organization produces a very different situation from the theory X approach. The result is likely to be a dynamic environment within which the growth potential of individuals is given scope to develop, and human reserves are more fully utilized.

Professor McGregor felt that full acceptance of theory X was not critical provided we appreciated the potential restrictions of the X situation. A theory Y environment provides stimulation for intervention and thought within which brain power in particular would be *motivated* to greater effort and effectiveness.

'N.Ach'—*the urge to achieve*

David McClelland, Professor of Psychology at Harvard, wrote that, 'psychologically, most people can be divided into two broad groups. There is the minority which is challenged by opportunity and willing to work hard to achieve something, and the majority which really does not care all that much.'

The minority, who do care, have 'n.Ach', the urge to achieve. It is interesting to take a look at some of their characteristics, as identified by Professor McClelland :

'They set moderately difficult but potentially achievable goals
   for themselves.'
'They choose to work on a problem rather than leave the out-
   come to chance or to others.'
'They have a strong preference for work situations in which
   they get concrete feedback on how they are doing.'

'They choose to work with strangers known to be experts on a problem to be solved, rather than non-expert friends. In contrast, those with higher n.Aff (the need to affiliate with others) prefer to work with friends.'

N.Ach people have a substantial need to do better, to improve the performance of their jobs. Organizations which attract such men tend to have high success and growth rates from the sheer pressure within.

A specification demanding an n.Ach man may reduce the number of possible candidates, but it is likely to increase the potential contribution from the job. It will also increase the price, for in the market place n.Ach is a quality in demand.

People with a strong need for power are significantly different from n.Ach. 'N.Power' people seek attention, recognition and need to be seen to be in charge. They are less concerned with real achievement and tend to be poorer performers.

Job enrichment

Much of the work on the application of motivation theory involves restructuring of jobs to make the content of each job more satisfying to the incumbent. This process is known generally as job enrichment.

The process of job enrichment involves the removal of those parts of the job which are below the general ability level of the incumbent (to be taken over by more junior staff) and the addition of other work within the capacity of the incumbent (generally taken from his supervisor or manager). In the process, the general level of work is raised to a level providing greater stimulation for the job holder, who responds by working well at his more satisfying tasks. The probability of his leaving is reduced and he is absent less frequently. As incidentals, his job may justify upgrading and his salary increase; and the number of jobs required in his department is likely to reduce.

To enrich a job is to reduce the boredom and increase the interest, by bringing the demands made on the incumbent more into line with his abilities.

Enrichment is therefore individual, but is only applicable in situations where the total content of a group of associated jobs can be reviewed, and the duties themselves regrouped to provide more satisfying work. The content of the amended jobs must be related to the varying abilities of the individuals within the group, or otherwise employed.

There is greatest need for enrichment in assembly line type jobs which have been broken down to the point where one man does one limited operation a thousand times a day, but where he is capable of much greater 'responsibilities'. It has applications in almost any job situation.

Opportunities for application are present when :
1   A particular sort of work is done by many people.
2   Some of these people are underutilized.
3   Productivity is low.
Enrichment affects salary administration in several ways. The enriched jobs themselves justify higher salaries, but the regrouping of duties may affect different jobs in different ways. It imposes a requirement for organizational flexibility, and therefore flexibility in salary structures. In fact, frequent review of salary structure is likely to accompany any enrichment programme.

The paragraphs which follow show some examples of salary administration action as a result of enrichment of various categories of jobs.

1 The role of a salesman varies widely. In a company selling engineering components for use in large equipments within the industry, ten area salesmen reported to the Sales Director, a competent and experienced technical man. The salesmen were paid on a commission basis for bringing back orders. They had a product manual and useful product knowledge, but if a customer complained about quality, delivery, or almost anything else, or asked about a possible new application, the problem had to be passed back to the office, where action was slow and uncertain. The loss rate of salesmen was high.

Taking one area initially, the salesman was told, 'You will *manage* this territory in future : whatever decisions need to be made, you make.' He was given far more information about costs and pricing, about technical service, applications, and so on.

Over a number of months, the following became apparent. Sales levels were significantly higher. Average prices were higher, in spite of the discretion given on discounts—they were given now only when necessary, not automatically. Customer relationships were much better—poor quality products were taken back and replaced quickly—technical application problems got dealt with by the salesman, who made sure he got the answers required fast.

Later, the same general pattern was repeated in each area. Staff turnover dropped to zero. Profitability increased considerably. One salesman said that he felt he was important now, not just to his employer, but also to his customers—a typical 'enrichment' reaction.

In this case, the remuneration side was adequately covered by improved commission; but the commission was reviewed openly at the next sales conference and a changed basis developed and adopted which reflected the greater concern for service and less emphasis on 'sales only'.

2 In a management situation, an MbO (Management by Objectives) exercise revealed to the top managers that the company's potential was being slowed by their own lack of delegation.

Enrichment took the form of the top jobs blossoming out into forward planning and the development of simple reporting for control purposes; and the getting rid of all routine decisions.

At the next level, middle management began to act much faster as they were allowed to make their own decisions within new policy guide-lines. This in turn affected the jobs of their subordinates.

This 'Universal' enrichment progressed with the phase of the MbO exercise, which quietly altered the managing style of the company.

The effect on salary structure was considerable, for the real content and contribution from almost all management jobs was upgraded, and this quickly began to have impact on values. The valuation of management jobs rose—as a result of changed content—by an average of 20 per cent in addition to the normal rise in market values over a three-year period.

3 As a third example, consider the situation in a large office dealing with a high volume of mail from customers. One girl operates a machine to open envelopes, a second removes the con-

tents, a third records receipt, a fourth sorts them alphabetically, a fifth reads all those from surnames beginning 'A' and passes them on for various sorts of action, a sixth does the next piece. Everyone does one tiny boring bit—over and over.

The enrichment process took some time, but gradually the point was reached when one girl received a letter, opened it, read it, investigated the query, got the answer, wrote the letter—and signed it personally. If any further queries came back, they would certainly be addressed to her. She was fully responsible.

The number of girls and supervisors employed was substantially less. The level of earnings of the girls in the now responsible jobs was higher than for all earlier positions except supervisors, the level being clearly justified by the range and complexity of the responsibilities now held. The total costs of the department were down by almost one third.

As this book is about salary administration rather than job enrichment, I must refer interested readers to the writings of Herzberg and Gellerman, for greater detail on this fascinating aspect of man management.

Chapter 3

Market Values

Introduction

Market value theory (of job value determination) assumes that the economic laws which apply in other commodity markets with variable supply and demand will also apply to the evolution of salary values. In the case of salaries, there are supplies of individuals with widely varying abilities, and demands for wide varieties of people. The supply of and demand for each particular category influence what is currently paid, within constantly evolving patterns of values.

Let us be more specific; there is a supply and demand situation covering individuals competent to undertake each and every type of job, at specific standards of performance, and in particular environments. These 'situations' are related where individuals meet specifications and are competent to hold positions under several headings, so that market value patterns are related to the extent to which individuals are mobile. This mobility is normal within 'job families'—families of jobs requiring similar basic training and experience.

The actual market value of a job in a specific situation is indicated where the asking or acceptance prices of individuals and offer prices of employers coincide. It is likely to be an 'area of money' rather than a precise figure.

Individual values arise from the demand for the particular packages of skills which individuals have, the demand for these skills, and the willingness of individuals to offer their skills for the various possible uses and users.

It has been suggested that market values serve the function of drawing resources towards those applications which offer the highest economic return, by pressing individuals to utilize their personal resources in the most efficient manner. This rather assumes that the highest pay goes with the highest return to the employer, which is not automatically so; and also that remuneration is the overriding factor in job choice, which it is not.

Individuals are mobile within the demand area for their skills. While some will simply sell to the highest bidder, the thinking manager will tend to be selective about the position he is willing to fill and the environment in which he works, taking into account factors which provide him with satisfaction and the pace he finds acceptable. Also, companies have different styles of management, and the styles favoured and used by an individual and his would-be employer may prove incompatible.

Thus, mobility is far from 'free' and the market value clarity becomes muddled—both by lack of knowledge, and by the vagaries of personal career preference. (But not to the point where we cannot be quite precise about values if our man specification is clear and properly related to job and environment data.)

Where there is normal mobility of personnel—either horizontal or by career progression—there are likely to be relationships in earnings levels for comparable groups of personnel (*market groups*). In the open market situation, demand is likely to be met by movement of people within the related group, with possibly some adjustment of value levels within the group.

A shortage within any group can only be met from within or from closely related groups. Other groups may be completely unaffected, or marginally affected if mobility between fringe areas of groups is practicable. For example, a shortage of management accountants may raise their values, but would be quite unaffected by a glut of architects. The shortage can only be met by similarly qualified or experienced individuals transferring to the shortage area, or alternatively by the demand dropping in the face of rapidly escalating values.

Personal values

These analyses lead to the conclusion that *it is individuals who have market values*. It is through their availability and willingness to do various types of jobs that job market values emerge, and *it is the combined pattern over hundreds or thousands of people with related skills and abilities which produce the market group.*

An individual may vary his asking price for different types of post or different work situations. He is likely to have preferences for certain of the types of work for which he may be employable, these preferences being related perhaps to his career objectives. Also, he may favour certain types of company or location. It would not be exceptional for him to raise his asking price by a substantial amount—possibly by as much as fifty per cent—as the premium he would require to take on a relatively unwanted assignment.

The individual who meets a particular specification and is interested in a post is likely to be in competition with a number of comparable candidates. Their asking prices are likely to be reasonably similar and unlikely to be a major influence in the selection process.

Personal values of key men

In any organization, the critical decisions are made and influenced by a small number of people. It is these people who control the commercial destiny of the company and whose value is of a different order from all subordinate staff.

In examining the market value aspects of this situation, one recognizes that the intellectual calibre and commercial judgment, the drive, and the dedication of this group is generally of a higher level than of others in apparently comparable jobs, and that such people occupy the upper rungs of any relevant distribution of salaries.

It is not a simple matter of certain obvious posts being key posts, but rather is it a matter of certain individuals becoming recognized as key contributors—the people who have the real contribution to make on critical issues when the time of decision arises. Within a Board group, which people have the knowledge? On whom do the others lean? Who has the guts to take the decision? It may not necessarily be the man who holds the purse-strings, nor may he be in the formal seat of power. He may quietly influence the situation by achieving agreement on vital matters, but in contrast be trodden down when the decision concerns the location of new cycle sheds.

Within our organization, we must identify him and ensure that he stays, for his is the brain power which ensures our survival. And within the organization of our competitor, if we are able to identify and draw off his key personnel this will increase our advantages enormously.

In the end, commercial advantage exists in the people employed more than in any other factor when competing companies can so nearly match each other's resources in every way.

Manning standards and salaries

I refer once again to the *value analysis attitude to manning standards and salaries*. There are situations that require high-priced specialist help where economy would be false. There are many more situations where the job and man specifications are over-stated as a result of lack of proper data or of competence, and where cost reduction is possible following proper analysis of manning requirements. This practice is important nationally, in high demand areas where the waste may have larger implications beyond in-company costs. As an example, when we were seeking a Managing Director for a company with very straightforward technology, one of the very best applicants was a man who was outstandingly well qualified technically in addition to his other qualities. Our decision against employing him was a reluctant one, but was influenced by our realization that his talents would be used only partially. (The possibility of technical boredom was also foreseen.)

New management techniques coming into use result in high demand for individuals with knowledge or experience in them. Values of these individuals, therefore, increase at a fast rate in line with demand and with individual rates of learning and ability to apply. The rate of increase in values is likely to be much faster than in parallel, but more established activities.

This mechanism operates as a selection technique. Many people are attracted to new activities by the high potential earnings, and the most able are (naturally) chosen. These people justify their fast rate of salary rise on general ability, but also increase the rate at which know-how is developed around the new techniques. In the second stage of development in the use of new techniques, the individuals involved are still 'pathfinders' with opportunities for creative thinking. Later the proportion of routine standard applications will increase with resulting changes in manning requirements, and significant value differences between the 'new thinkers' and the 'doers'.

But in the second stage, high calibre people with fast learning rates and high application ability are attracted by potential job satisfaction combined with high earnings at young ages. Any impression of excessive payment proves false if reasonable comparisons are made with individuals of comparable ability who are in other functions. Values will not be identical, of course, and comparisons are based on rather arbitrary measures, but the variations may not be as great as were initially suspected.

High calibre, extremely ambitious people tend to gravitate to (or to be attracted by) situations where their values may advance very rapidly by some means or other. Such positions tend to provide full and satisfying use of their abilities. A frequent chosen career today is that of a specialist in a 'new technique' area where demand will rapidly suck the competent individual up a narrow tube. The act of broadening rapidly and consolidating at the top of the tube, as a basis for further advance, is a problem to be faced later.

Tight market situations

The demand for computer staff was strong for some time and has enabled us to study the pressures of a tight market quite carefully.

The rise in pay levels was not slow and steady, but built up into a series of steps. As demand grew, sooner or later one employer would raise his pay levels out of desperation—usually by around 5 per cent. He gained an immediate slight advantage and was able to recruit again. Other employers found that they had to match his new rates in order to retain their staff and compete in the market, and they made immediate adjustments to the salaries of relevant staff they wished to retain. Within a very short period of time a new equilibrium was reached, with some of the immediate pressures removed (and the most desperately placed employers in a slightly improved position). It would then be some months until pressure built up to the next stage, and the surge was repeated.

The supply is not relieved by this process, but more people with relevant skills are attracted by the visibly rising rates. These newcomers may not be fully effective for months or even years, but they fill some holes in the structure and release fully skilled personnel for jobs demanding these skills. The specialist is utilized to maximum advantage and his job is trimmed of all the non-specialist aspects. The pressure is relieved at each 'value surge' by the influx of new people and the reshuffle and better utilization of the existing force.

More recently, training personnel at all levels have been in considerable demand—which has far outstripped supply. Large numbers of other people have been drawn into the training area, but activities have changed considerably around the available skills of the influx. For example, we have, in proportion, vastly more training administration, and the effective training work is being done by the original specialists. It will take several years for the cream of the influx to acquire the necessary skills and experience to supplement this effort properly.

At senior management levels, this same process operates, but on a much more individual basis, and rather more slowly. Where skills are in short supply and head-hunters move in, a sharp increase in salary levels—and executive mobility—may result. Close touch with the market in these circumstances is essential.

Values are not precise

Market values are not precise and the 'market' is far from perfect, largely because it is not understood. Some companies take an old-fashioned view of 'equity', linked to traditional remuneration differentials. But jobs change, and as the availability of newer skills usually lags behind the demand, pushing up values, the change in market value relationships may be very marked over quite short periods.

Even where employers properly appreciate the factors which influence values and relative values, they may not always know clearly what they require from the holder of a post. As a result, a price may be inexpertly established, based on a good specification perhaps, but overlooking factors which may have a significant impact on man specification and job value. Environmental factors and quality of performance are particularly relevant.

As a result, a job with few difficulties attached (for which the man specification should be straightforward), may be filled at a high salary appropriate to a competent specialist in the field because it is vaguely assumed that all such jobs are of comparable difficulty and value. Had the job difficulties been much greater and in line with the pay level, the man appointed might probably have failed, although no one in the company would have understood why.

By these faults in the system, anomalies can exist, and do so in substantial numbers—usually in the form of overpayment in overvalued posts. At the opposite end of the scale, the high calibre man will sometimes accept underpayment to take an underrated job which he recognizes is more complex than has been assessed and will give him sound experience, and possibly lead to appropriate payment in the longer term. He accepts the situation that he is mobile and can cash his 'experience cheque' by taking a higher priced position if his contribution continues to be underestimated.

For lower level posts, local market value patterns have been clear for some years (although increasingly modified by staff union activity and influence). For senior posts, the value picture is becoming increasingly clearer with growing executive mobility, but the range of factors which influence values is more complex than lower down the scale.

No absolute values

The fundamental assumption in market value theory, is that there is no absolute scale of values, only a constantly changing set of relationships. The current pattern of differentials is no indicator of future patterns, except that vertical, hierarchical relationships within job families (such as production engineering or cost accounting) appear fundamental and subject only to variation in width of differentials.

The market produces, not a precise value, but usually an 'area of money' within which agreement between employer and employee may be reached. It covers specifically remuneration, but assumes certain standards of related benefits, variance from which may affect the financial value.

Environment and values

Consider the situation of a Personnel Manager who is required to operate with a Board who belittle the personnel function. They consider it has nothing to offer them, but accept that it is a necessity. They need someone to complete employment returns and to undertake initial recruitment and welfare work.

In filling the post, there are two possibilities. More than likely, they are going to attract an individual who will provide a routine service, but make no creative appraisal of their problems and needs. In other words, he will fulfil their requirement and be paid accordingly.

Alternatively, they may attract an individual who is a trained and creative thinking Personnel Manager. Finding himself in this post, he will be immediately frustrated. His only hope of success will lie in educating his Board—in getting across his concepts of his function and obtaining acceptance of the impact that these may have on the future of the business.

If he is able to do this successfully and alter the attitude to his function, then his value as a pioneer is clear-cut and he justifies his salary level. Otherwise, his value is related to what he might achieve in some other environment, and he is over-paid in his present post.

The speaker who said 'part of the function of the price mechanism is to remunerate individuals for the serious disadvantages which arise in some companies and occupations' was thinking of one aspect of environment. Where there is major reorganization or serious commercial difficulty, the pressure on an executive, and the career risks to which he is exposed, may raise his asking price to a significant degree.

These criteria are obvious, but the environmental problems of attitude are more difficult.

Any executive post exists in an 'environment'. Whatever the abilities of an individual may be, his current value is related to his present situation, and is determined by his ability to cope with this environment. Put another way, it does not matter what volume of professional knowledge any individual may accumulate, his value lies in his ability to apply it to the production of successful results and this ability may be restricted by unfavourable environment.

Environment is attributed partly to the industrial and competitive situation in which the company exists, but more to the attitudes of the organization's key executives. These people may belittle, or simply not accept, the value of—or a concept of—a particular activity. If this is so, the difficulties faced by the relevant manager are significant and the calibre of individuals capable of achieving successful performance is almost certainly out of line with the valuation placed on the role by the company.

In other situations, difficulties may be related to a changing commercial environment. The need for personal qualities or abilities capable of overcoming the difficulties may have a substantial impact on the man specification and job value.

Structure of market values

The overall pattern of market values can best be understood by looking at the company pyramid structure as shown in Fig. 3.1. At top and bottom there are market groups common across the entire organization, while in the middle area functional differences create vertical divisions between jobs with unrelated values.

Across the lower rungs of an organization, we have stratified layers of clerical, secretarial and lower technical staff who are able to be moved with reasonable freedom to comparable jobs anywhere else in the company.

As we get to the top end of the clerical scale, and into the junior technical regions, movement is less free. The senior clerk has acquired special knowledge over a period of time in some aspect of the business, probably in one particular department or function, and his value is linked to use of this skill. He would be less valuable if employed elsewhere. It might take him two or more years to acquire comparable skills in some other senior

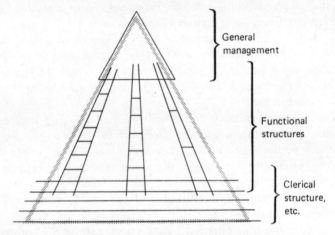

Figure 3.1 Market value structure related to company pyramid

clerical activity. His current market value is not linked to clerical work generally, but to the specific area in which he has functional skill.

Similarly, the junior technical assistant steadily acquires skills which tie his value to a particular area and he is not free to change streams or return to square one, without some reduction in his employed value. This elementary 'streaming' is the first stage of division into the major market groups, allied to the broad functional division of companies into production, marketing, finance, and so on.

It is only when we get to the top of the pyramid that the market groups are linked again through those posts which fall into the 'general management' market group. (Within this market group, there are sub-groups linked to different industries and their requirements for differing types of managerial or technical skills.)

Under the top man come the heads of functions, called directors or managers, of marketing, production, personnel, and so on. In so far as these posts involve participation in the general management of the company, the values of the jobs and the incumbents are influenced by the pattern of values within the general management market group. There may not be a clean, hard line, but certain jobs may exist on a fringe between two market groups, with precise values depending on the blend of activities.

The functional market groups in the middle have vertical structures. They have links at top and bottom with other structures, but relatively little association with other groups in their middle areas. For example, the value relationships between a middle level engineer and a 'comparable' accountant cannot be assessed on any common ground. It is virtually impossible for either to be moved into the other job, and the basis for payment of one cannot logically influence the pay of the other. (At least, not logically in economic terms.)

It is a critical facet of market value theory that values will be related only where there is normal freedom to move within short periods of time to the other job group.

Each of the market groups within a company is likely to divide into a series of work levels, or grades, or value levels, with a progression of skills, experience, ability to apply, and so on between levels and justifying salary differentials.

The groups may also divide into a series of related streams which may link at points within the structure. For example, within a function some staff are employed in general roles and others in specialist capacities, and established 'generalists' and 'specialists' are not easily interchangeable due to different knowledge and experience backgrounds (apart from possible other factors).

Studies show that specialists are often in short supply in relation to demand, and command comparatively higher values (on an age × service basis) than *apparently* equivalent generalists. My view is that different types of people are attracted to special-

ize and that value differences reflect differences in capacity—
as the value advantage which the specialist attracts is normal
and the supply situation does nothing to correct.

It does not follow that all individual specialists are of higher
calibre or are paid more than generalists. The overlap on both
counts is considerable. Assumptions made on average figures
without analyses of justification would suggest that differentials
'normally apply' between these two parts of the job family.

Similarly, knowledge of 'newer' skills tends to attract a
premium due to insufficient supply of experienced men. Where
the demand is likely to remain strong, the calibre of individuals
attracted, in terms of learning and application of skills, may be
high as this represents an attractive opportunity to progress exceptionally rapidly upwards.

Family structures

The pattern of salaries within a primary family such as 'finance'
would divide between straightforward operational accounting
(book-keeping), cost accountancy, budget specialists, financial
analysts, and so on. The extent to which these divisions need to
be recognized within a structure depends only on the degree of
specialized knowledge which may separate groups of posts from
the general run.

I have not endeavoured to provide a comprehensive analysis
of primary and subsidiary market groups, as even in very large
organizations it would be unusual to identify and use more than
about thirty groups, while the single product line unit would
probably identify no more than ten for practical purposes.

For example, a typical list might be :

General management	Inspection
Marketing	R&D (possibly separate research)
Field sales operations	Accounting operations
Sales administration	Finance
Production operations	Personnel (including training)
Industrial engineering	Medical
Production planning	Clerical

Structure and individuals

Approaching market groups and sub-groups from the direction of the individual, we might start by saying that accountants are clearly different from engineers. Looking more closely at accountants to see why they are not freely interchangeable, we establish :

1   People entering accountancy as a career may have similar educational levels.
2   They then embark on varied professional qualifications—these prepare them for varying types of positions.
3   Experience at this time and immediately afterwards will be in various aspects of accountancy.
4   Experience will be in varying industries. Both points (3) and (4) may present a further narrowing factor.
5   Choice of managerial or specialist application adds a further factor—and there are many others.

Thus, the man who has obtained his ACWA in an engineering company is not able to replace the man who obtained his ACWA in a tobacco company. Should he wish to transfer, he would need to go back a stage and learn about tobacco processing, and the application and problems of cost accounting in this industry, in order to join this clear market sub-group.

Similarly, of two ACWAs in engineering, one may be in an operating situation while the other is in a central staff team. The two are not interchangeable and, at best, they would take time to acquire the knowledge to do the other's job.

Market values are common at points of free interchange, but begin to take separate existence where knowledge required to do jobs becomes different. They begin to become unrelated where the 'learning time' required for transfer exceeds one year. By the time 'learning time' reaches five years, the two categories may be taken as independent market groups with no normal interchange.

To simplify this, the qualities of a distinct market group would appear to be :

1   Common education and training requirements.
2   Experience patterns which are sufficiently related to ensure interchange at any level within about a year.

3   Reasonably common ability standards.

This last factor is widely relevant. It is frequently possible for an exceptionally able man to acquire know-how speedily and to transfer between market groups, where the normal run of personnel within those groups might prohibit this. Factors (1) and (2) therefore apply subject to normal manning/ability standards. And ability standards may also represent the basis of a division between families, e.g. certain computer and management sciences staff in relation to other personnel with similar initial training.

A difficulty many people have in understanding market value concepts is that values are not precise, and that market group boundaries are not precise. There must always be exceptions and anomalies because the whole pattern is built on personal choice, and by no means every man chooses to go to the highest bidder, or to follow normal, 'traditional' career paths. Further, job content and environment are infinitely variable, and values too. We do not have a concrete structure, but rather a concept which provides a rational explanation for the patterns we find. Those who do not normally think conceptually must anticipate difficulty in comprehension.

Visual presentation is not easy. Relationships between market groups are multi-factored and would need to be presented in multi-dimensional form. An extreme simplification of two dimensions (or 'microscopic section') might show a series of separate groupings, in loose clusters, sometimes overlapping so that individuals are incorporated into two groups and sometimes touching to show a transfer point, and also loosely connecting the main clusters. Movement at one point in the total 'pool' might have some ripple effect on near-by groups, but would always tend to be local.

The changing pattern

There is no absolute scale of values. Relative values alter continually with changes in supply and demand and with the pressures from organized groups. One can see most clearly the massive changes which have taken place by looking back over a period of about fifty years, during which time the relative values placed on white-collar workers compared with blue-collar workers has changed dramatically. With this in mind, there can be no logic in claiming that because group A was paid more than group B in 1950 or 1970, that the earlier relationship should be reinstated. Such a proposal is comparable with demanding a return to horse-drawn transport or the abandonment of trade unions.

In any one year, values for small demand categories may move by a small amount or not at all, while high demand categories in very short supply may rise in value by considerably in excess of 10 per cent. Over a three-year period, it is conceivable that two jobs which start on level pegging will open up a differential in excess of 30 per cent. As this has side effects in terms of altering the calibre of individuals attracted, it is unlikely that the former relationship will ever return.

This is typical of the whole pattern. Value relationships between families or market groups move in unrelated ways. Even within market groups, the value differentials between levels will gradually widen or close with market pressures. Also, as has been happening slowly but steadily for several years, differentials between the most able and the general run can widen (or alternatively contract) to reflect demand for exceptional ability.

'Traditional' career movement

We talk of 'career patterns'. In the UK, individual career progression lines fall into traditional or accepted-normal patterns to a significant extent. Flow of people across these normal lines is not substantial and attempted movement may even be difficult. The result is an additional pressure factor in the formation of market groups with clear boundaries not normally crossed.

This can be illustrated very clearly from analyses I have undertaken in the personnel field, where for several years there was clear separation between Personnel Officers in general personnel activities, and those following careers in some specialized aspect of personnel management.

The extent to which there could be movement between the streams was very limited. Once a Personnel Officer had begun to follow a specialized track, his market value rose very fast and he could not afford to switch into more general work as his value in wider activity would be substantially lower. Additionally, his narrow experience was unacceptable to a possible employer with a vacancy for a more general operator.

The generalist moving towards specialization had similar difficulties. His early operational training encouraged one style of thought and action, while specialized staff made differing demands which he often felt incapable of meeting.

The career pattern through the middle area between the newly fledged Personnel Officer and, virtually, Personnel Director seemed quite separate, with a minimum of opportunity to transfer—usually limited to planned development in big organizations. Then at the top, where personnel management comes more into the general management sphere, salary patterns re-unite and there is common ground, although somewhat dominated by people from the tighter thinking and planning discipline of specialized staff work.

It is the responsibility of the Salary Administrator to make sure that market values are properly related at the various link points where career lines divide or reunite. To do this, he must understand the career patterns which are relevant in his own organization and ensure that his salary structures are related.

The controlled market

The free market in which market values emerge in the way described earlier in this chapter is a diminishing area. In particular, unions have extended far into staff categories, and a greater proportion of the employed population is within the Civil Service, local government, nationalized industry zone where group negotiation is required. The overall supply and demand situation still has some bearing, but other pressures are generated by the 'power groups' involved.

Today, many managers are members of trade unions or staff associations, and their salaries are at least influenced by these bodies. Below management levels, there are progressively fewer employees whose pay is not influenced by negotiation in some way.

At the present time, the 'natural' relationships of a free market have been replaced by an assembly of temporary and disputed relationships and a scene where progressively stronger and more militant unions attempt to achieve higher levels for themselves while socially justifiable and desirable claims of other groups are held back to low levels.

Management remuneration remains largely clear of these influences but we need an appreciation of the forces at work and the reaction of companies to the mix of current pressures.

Where unions negotiate a local rate, and a short supply situation exists, some employers will supplement the agreed levels of payment in order to attract more easily the people they need. The 'going' rate for mobile employees is determined by the degree of demand and the level of supply, and negotiated general adjustments do little to change supply and demand. Locally adjusted rates explain the 'wage creep' which is a significant factor in national wage movement.

Where the supply is adequate or exceeds demand, pressure for supplements to attract people disappear. It does not follow (or rather, has not followed in the past) that wage claims and negotiated general adjustments will not continue. Costs of living may be rising and the levels demanded by existing employees creep up in parallel. This appears to continue even when supply grossly exceeds demand and there is substantial unemployment, although employers' willingness to concede adjustments at such times is probably lessened. Market values (accepted minimum rates) appear to move up for unionized groups in line with cost of living changes as a minimum.

Where a union is very strong; where it has substantial membership and exists in a position of short supply, it is able to add pressure to natural movement in market values and artificially speed up the rate of inflation—especially in respect of low calibre personnel whose personal values would progress far more slowly in a free market. These personnel become overpaid in relation to free market values, unable to move, and an annoyance and embarrassment to employers. Significant feelings of unfairness are generated among managers by narrowed differentials.

A strong union able to exert an exceptional influence on a company through a small group of employees may get carried away and push excessively hard for higher incomes. Employer reaction to this comes partly in the form of the development of alternative methods to reduce staff requirements. A particular example is seen in the efforts to minimize the need for detail (copying) draughtsmen and those on simple, near routine, design work where much activity can be computerized.

If the demand for relatively simple skills is such that values rise to a point where some alternative method becomes economically sound, then demand will be reduced and values steadied by change of system.

One example of this has been in the pressure to use computers for minor design and re-drawing work, as a substitute for highly priced draughtsmen, as mentioned above. Over a decade, draughting work has gradually changed in the face of union pressure for higher rates. Much of the simpler work has been automated by various means and the man at the drawing board is increasingly a design engineer. Over a further decade his drawing board and much of his basic design work may also become automated as a result of continuing pressure on salary levels, as work level is related back to pay level. Perhaps we should accept that this provides a valuable spur to progress. These same economic pressures almost inevitably force the pace of automation in many activities.

It is interesting to reflect on the ultimate development of this line of thought, but in the shorter term, if excessive (faster than 'natural' market) pressure on incomes provokes a management response, the demand for people in the relevant groups must be slackened, the market weight of wage demands reduced, and the pressure for altered manning standards increased.

At the other extreme, union organization encourages some managements to resign their responsibilities for ensuring that salary levels are adequate to retain staff of satisfactory quality. They see their role as having been changed to keeping union claims in check. I have seen this situation carried to the point where poor union organization was battened down and salary levels held down over several years to an impossibly low level with disastrous impact on staff turnover and quality.

In virtually all 'power group' situations, market value theory continues to operate through the calibre of people attracted and retained in the occupation group. The fact remains that in the long term we get what we pay for.

This is not an argument for retaining or returning to any pattern of differentials of earlier times. The content of jobs change imperceptibly over periods of time as knowledge grows and methods change, and *last year's wage differentials are no guide to next year.*

Large employers

While trade unions may have a special effect on the market situation, so too may the very large employer. This may be particularly true in the case of technical staff and management where a single employer may have a dominant position in the labour market for a particular market group, or may influence the general level of that market.

However, the situation remains a free market one, for the small employer may attract the better people by careful setting of his salary levels, or by establishing a calculated management environment in contrast with a known frustration pattern in his big rival.

Wage 'freeze', 1975-77

Historically, periods of wage freeze represent hiccups in the evolution of market pressures and changes of rates and differentials, followed by re-establishment of the natural order of things.

Chapter 4

Salary Administration
and the Trade Unions

Salary administration has been called a management tool. In today's society, policies and procedures that affect people are increasingly discussed with those they affect, and nowhere is this more critical than in the field of remuneration and benefits. It is normal today to discuss and negotiate minimum salaries for groups of jobs up to middle management levels, and this negotiation is extending towards full involvement in job evaluation and grading; setting salary structures rather than just minima; covering higher salary levels; approval of salary review decisions; and so on. And the official representatives for this purpose are generally trade union representatives, with only limited roles for non-union spokesmen.

The Salary Administrator must keep a continuing look-out on the views expressed by the unions which may affect his actions and policies, for example, on job evaluation. The TUC has published a booklet on *Job Evaluation and Merit Rating*. From this we can see that unions are generally in agreement on the need for the maximum amount of trade union involvement in company and industry job evaluation schemes. ASTMS indicate that their attitude is to a large extent dependent on the amount of union/employee participation in the early stages of the exercise, in drawing up the actual scheme and in selecting and weighting the factors.

The GMWU note, among other factors, that job evaluation schemes often mean long and involved negotiations enabling the trade union to increase its influence on management and prove its usefulness to its members.

These comments provide pointers to the Salary Administrator. The starting point for the development or updating of a job evaluation scheme will gradually shift from invitation and design of a scheme, and selling to management, to introducing the concept to trade union representatives and developing each stage from that point.

The type of scheme to be used will also be affected. APEX do not recommend any particular type of scheme and recognize that company circumstances differ, but most unions and negotiators find that points evaluation schemes provide a sounder basis on which to negotiate than schemes which rely more on management and Salary Administrator expertise. It also justifies the comment on 'long and involved negotiations', both in establishing factors and weightings, and subsequently processing large numbers of jobs.

The TUC recommend that there should be careful attention to the technical factors of each scheme, to establish the most appropriate one for the situation. They also suggest a measure of joint control over the exercise, and list various other points and safeguards.

Similar policies or statements of generally held viewpoints could be developed for each aspect of salary administration, but these can be dealt with in the relevant chapters of the book. What we should be considering now is *Participation*, what it means in theory and what it means in practice.

Participation

In a company that practices participation in a full sense, day to day, employee involvement in job evaluation, appraisal and salary determination should present no problems. This may be idealistic, but let us examine the viewpoint further.

We are talking about a situation where there exists an openness and trust between management and staff; an acceptance of fair dealing and honesty, and a willingness to talk frankly. In such a situation, open discussion of and participation in job grading becomes possible; employees participate in establishing performance standards for their own jobs; take lead roles in evaluating and discussing their own performance and even reviewing their own salaries.

This process ceases to be practicable if the management style is at all autocratic, or if there are clouds of secrecy surrounding the administrative systems.

The process is not practicable if employees or their representatives take stands against differential payments for perfomance, or in any way restrict open discussion between a manager and his staff. Most of all, the ideal is crippled by lack of trust on either side. At this point, it becomes difficult to convince people that their salaries are being administered fairly. Salary plans need to be designed to run with 'minimum requirements for trust', with remuneration linked as closely as possible to specific measurables. The practical difficulty of forecasting, and 'selling' these specific figures in industries which face continual pressure for change makes this approach extremely vulnerable, with some staff benefiting and others suffering from unforecast changes of trends.

At extremes of mistrust, difficulties in setting realistic performance standards, and may reach a point where salary ceases to have any value as a motivator. An economist has suggested that the large corporations will become means of distributing wealth to employees in the same way that governments distribute wealth to the unemployed, that pay is on the basis of 'membership' rather than on contribution where it is difficult (or advisable not) to base pay on performance.

Having gone rapidly from the idealistic to the cynical view, I accept that practice will fall somewhere between the two. The quality of any participative exercise involves both parties aiming to achieve the best for all concerned and not fighting for their sectional interests alone. Where management beat down union representatives, the company (by which I mean everybody concerned) loses out because the better people will tend to go elsewhere and weaken the company. Where tough unions 'win', the results will be just as disastrous as the company's products become uncompetitive—but we are familiar with that already in the UK. Participation involves achieving a balance between all the interests involved including the State and the community, and it must fail where any 'participating' group sets out to 'win' for itself. Only time will tell whether or not we have the intelligence and the self-discipline to make participation work.

The trade union and salary administration

Salary Administrators have a particular need to be aware of the environments in which they exist, and to anticipate the possible form and direction of new interests in their activities. It is natural that they will have an interest in the trade union scene, which they may observe with something between an expert and a layman's eye.

The union movement is large and complex, and may be expected to have all the normal internal problems and pressures of large organizations. The officials with whom the Salary Administrator may deal will be as concerned about the internal union reactions to what they may say and do, as they will be concerned about the local members' reactions, and the reactions of the employer. Negotiations of any sort will not take place in the tidy backwater of internal company factors alone, so always look briefly at the other factors which an external, full-time official may bring in.

The primary pressure on full-time officials, if they are to survive in their posts, must be to satisfy the membership. They cannot afford to forget that the finances of the union are directly related to the size of the membership; that several other unions may be competing for the same people; and that an aggressive and apparently effective union may have greater recruiting power. The interests of members are critically important, and may override questions of national interest, concepts of 'equity' and certainly the interests of the employer.

Pressure comes also from the changes in involvement of grass-roots union membership, where greater initiative and local participation tends to exclude full-time officials who may have been expected to provide leadership at earlier times in their careers. Political progress, both with a small 'p' concerned with the natural politics of a large organization, and a large 'P' to cover various party affiliations, add to the burden and may influence the behaviour of an official at any time.

Against this background, the Salary Administrator may endeavour to be as fair as possible with the in-company employee representatives, where the influences and pressures will be substantial, but not necessarily entirely, in-house. If he is able to work on a participatory basis with moderate, thinking men, with whom an atmosphere of mutual trust has been developed, there is freedom to discuss any potential problems and negotiate a settlement. However, it would be foolish to overlook the existence of others, less sensitive, tied to some political dogma, but forceful leaders of their fellows. Then the development of trust and freedom to discuss may be inhibited.

It is for the Salary Administrator and his associates to assess the quality of relationships and to develop the best achievable in their situation—and each situation will be different. They must always remember that they are concerned with the total interests of the company and its employees, and recognize that they cannot take up narrow viewpoints of the problems facing them. The Salary Administrator steps out of his functional position and takes on the role of General Manager in assessing the proposals presented first to him.

The professional manager and the trade union

Except in the smaller companies, managers today are largely employed managers—professional managers. As such, they are there on merit, and have as much right to belong to a trade union as any other employee. In practice, many of the more junior managers (foremen and supervisors) are members of a union, and so are many of their more senior colleagues.

The 'them and us' attitude of some older unionists has become a bit dated by this development, but common membership of unions does not alter the responsibility of a senior manager to protect the interests of the company that employs him. In fact, if he has been made a director, he can be held accountable in law, and the fact that he may retain an allegiance to his old craft union and be a member of their supervisory and management affiliate is irrelevant.

The professional manager has to look on the business he manages with an 'owner's eye' so that the money he spends is dealt with as 'his money' and he is properly concerned with wise spending and investment. If he does not, his ability to attract capital in the open market to finance the business will be impaired. Then, not only will he have failed as a manager of that business, but he will have placed the job security of its employees in jeopardy. The second part at least will not improve his image as a good trade unionist.

My point is simply that, unionist or not, he has a responsibility to ensure that wage settlements and participation do not adversely affect the economic viability of the company. Also, unionist or not, he should be adequately paid for his responsibilities.

Part 2

Operations

Chapter 5

Job Analysis

Job analysis is one of the cornerstones of salary administration. Without proper knowledge of the make-up and content of a job or jobs, any evaluation will be based on unknown quantities and must be unacceptable to the Salary Administrator.

The process of job analysis consists of breaking down a job to the point where each part can be seen and identified; the purpose of each part made clear; the overall function defined together with its relationship to the function of other positions; and the essential requirements to be looked for in a holder of the position determined. Maintaining this picture is a key practical stage. in any Job Classification Structure and Salary Administration Plan.

The value of job information and analysis

Job analyses have many purposes and applications other than for salary administration. They are, for example, widely used as an aid to selection and placement of staff, and as a guide to skills and responsibilities when building a training programme. Job analysis is as fundamental to organization and methods studies or work study as it is to salary determination, and is fundamental also for the establishment of normal staffing standards and the definition of good organizational structures and responsibilities.

These additional or alternative uses should always be taken into account when planning any job analysis operation, both with immediate application in mind as well as all future ones.

The effort and expense of a major job analysis exercise are not likely to be undertaken a second time in a short span of years by most organizations (although job information 'dates' quickly).

If a method of obtaining job information already exists, examine it. What is the method by which those responsible for selecting new staff obtain information about the vacancies they have to fill or advise on? Is the information adequate for salary administration purposes, or perhaps inadequate even for the recruiters to carry out their function properly? If so, the job analysis programme, whether it is to be a company-wide exercise or merely a local affair, can be slanted to provide the specific additional information required for selection purposes.

Or perhaps detailed information about each vacant position is already obtained on a one-off, throw-away basis, possibly at quite considerable cost and effort. The job analysis programme can ease such a situation by providing for full and proper records of information previously collected haphazardly. Economy of this type may well provide part of the cost saving so often looked for if a 'justification report' has to be produced to support expenditure proposed on job analysis.

The application of job analysis to the training function is feasible both in the manual worker and in staff job areas. Breaking jobs down into individual skill requirements provides a basis for grouping various jobs requiring similar types of skill, and indicates obvious sources for selecting suitable people for training.

Organization and methods studies and establishment control studies require a detailed breakdown of the jobs in the area concerned. The analysis of job information provides the basis for rationalization and simplification, by clearly indicating duplicated or overlapping activities.

Organization planning is basically similar, but the end product is concerned more with the higher levels of the structure; with the logical allocation of responsibilities based on a detailed analysis of existing organization and activities, and the present and future requirements of the total unit.

Internal selection procedures may incorporate the use of punched-card personnel records to identify people with appropriate qualifications. This is done in association with a study of the job specification which identifies job requirements such as education, experience, supervisory ability, languages, etc., and searching by punched-card analyses for employees who have similar or identical characteristics recorded on their cards.

Other uses for recorded job data occur where a safety factor has been used in the evaluation plan. Details of possible safety hazards or causes of industrial sickness should be extracted from the job specifications and passed on to the Safety Officer for analysis and preventative action. The Chief Medical Officer will also be interested.

Other users of the data contained in job descriptions and specifications are Personnel Officers responsible for recruitment, and also consultants where these are employed.

Internal auditors as well as organization and methods staff constantly derive immense help in their studies from job analyses. Co-operation is invariably on a two-way basis with these people on job studies.

The collection exercise

The range of information which will be needed for a particular study can be determined on the basis of the anticipated requirements as described above. Before describing the actual collection of this information, we have summarized some of the basic pieces of information universally required.

Job identification

The basic data which will invariably be needed are the employee's name and job title, the names of the company, division, department, section and subsidiary unit as appropriate, identification of the reporting relationships of the job and particularly the position to which the job holder reports.

The specific detail required here may vary, but the purpose is to identify the job positively, and to determine its position in the company organization. Space may be allowed on the job analysis form for coding data for cross-reference or record purposes.

Job title

A title may well be almost meaningless in a company with no tradition of standard job titling. The most common general fault is the excessive use of words such as 'Senior', 'Leading' and 'Chief', and of supervisory and managerial inflation.

Where titling has become out of hand in the past, the situation should not be allowed to continue indefinitely. A study of job titling should always be based on detailed job information : no other basis for the amendment of titles could possibly give meaningful results. Such a study requires a considerable volume of cross-checking and matching of similar jobs, a gradual identification of identical jobs, and a gradual achievement of common titling standards.

A further factor to remember when changing titles is the emotional implication of apparent loss of status which may result.

Organizational position

The name and title of the individual to whom the job holder is responsible is equally important basic information. Wherever possible an organization chart should be attached to, or associated with, job information to establish clearly the place of each job in the structure.

The job summary

Allow space for, say, fifty to one hundred words to summarize briefly the purpose and objects of the job; to explain why the position exists.

The ultimate purpose of a senior position can usually be clearly defined and this definition can be immensely helpful in indicating briefly the reasons for the total range of duties or job scope.

For example, the mandate of an Industrial Engineer might read : 'To increase productivity and reduce costs in PQR department by increasing the effectiveness of existing resources, i.e. men, materials and machines, and reducing waste.'

Or, the Comptroller of a subsidiary company might have as the purpose of his position : 'To advise the subsidiary company management of the meaning, implication and effect of all existing, planned or proposed activities of the subsidiary from a financial viewpoint. To develop, recommend and supervise financial policies, within the overall policies defined by the parent company, etc.'

This question is almost superfluous when asked about lower-level jobs, as little information is likely to be gained which will not be brought out elsewhere. For example, an Accounting Machine Operator in a payroll department might say her purpose was 'To process all payroll amendments and overtime lists, to produce the payslips and payroll summaries for all employees on payroll . . . each week.'

A Copy Typist might be covered by, 'Provides a service to a group of Sales Office Clerks by typing a limited variety of material from rough drafts.'

Statements such as these make absolutely clear the purpose of the job, provide a guide identification and make interpretation of all the detail which follows very much easier.

The value of this statement appears to reduce in direct proportion to the number of words used over about thirty, perhaps fifty for management positions, as extraneous detail is inevitably brought in.

Actual duties

The breakdown of the actual duties of a job into separate elements is the major purpose of the job analysis.

What does the job actually consist of? What does each part of it consist of? How is it done? For what purpose is it done? The extent of the detail required under the heading will vary substantially according to application. A precise summary of duties may be adequate for evaluation for recruitment purposes, when combined with specific personal information, but a methods study would require every stage of each operation to be minutely defined and timed, with full details also of the irregular incidents which are part of the job but which occur perhaps only once a year. The exact amount of detail should be determined from the analysis of job requirements but, as determination of the job duties absorbs the major part of time spent on analysis, care should be taken to avoid collection of too much or too little information. A more detailed comment on the writing of this part of the job description is included under the heading 'Style' later in this chapter.

Means of collection

The physical collection of job information may be carried out in a number of ways. The method chosen is likely to be based on the company outlook on the subject and the precise application of information. For example, an organization which intends to make heavy use of managers' knowledge by their participation in a job ranking exercise is likely to encourage participation by staff and supervisors generally, by using a questionnaire method of collection to which all will contribute.

However, where management interest or trust is less developed, a team of analysts or consultants may be called upon to collect information by interviews with job holders, or with their supervisors and managers. Whichever method is used, the Salary Administrator should have some experience of basic job collection by interview in order to appreciate fully the difficulties of information collection and the way individuals feel about their jobs.

The attitudes of the supervisors and staff likely to be involved and of their representatives need to be considered carefully. In many organizations these may present no problem provided the purpose of the studies is presented openly, and an atmosphere of mutual trust exists.

However, this is not always the case. If there is a background of suspicion, this may be difficult to overcome. If there is a general feeling of antagonism, then any form of participation in a job analysis study will prove difficult to obtain. Or there may be dogmatic objection to the concept and a view that classification can be negotiated without any local job analysis whatsoever. In such a situation, you have to accept that the quality of your analysis and any subsequent grading will be limited by the quality of data you are able to assemble, and must allow more flexibility in subsequent usage for the probable error.

Job analysis and grading requires first-hand information and positive co-operation if it is to carry confidence.

Job information by interview

An interview between the job holder and an experienced Job Analyst, followed by discussions with the immediate supervisor, may be considered to produce very complete and accurate job information. Unfortunately, this method of obtaining information is very time-consuming and, from time as well as expense viewpoints, must often be rejected. It should, however, always be used in cases where a significant dispute occurs, so that the fullest possible picture is available.

Let us assume that this method is to be used in a large department and examine the procedure.

The first, and vital factor, is one of *communication*. The initial approach must clearly be to the department manager and through him, never directly, to a subordinate. The Job Analyst should explain the full reasons for the study, the form it will take, the requirement from the department, the form of the anticipated results, and probable subsequent effects as far as these can be forecast. At this stage, all the cards should be on the table. The Salary Administrator is in the position of providing a service and should have no need for an 'ace up his sleeve'.

The first meeting should be followed by a wider get-together involving the heads of sections or supervisors in the department, the Salary Administrator, and his assistants in the study. The purpose is to brief the group on the study, obtain their general support and map out a detailed programme. After this the Analysts approach each supervisor as scheduled.

Each Analyst spends a few minutes talking generally to the supervisor, getting to know him, hearing his pet grumbles, and immediately assessing important problems to be faced. Then, quickly, he gets down to business by drawing up an organization chart with the supervisor, showing all employees, their job titles, the cross-reporting relationships—including those with other sections, until the basic form is clear.

Then he asks which individuals will provide the best sources of information on their jobs, perhaps one or two examples from a group of staff doing identical work, but probably every individual where the jobs differ. The supervisor should always be encouraged to contribute as much as possible to the planning of the exercise in his area, to feel partly responsible for it rather than merely an observer. His interest and enthusiasm, if generated, will pass on to his staff in the individual interviews which follow.

The supervisor should always be asked to introduce the Analyst to each individual whose job it is to be studied, to explain briefly what is to be done, and to encourage the employee to participate wholeheartedly. He then leaves them to get on with the interview.

This should always take place at the employee's point of work. The advantage of privacy in a specially requisitioned office, is outweighed by seeing the actual situation, the tools, papers, ledgers and so on which go to make up the job; also by hearing events and telephone calls that come up during the interview. It may be uncomfortable sitting at a desk corner in a passageway through a noisy general office, but the employee does his job under these conditions and this should be appreciated. If the person interviewed is at a more senior level with his own office, then privacy is obtained as a matter of course, as well as the proper location.

A cigarette, some small talk about the office, perhaps about last night's television, a little about the employee, his service, his views on the department, the company, the personnel department and so on, these begin to pour out as the worker relaxes. He may query the system of evaluation, challenging both the idea that an outsider can understand his job after a short interview when he took years to learn it, and also the idea that it can be evaluated by any sort of system, or compared with engineers and accountants.

A five-minute basic talk on job analysis and evaluation will generally settle his mind—an explanation of the systematic approach, the considerable influence of his supervisor and department head who know the work rather than the 'isolated and unknowledgeable' personnel view alone, the extensive cross-checking to ensure fairness in the finally agreed grading, and the emphasis on constant reappraisal to pick up job growth and organizational change.

Inevitably, some 'barrack-room lawyers' and others will challenge everything one says, and these people must be treated patiently, but cut short as gently as possible and encouraged to get on with the study.

'What is the basic purpose of your job? What does it do for the organization? What would happen if it did not exist? Use your own words to tell me how you see it so that I can get a basic feel of it and its place in the department.'

The interview is under way. The Analyst must guide its course to cover all possible queries, but doing as little talking as possible. He listens carefully, following up each suggestion or hint of an extra responsibility, also any irregular activity. He queries carefully each reporting relationship, the decisions which the job holder can make alone and checks on all other factors which may be relevant or influence the value of the job. At the end, which may be anywhere between one hour and a full day later, depending on the level and complexity of the job, he thanks the employee and returns to the supervisor for an introduction to the next subject.

Usually an Analyst will talk to between two or three, and up to a dozen, employees before going off to a quiet corner to sit down and write out full descriptions in standard format and style (see Fig. 5.1) from all the rough notes obtained during his interviews. His skill in transferring the basic material to a polished product rises with experience, but even the most competent Analyst will not be able to produce more than a few long descriptions a day for any length of time before quality begins to suffer. This 'writing up time', of course, is additional to the interview and any waiting time.

The next stage is to begin the cross-checking of the stories given by the job holders. As the job descriptions are accumulated for a whole department, the duplication of duties and responsibilities also begins to emerge and this provides an initial probing area for queries. Subsequently, the Analyst sits down as soon as possible with each supervisor to work through the descriptions of all his staff and then to study the supervisor's own job.

Invariably in this checking stage, errors are found as a result of individual inflation or deflation of jobs, and because of the normal inefficiencies of organizations. Whether these queries should be referred back to the job holders or not is a matter of opinion. Weak supervisors tend to avoid the issue if possible, but the authors feel strongly that an employee who claims a responsibility in a formal study of this sort and who is not subsequently corrected if his claim is untrue may reasonably assume that his statement has been accepted officially.

The cross-checking of descriptions proceeds through the various hierarchical levels, accumulating the descriptions of supervisory posts during this process. As managers are rarely aware of the detailed content of posts two or more levels below them, they should not be pressed to review and amend these descriptions. In any case, the manager of a large department would find it difficult to devote sufficient time to a comprehensive study of the jobs undertaken by all his junior staff.

However, the manager is likely to interrogate the Analyst, and to rely on his comments on the accuracy of the descriptions, and also on the effectiveness of his organization and its faults, which may also have been queried at the checking stage above. At this point, the overlap with organization studies is significant, and the potential contribution of the personnel man, particularly those concerned with job analysis, becomes apparent.

The questionnaire method

Where time and budget do not permit the luxury of an ample supply of Analysts, the questionnaire method of collecting job information is an effective substitute.

The form of the questionnaire should be as simple as possible without omitting any of the information and should describe clearly what is wanted under each heading. This requirement is discussed below and Fig. 5.2 shows a form of this type. Once the form has been designed and general approval for a job information collection exercise obtained, the procedure to be followed is not unlike that used in the interview method. Most important to success are: comprehensive briefing of all participating employees; the initial private talks with department managers; the group briefings of other supervisors; and encouragement for supervisors to brief their own staffs.

The story given to each level will vary slightly to recognize the differing viewpoints of recipients. The manager should be told in full about the form of the end results as a management tool, while the clerk will be told that the company is carrying out a continuous audit of jobs to ensure that it pays fair salaries and also retains a rational organization structure. This variation is justifiable only as long as each story is convincing and appropriate to the group of staff. We all know that employees fill in inadequate communication with rumour which is invariably to the company's disadvantage.

The completed questionnaires together with rough organization charts should always be fed back to the department manager through his various reporting lines. Each supervisor, from the immediate supervisor of the post, through any more senior levels, should vet the completed forms and satisfy himself that each represents a true picture. He should query points which appear unsatisfactorily presented and negotiate amendments.

Beyond the basic job data provided by the job holder, information on the job specification will be added by supervision. Higher levels of supervision have a special responsibility to ensure that these data are reasonable, and that common standards are used on all forms in a department. Informal discussions between managers to establish 'bench-mark' posts provide pegging points in the achievement of common standards of information.

The end result, by this technique as with the interview method, is a complete set of job analysis sheets in the hands of the manager and the Salary Administrator.

Format

Each organization should develop its own standard format for the collection and presentation of job information, taking into account the special requirements peculiar to its own situation. Variations will evolve according to the type of evaluation to be used, and its application to purposes other than salary administration. It may also be decided to use different formats for executive staff positions, or for different job families.

Basically, the format selected is not important, provided that it supplies the information required by the company's system. There are obvious advantages in planning standard layout and presentation as far as possible.

Some of the very many layouts in use are examined below.

Simple analysis format

A minimum amount of job information may suffice for the classification of clerical and office machine operator jobs into an established structure in which the levels are already defined. For example, in a structure of this sort, one of the defined levels might include: 'Copy Typist—types a limited range of material from rough drafts. Normal speed not less than thirty words a minute. Corrects obvious errors in drafts, but makes no other decisions.'

A simple job information sheet which indicates *a trained typist largely engaged in typing drafts for a clerical group and occasionally helping out with minor other duties*, is adequate for classifying the job against Grade Level Descriptions without any need for a more detailed analysis.

Simple job information sheets may also cover a recruitment specification: 'Age about 25, HNC (Production Engineering), from two to three years general work study experience; to lead a small group engaged on time study and ratefixing in production shops engaged on the sub-assembly of small mechanical units, and negotiate new piece-work prices under guidance from the Company Work Study Engineer.'

While this specification leaves a number of things not clearly defined, it contains sufficient clues for an experienced Personnel Officer to place the job level and type of man required.

A simple format of this sort has a very limited use and probably has no application at all for senior or management position information requirements, or to the establishment of job classification structures.

Normal analysis format

'Normal analysis' in this context is taken to be an analysis which provides an adequate amount of detail for a full job classification or evaluation exercise. Such an information sheet has no set number of words or length, as these must be determined by the complexity of the job and the system of evaluation which applies. The format of the information sheet must define every piece of the job and each relevant factor which may influence the rating of its relative value in the structure and place in the organization.

Figures 5.1 and 5.2 are typical forms used by major companies for analyses of this type.

Figure 5.1 is of a type which may be used where a points system or factor comparison method of evaluation is to be used, and the job information is accumulated under the required factor headings. Owing to its complexity, a format of this sort would require interviews between a job holder, his supervisor and a Job Analyst. In addition to its complexity it is impossible to incorporate all combinations of questions on information requirements at the head of each factor section on a question-naire type of form.

The type of job information form which can be handed out for a job holder or his supervisor to complete is shown in Fig. 5.2. This is a much simpler form which will provide information for a less fine system of evaluation—a system in which the whole job is examined at the same time rather than by separate scrutiny in minute detail of its various aspects.

The type of form and method of collection of information to be selected by an organization are largely related to the subsequent applications as discussed earlier in this chapter.

Detailed analysis format

Detailed job information is always needed for specialist studies and 'extra' detail required may be obtained for the organization and methods department as required. Studies as detailed as this are not normally part of salary administration. However, where they were used for some form of organization study, the results might well affect job grading and individual salary levels.

'Objectives' format

For senior managerial and senior staff appointments, the basic statements of the job may be backed up by a summary of short-to medium-term objectives, and of the performance standards expected. Most jobs at these levels can be described clearly enough in general terms, but the actual 'work done' reflects the effort on current problems and objectives. By providing a statement of forward objectives, the nature of the job as 'positively directed' or 'chaotic fire-fighting' is revealed, and the perfor-

Figure 5.1 Job information record form: a type used for points evaluation with factor headings

EXCELSIOR ENGINEERING COMPANY LTD:
JOB INFORMATION RECORD

Job title:

| Department: |
| Division: |

| Reports to: |

Score summary

Factor	1	2	3	4	5	6	7	8	9	10	11	12	Total	Grade
Degree														
Score														

Part A: Give a brief statement of the function of the job	
State briefly the major aspects of the work	

PART B:
(Refer to the factor evaluation schedule before scoring each factor)

Factor 1: EDUCATION What is the optimum educa-cation required?	
Factor 2: EXPERIENCE What is the minimum period of experience which the average person would require?	
Factor 3: SUPERVISION Evaluate the degree of direc-tion or supervision which the job holder normally exercises	
Factor 4: DECISIONS Consider the responsibility of the job holder for various decisions	
	(Continuation not shown)

Figure 5.2 Job information form: questionnaire type

JOB INFORMATION FORM

(This form should be completed by the person holding the position.)

Name..

Job title..

Organization..

FOR SALARY ADMINISTRATION USE ONLY	
Job number	Job grade

Monthly/Weekly staff ....

Regular day work/Shift work....................................

Normal hours (excluding overtime)..............................

Approx. hours overtime to be worked per week...................

Description of duties: (Describe each duty clearly, defining the tasks which make up each duty. Start with the most time-consuming duties and finish with the minor duties. State whether the holder of this job directs or supervises the work of other employees and for what duties. In the column at the left state the approximate percentage of time normally spent on each duty.)

Percentage of time

(Signature of supervisor ....   Date ....

EDUCATION: What are the *minimum* technical, commercial or academic qualifications necessary for the proper performance of this work? For example, G.C.E./ O.N.C./H.N.C./University degree/etc. State subjects required.

EXPERIENCE: *In addition to the educational* qualifications defined above what *minimum* experience is essential before appointment to this job?

SUPERVISORY RESPONSIBILITY: State the number and categories of employees supervised by the holder of this job. Where a section or larger organization is supervised an organization chart must be attached.

JOBS SUPERVISED	No. IN CATEGORY	JOBS SUPERVISED	No. IN CATEGORY

ASSETS AND MATERIALS: For what plant, machinery, equipment, tools, stock, valuables or cash, is the job holder responsible? State approximate value.

CONTACTS: Describe the purpose and frequency of personal contacts with others both within and outside the Company.

PLANNING AND DEVELOPMENT: What policies, plans, procedures, equipment or standards is the job holder responsible for initiating, developing, or improving?

DECISIONS: What decisions may the job holder take without reference to higher authority?

SUPERVISION RECEIVED: Describe the nature and frequency of direction and/or supervision received by the job holder.

(Signature of Department Head).. Date................

mance standards expected forward play a part in indicating the man specification required. Chapter 10 on position grades and objectives provides more detail of this method and its applications.

Style

A standard style together with a standard format for the writing of job descriptions greatly simplifies subsequent interpretation and valuation.

Any authority evaluating or auditing a large number of job gradings would be greatly confused by haphazard individual job descriptions, but would find his task relatively straightforward if all the job information was presented in an identical format and style. Any series of laboratory experiments requires standardized laboratory conditions to exclude unknown variable factors. Although job evaluation is not scientific in the same sense, it is basically systematic and is similarly assisted by minimizing unknown variables arising from style and format differences.

Assuming that the format has already been established, the following notes provide a useful guide to standardized presentation of information. The job description should:

1   Give a clear but concise description of the whole job so that anybody can understand its purpose and content.
2   Describe each main duty clearly in a separate paragraph. Each task that goes to make up the duty should be shown logically in order. Start with the main or most important duties first.
3   When describing the duties that go to make up each duty consider the *What, How* and *Why* of it. *What* is the duty, *how* is it done and for *what reason* or end product. If this simple formula is always used in all descriptions, they will always be clear.
4   The style of writing should be crisp and clear. Use should be made of the third person, active present tense to start the description of each duty. All unnecessary words should be omitted.
5   Names of other jobs, organizations, plant and equipment

should start with capital letters to highlight their importance.

6 Have recorded against each main duty the percentage of total working time spent on that duty. Naturally, this will only be approximate, but it is a vital piece of information. For example, if a man is copying out information from one form to another for 95 per cent of his time and acting as Cashier for 5 per cent of his time, this gives an entirely different value to the job than if the percentages were reversed. The actual figures given are unlikely to be accurate and should be used only as a guide, when evaluating.

7 Indicate how much direction and supervision is both given and received.

Where the job holder directs other people, start off the duty as follows : 'Directs the work of a clerical section . . .'.

If he oversees the work of a group of manual workers this should be stated : 'Supervises a group of skilled Fitters . . .'.

Similarly, the amount of direction or supervision which the job itself requires can be indicated as follows : 'Under occasional direction from the General Foreman, supervises a small group of Machinists . . .'.

The above style is appropriate for the majority of staff jobs in a company. However, a more sophisticated style may be used as in Figs. 5.3–5.5 (job descriptions of a Secretary, an Engineering Section Head and a Division Finance Manager).

These examples show a variation in detail and format at different levels. However, individual company usage will inevitably lead to a great diversity of format and styles, of which these represent only a glimpse. Chapter 10 on Position Guides examines the more detailed statements of job objectives which may tie into correct business plans and provide a basis for individual appraisal.

For large, well planned organizations, particularly, the development of manuals of standard descriptions is gradually increasing in the United Kingdom. These manuals consist of full sets of descriptions for all basic jobs, descriptions which tend to be rather general in character in order to take departmental variation of, say, Records Clerks into account.

Internal publication of a manual on these lines would form a significant contribution to general acceptance of common job

Title: Secretary

Number: ...27. 5   *Grade:* 5

Division: ....

Reports to: Department Manager   *Date*........................

Summary:
To assist an executive in dealing with the routine business of his office; by dealing with his correspondence, typing and maintaining records.

Duties and responsibilities:
Records daily all incoming and outgoing correspondence. Distributes incoming mail to supervisor and/or other executives according to subject matter.

Takes shorthand notes from supervisor of correspondence, memoranda, minutes, etc., and of telephone or other verbal messages.

Transcribes shorthand notes and prepares letters, etc., for signature and mailing. May by arrangement sign for supervisor in his absence.

Prepares, collates and presents papers prior to requirement at meetings, interviews, etc. May make appointments for supervisor in his absence.

Maintains a record of all live correspondence, etc., and operates a follow-up file on overdue items, long-term appointments and items for review.

Makes all transport and accommodation reservations and obtains tickets as required. Maintains record of Personal Account expenses and deals with queries arising.

Supervises Shorthand Typist and/or Clerk Typist.

Plans and maintains comprehensive filing system.

Specification:
Educational standard: G.C.E. 'O' level.

Minimum experience: three years as Shorthand typist,
                      two years as Secretary.

Figure 5.3 Job description (of a Secretary)

Position: Section Head—Development Engineering.

Organization

Basic function:

To direct and co-ordinate the design and development and engineering of a major part of a Division's present and future product lines ensuring that the products are suitable to manufacture and competitive technically as well as in respect of quality and price.

Reports to: Chief Engineer.

Duties and responsibilities:

Supervises a large group or two or more smaller groups of engineering and related personnel in the design, development and engineering of a major part of a Division's present and future product lines.

Initiates designs from specifications and general layouts agreed by the Chief Engineer. Guides and co-ordinates subordinates in detail design, development and engineering required to achieve the objectives, which may include the technical and cost improvement of existing products and the development of future products to meet known or estimated market requirements.

Discusses periodically design in progress with senior production engineers to enhance the product's suitability for manufacture.

Directs the preparation and issue of technical information concerning the products to such as manufacturers and customers as necessary.

Represents the Division in committees set up for the exchange of technical information.

Contacts senior customer engineers to discuss specific technical problems, as necessary.

Figure 5.4 Job description (of an Engineering Section Head)

Job title: Finance Manager	*Group:* 2
Section:	*Job holder:* ....
Department: Finance	*Date:* ....
	Area: ....

Job summary:

Directing, supervising and co-ordinating the work of Finance Department; carrying out special studies; participating as member of management team; responsible for administration of Division; responsible to Division Manager.

Work performed:

Directs, supervises and co-ordinates the work of Finance Department staff in the following duties.

Accounts Section. The preparation of quarterly and final accounts; quarterly Operating Costs statements; forecasts of expenditure and profitability of sales; the calculation of selling price build-ups and other related work.

Cashier's Section. The receipt, safe-keeping and payment of funds; and the calculation and payment of salaries, wages and allotments.

Methods and Office Services Section. The investigation into and co-ordination of all clerical methods applied in the Area; all legal business relating to Division's property and operations, and the operation of all Office Services.

Audit Section. The planning and implementation of the Internal Audit Programme.

Private Accounts Office. The calculation and payment of Senior Staff Salaries; the maintenance of Pension and Provident Fund records, and any other accounting work of a private nature.

Receives all statements, returns and other documents of major importance prepared by his Department and scrutinizes for presentation and accuracy before approving.

Deals with frequent queries relating to Department's work from his Department Heads, from other departments of the Division, and from outside parties.

Attends management meetings to assist in deciding on policy matters, and keeps Division Manager informed on all major matters affecting the Division's finances.

Ensures that Division's financial policy is suitably implemented.

Maintains liaison with senior officers of local banks to facilitate Division's business.

Is responsible for the administration of his Department, including the welfare, discipline, training and career development of staff, makes reports on all his staff as and when required.

*Figure 5.5 Job description (of a
Finance Manager)*

titles for specific posts. This understanding is of considerable value in a multi-locational or multi-divisional structure in which there is any degree of internal movement (see also Chapter 6 on this subject).

Application to organization planning, career planning and succession

The function of salary administration, particularly of salary planning, is closely related to career planning, to succession planning, and to organization planning, which brings us back to the application of job information.

Organization planning has a number of facets, one of the most important of which is based on the analysis of job information and the development of optimum groupings of responsibilities, of optimum reporting relationships, and a minimum of overlap and duplication. Management organization planning on this basis, linked with the influence of management personalities, is one of the most complex and satisfying aspects of personnel work.

Analysis of job content and requirements against individual abilities provides a basis for training associated with career and succession planning.

This short summary has been included here for two reasons—to show briefly the application of job information to organization planning, and to show the close relationship between salary administration and other aspects of enlightened staff management.

Chapter 6

Job Evaluation and Grading

Job evaluation is a systematic procedure for analysing a group of jobs and establishing their value relationship one to another. However, so many different theories and systems have been evolved during the last few decades that the basic simplicity of the operation has been obscured by pseudo-scientific smoke-screens.

The major division is between

1   *Quantitative or points* systems, which attempt to measure relative values of jobs using scales based on chosen factors, generally using specialist evaluators, and

2   *Non-quantitative, job ranking schemes* which use management knowledge to assess one complete job against another, to determine relative value.

Quantitative systems such as *points evaluation* have become so elaborate and time consuming that in many cases they can only be established and maintained by large teams of experts and bring to mind a picture of a walnut being cracked by a steam-driven sledgehammer. To clear aside the smoke-screen and take a clear look at job evaluation, what are we seeking to achieve by its use? To establish the values and relationships between a group of jobs. Clearly, given normal industrial operating conditions, a study like this should be done as fast, as economically and as effectively as possible, and unless there is a large team readily available these criteria immediately rule out the quantitative evaluation systems.

This leaves non-quantitative systems such as the use of *grade level descriptions* and *job ranking* as the *recommended* alternatives, and so, having made our recommendation, we shall concentrate mainly on the use of these techniques throughout this book. However, it may also be helpful to describe in outline the use of points evaluation and factor comparison methods together with related operating problems for those who prefer, or have to use, such systems and this is done in this chapter.

Each of the great variety of job evaluation systems in general use today has its own exponents and supporters. Individual views are invariably biased towards individual experience and towards the requirements peculiar to the company interested in introducing job evaluation. This goes far deeper than merely building a scheme to fit the company. Rather it is a matter of choosing the method which will appear most attractive to the management of the company and most feasible in relation to the present skill of the evaluators, whoever they may be, and to the time available.

There are wide variations in the skills required for operating the different methods of job evaluation; in the knowledge and skill required from specialist staff, from managers and supervisors, from committees where these are used, and each of these attributes will be discussed in relation to each form of evaluation described in this chapter.

The evaluation system selected for operation in any organization is important, but not the sole reason for success or failure. In the hands of competent, experienced staff, successful operation of almost any system is possible, while inexperience is likely to ruin any method. The sections that follow examine each of the basic methods and discuss the characteristics which participating individuals must possess.

Grade level descriptions

The use of Grade Level Description for evaluating jobs is undoubtedly the simplest and fastest method of all, but unfortunately this method can usually be applied only to clerical and lower-grade technical jobs of a stereotyped nature with any degree of grading accuracy, as higher level jobs vary more widely in job content than can be covered by generalized descriptions. Basically, the method consists of deciding on the number of

Level	Typing	Clerical
5	Supervises a large typing pool, probably using audio equipment.	Directs and supervises the work of a Clerical Section. Carries out more complex work personally.
4	Supervises a small group of typists and assigns and checks their work. Carries out more complex work personally.	Carries out more complex clerical duties under infrequent direction only. May supervise the work of a few Clerks.
3	Carries out more complex typing work such as preparation, involved statements, under occasional supervision only.	Carries out a number of routine clerical tasks working under occasional supervision. May guide the work of a Junior Clerk.
2	Carries out routine copy typing working from a number of source documents. Works under frequent supervision and routine checks.	Carries out routine clerical work requiring some training and experience. Works under frequent supervision.
1	Carries out simple copy typing such as completing one or two simple forms, under constant supervision.	Carries out simple, routine clerical tasks such as operating duplicating machines, filing and sorting mail under constant supervision.

Figure 6.1   Grade level descriptions

grades or levels into which it is required to classify the jobs under study. Then, for each job family or sub-family, such as typing and secretarial posts in general and then, say, Typists' jobs in particular, a number of brief job summaries are prepared which clearly identify each level at which the job is performed (see Fig. 6.1).

Similarly, grade level descriptions covering all other jobs at each level are prepared and these are printed in sets for use by the staff who are to carry out the evaluation.

There are different methods of analysing and evaluating the jobs under study as was explained in Chapter 2. Either each employee can be asked to record a job description covering their own post, or evaluators in each department can work from their own personal knowledge of the jobs. In any case, each job description is compared with the relevant set of grade-level descriptions and the appropriate level or grade that approximates most to the actual duties and responsibilities is assigned. Finally, all jobs are slotted into a homogeneous grading structure which should subsequently be matched against current market rates in the form of competitive salary ranges.

The Institute of Office Management publication *Clerical Job Grading* which is widely used is essentially a form of 'defined level' job descriptions, using a series of six basic grades or levels which appear to have almost international acceptance and application.

Job ranking method

The ranking method of job evaluation is a simple method of job evaluation, but of all systems it requires the highest degree of professional skill from the Administrator and makes the greatest demand on management knowledge and ability.

Fundamentally, it consists of assessing the relative 'whole-job' values of a group of jobs and placing these in a rank order of relative importance. It accepts the impracticability of breaking jobs down into separate pieces which can be measured against a defined series of scales.

As with any method of evaluation it is preferable to work from job descriptions when carrying out a ranking study. However, if they are not available, or if only a small number of jobs are being ranked, it is still possible to carry out the exercise working from each manager's knowledge of the jobs in his organization, and from verbal descriptions of the jobs which he, or his subordinate supervisors, should easily be able to provide.

There are various ways of ranking jobs. The simplest method if you have job descriptions is to read all of them and then to

---

JOB RANKING FORM

Date......................   Number...............

Organization.....................   Location ....

............Dept. ....Section	............Dept. ....Section	............Dept. ....Section	............Dept. ....Section

Figure 6.2 Job ranking schedule – blank form

---

stack the papers physically in descending order of value. Where two or more jobs are considered to be of equal weight or value they can be clipped together. The next step would be to record the jobs in rank order on a form similar to that shown in Fig. 6.2.

Where there are no job descriptions, or where the stage described above is not considered necessary, the jobs can be listed immediately in descending order of value and jobs of approximately equal value bracketed together.

These procedures are followed section by section in a department, and rank order lists drawn up, as in Fig. 6.3. The next stage is to check across the lists of ranked jobs to line up those of approximately equal value in different sections of a department. This sounds more difficult than it is in practice. Good bench mark or key jobs which will help in this cross-alignment might be section head or foreman positions at the top and middle of

..............Dept. Purchasing Section	............Dept. Receiving Section	............Dept. Shop Section	............Dept. Clerical Section
Chief Buyer		Senior Foreman	
	Supervisor	Foreman	
Buyer	{ Chief Storekeeper Stock Control Supervisor	Chargehand	Clerical Supervisor
Assistant Buyer			Senior Clerk
			{ Clerk Shorthand Typist
	Records Clerk } Typist	Shop Clerk	Typist
			Junior Clerk

Figure 6.3   Job ranking schedule – partially completed

the ranking lists, 'first level' professional posts, and identical clerical posts at the lower levels. Once such similar 'weight' jobs have been identified, lines are drawn across the lists to group them together, which also starts the phase of forming separate levels or job grades.

To give a helpful definition of these grades or levels, we can say that all the jobs grouped at any one level are considered to be roughly equal in value, and that the jobs at any one level are considered to be clearly higher in value than the jobs in the next lower grade or level, but lower in value than the jobs in the next level above.

The exercise described above is carried out in each section and department of the company in conjunction with line managers, and ultimately the cross-correlation of jobs company-wide is carried out in co-operation with top management, including the functional directors who will be able to advise on the lining up of job gradings across the company within their own functions, particularly in a number of separate profit centres or operating divisions.

As the ranking study covers more and more company jobs it becomes possible to decide how many levels will be used in the company grading structure. This is a matter for individual decision, but we advise that the number of grades should initially be kept as low as is practicable and restricted to the number of clearly definable levels. Grading structures have an alarming habit of growing to accommodate 'special cases' but it is wise to start off with an effective, streamlined structure. About a dozen levels will usually be adequate in a major company, excluding the top management group which may either be covered by an extension to the structure, or by a separate range of grades.

The man who is responsible for the study should, as before, brief managers in the methods to be used, issue forms, advise and help continually on each phase of the work and generally co-ordinate everything. He will certainly have to help with the actual ranking operation, as some managers will not easily be able to separate jobs and job holders in their minds and will probably appreciate some tactful, unbiased advice on relative job values. When several section heads are brought in to assist a department manager with the ranking, arguments will probably develop over whose jobs should be highest. Some of the heat can be dispersed by an objective analysis of the jobs in question—this usually decides a logical rank order and cross-relationship.

A question which is always raised during a ranking study is, 'How can anyone possibly establish the grade relationships between say an Accountant and an Engineer?' Actually it is not as difficult as it sounds. Both are professional positions requiring a formal training and a qualification amounting to a university degree or the equivalent. The essential industry or work experience necessary since qualifying for each job can be compared, as can factors such as any supervision exercised in the current positions. In other words, the normal process of job analysis involving a study of the job descriptions and analysis of the specifications.

All jobs are susceptible of this same simple analysis and cross-comparison, and while speed of evaluation only comes with increasing experience of these techniques, competent supervisors and managers will be fully capable of taking factors such as these into account and saying definitely that one particular job is 'heavier-weight' than another, or that they are so close that the two positions should be equated.

The ranking of jobs in the specialist and supervisory position levels is more complex as a wider variety of factors have to be taken into account. However, the complexity and mix within any one department should not be too excessive for a department manager to cover. The correlation between a series of rankings for different departments across the company is normally carried out with some specialist assistance.

The head of a technical department will have to take into account the optimum education and training requirements for the various jobs under his command; weigh the relative supervisory responsibilities against the degree of responsibility for output of fundamental ideas required from a 'boffin'; consider the value of contacts—particularly customer contacts; take into account responsibility for assets, and assess the possible effect of decisions which the position holder may take; in these he is guided always by the Salary Administrator.

The factors which the Accountant and the Production Superintendent will take into account will be broadly similar to those of the Technical Manager, *but the relative importance of the factors varies substantially between functions.* At senior levels, the manager ranking the jobs of his department heads, and the Managing Director ranking the positions of his Directors, determine the rank order according to the relative weight of the contribution which the position holder is expected to make to the total management effort.

Top-level policy and such vague matters as the current bias on certain company activities clearly affect these rankings. A company going into a massive production expansion programme will require 'heavy-weight' production men able to handle the responsibility for planning and carrying out the expansion and

D

will tend to rate the production jobs above those of the market-ing people, who may have an easy selling job and be required to make relatively smaller contributions. But in tough market conditions a top-flight sales team is required which will tend to be ranked above a production team who may have an established and straightforward production line.

However, in each of the last-mentioned situations, the Pro-duction and Sales Directors might have been ranked equal; for example, in the former case, the responsibility of the Sales Director for identifying future trends such as more difficult markets and demands for changed products could clearly have a substantial effect on the company.

Today we can see the rise in importance of factors such as 'brawn' and 'willingness to do low-skilled or unpleasant work'— for example, in the case of some underground workers. It is this type of development which spells out so clearly the limitation of points schemes, for the factors to be used and the weightings to be given must be amended to ensure the end result continues to live with market realities. This continuing review and change of system provides the major reason for lack of credibility in points schemes, and is totally avoided in whole-job ranking.

Formal committees are rarely used in conjunction with the ranking method, although an informal committee or group of top executives, together with the specialist co-ordinating the operation, normally meets to thrash out the final correlation of senior jobs across the organization.

Once this is done maintenance of the structure becomes the responsibility of the specialist Administrators, acting for top executives. The day-to-day upkeep is, for the most part straight-forward, with new and changed jobs easily slotted into the established structure by comparison with gradings of similar or equivalent jobs. However, from time to time disputes will occur and if they cannot be resolved between the Salary Admini-strator and the local manager concerned they should be referred to the Personnel Director and, if necessary, ultimately to the Managing Director. In any dispute with a union over job evaluation, the use of factors and points can help remove the emotion from the grading of a job (or man!) by concentrating attention on comparison of facets of the jobs concerned.

Factor comparison

The factor comparison method of evaluation is a modified version of the ranking method which is considered by some Administrators to ease the way for participation by non-specialists. Factor comparison has two distinct sub-forms which might be said to represent steps away from the basic ranking system towards points systems of evaluation.

The basic forms of factor comparison consist of ranking the group of positions under review as in the basic ranking system, but in carrying out this ranking against a series of factors instead of in respect to the whole job.

For example, a scheme covering clerical jobs might use five factors :
1 Minimum education required.
2 Specialist training or experience required.
3 Importance of decisions which must be made.
4 Confidential nature of work.
5 Supervisory responsibility.

The individuals carrying out the ranking are asked to place the jobs under review in rank order for each of these factors. For example, a Secretary would probably rank above a Typing Pool Supervisor under the heading 'minimum education required', but obviously lower under 'supervisory responsibility'.

Each member of the team produces a simple table of rankings as shown in Fig. 6.4.

Normally, about three individuals should carry out this exercise and the results should subsequently be averaged under each factor. On the basis of the results, arbitrary conclusions of overall rank order may be drawn. With this method, it is more difficult to evaluate large numbers of jobs at one time. Usually 'bench-mark' jobs are selected from the various categories to be covered and these are ranked first. Once agreement is reached on the relationship between 'bench-mark' jobs, a series of further exercises to rank the remaining jobs completes the classification by slotting them into the established basic structure.

Committees are sometimes called for basic factor comparison evaluation, particularly for the initial ranking of 'bench-mark' jobs. The committee approach is said to provide opportunities for the discussion of differences of view, and to gain subsequent wide acceptance and appreciation of the basic ranking of the key jobs.

A variation of this method of evaluation is the weighting of the various factors—the assignment of a points value to each factor to enable the factor rankings to be converted to an overall arithmetic result. This arbitrary weighting has the same fundamental weakness, i.e. of appearing to produce accurate results

Job	(1) Educ.	(2) Training	(3) Decis.	(4) Confid.	(5) Sup.
Secretary	1	1	1	1	2
Typing Pool Supervisor	3	3	2	2	1
Billing Clerk	2	4	4	2	3
Punch Card Machine Operator	4	2	3	2	3

Figure 6.4   Factor comparison table

but without guaranteeing them, which is discussed below under the heading 'points systems'.

Finally, a disadvantage of ranking by factor comparison as compared with basic whole-job ranking is that the factors required for different types and levels of jobs can vary so much that comparisons have to be restricted to smaller ranges or groups of jobs. This results in a series of small disconnected structures rather than a complete structure covering a whole organization.

Business criteria evaluation for management posts

A technique which we have developed for evaluating management jobs or for comparing and validating the grading of senior posts can be termed 'Business or Functional Criteria Evaluation'. This is a form of factor comparison where the factors are for

	Div. 'A'	Div. 'B'	Div. 'C'
Turnover	£10 million	£4 million	£1.0 million
Assets	£6 million	£2 million	£0.5 million
No. of products	120	50	20
Complexity rating	Highly complex	Complex	Uncomplicated
No. of employees	1,000	600	200
Grade Z	General Manager		
Grade Y		General Manager	
Grade X			
Grade W			General Manager

Figure 6.5 Business criteria ranking

specific groups of senior positions, usually in one function at a time.

When considering gradings within a group of jobs such as general managers, or all the management jobs in a marketing organization, the basic procedure is to identify all the main criteria which are relevant to evaluation of the group of posts under review. We then assess the relevant level of each job

As per **Figure 6.5** — but weighted and scored

Criteria	Weighting	Div. 'A'	Div. 'B'	Div. 'C'
Turnover	£m × 5	50	20	5
Assets	£m × 5	30	10	3
No. of products	÷ 10	12	5	2
Complexity rating	1 to 10 scale	10	6	2
No. of employees	÷ 100	10	6	2
	Total points	112	47	14

Grade Z	General Manager	
Grade Y	General Manager	
Grade X		
Grade W		General Manager

Figure 6.6 Business criteria with weightings

against the criteria, either in ranked order, or, if preferred, against weighted scales for the criteria (see Figs. 6.5 and 6.6.). A simple weighting can be used to arrive at a points score as drawn up in Fig. 6.6. This is preferred by some Analysts and by less analytically-minded company managements. It is easy to develop, to use and to explain. With careful development, it can be quite accurate as a guide for arriving at appropriate job grades merely by reading off the grade from a points table as shown in Fig. 6.7.

Job grade	Points range
Z	76 –155
Y	36 – 75
X	16 – 35
W	5 – 15

Figure 6.7 Points table

We list, for the major functions, a selection of the business criteria likely to be most relevant. In operation, we have found it important to select no more than about five for any particular exercise, recognizing that this places some restriction on the range of positions tackled at one stage. Typical functional criteria, then, might be :

Marketing jobs Factors include total sales volume (value of units), UK sales, export sales, number in sales force, sophistication of marketing operation, number of products, complexity of products, share of market, quality of competition, etc.

Personnel posts Factors include number of staff, number of hourly employees, number of sites or factories, union problem rating, recruitment difficulty rating, growth or static situation, welfare or management orientation, sophistication of practice, etc.

Technical management jobs Factors could include the number and range of products, product complexity rating, pace of technological change, pace of product improvement, quality standards, number of qualified engineers, number of other employees, R&D budget.

Manufacturing management jobs These could be evaluated against value of goods produced or processed, number of products, value of inventory, complexity rating, number of employees, number of factories, geographic problems, employee relations rating.

Finance management jobs These positions would consider role sophistication, level of finance knowledge applied, budget standards, cost control standards, management accounting activity, use of newer techniques required, span of service, numbers of qualified and other subordinates, financial control up or down.

Checking management jobs against the above-mentioned criteria on prepared schedules is a very satisfactory way of selling the final job gradings to a Managing Director or the Board. This type of quantitative approach has a definite acceptability to top level executives without falling into the trap of pseudo-science by attempting to measure the unmeasurable.

Points systems

Points systems are probably the most widely used method of evaluation in the United Kingdom (although this is certainly no longer so in the United States), and they are also by far the most heavily criticized.

These systems attempt to bring science and accurate measurement to a situation in which the relevant criteria, factors, are not always clearly defined, and scales of measurement can only be arbitrarily established. Blind faith in the accuracy of any points system of evaluation is clearly and utterly misplaced. However, intelligent application and manipulation of the better schemes by skilled and experienced Salary Administrators can produce acceptable results.

Like the factor comparison system discussed previously, these

Figure 6.8 *A points system of evaluation**

Under this system, each post is evaluated against each of the following twelve factors, and points scored against each factor are accumulated towards a total number of points. As grades are linked to non-overlapping ranges of points, the total number of points determines the job grade.

FACTOR 1. EDUCATION: WEIGHTING 12 PER CENT

What is the optimum education required to perform the job being evaluated?

Degree		Points
1.	Ability to read and write simple written messages and instructions; to maintain simple records, and to carry out simple arithmetic calculations	8
2.	Ability to write routine letters and reports; to carry out routine clerical work including shorthand and typing, and to carry out routine calculations including decimals and fractions	17
3.	Ability to write letters and reports on a number of subjects, to carry out more complex calculations, and to prepare statistical statements	25
4.	Ability to carry out work requiring good practical knowledge of subject such as accountancy, statistics and business *or* some technical training in scientific subject	34
5.	Through knowledge of subject such as book keeping, costing; *or* technical school training, or its equivalent, to O.N.C. level	43
6.	Knowledge of a science to university degree level (or equivalent)	51
7.	Post graduate training in a specialized field. Ability to carry out or direct creative work	60

FACTOR 2. EXPERIENCE REQUIREMENT: WEIGHTING 16 PER CENT

What is the minimum period of experience which the average person would require in addition to the educational requirement stated in the Education Factor (no. 1)?
This period should be the minimum of unduplicated experience.

Period		Points
1.	Up to 1 month's experience	10
2.	Over 1 month's and up to 3 months' experience	20
3.	Over 3 months' and up to 6 months' experience	30
4.	Over 6 months' and up to 1 year's experience	40
5.	Over 1 year's and up to 2 years' experience	50
6.	Over 2 years' and up to 5 years' experience	60
7.	Over 5 years' and up to 10 years' experience	70
8.	Over 10 years	80

*This system, in line with most other points systems, is not intended to cover top management posts.

FACTOR 3.   SUPERVISORY RESPONSIBILITY: WEIGHTING 10 PER CENT

Evaluate the degree of direction or supervision which the job holder normally exercises.

Degree   *Points*

1. Little or no supervisory responsibility other than showing others how to perform duties   8

2. Supervises a small group of hourly rated employees *or* one or two clerical staff   16

3. Supervises large groups of hourly rated employees *and/or* a small group of clerical or junior technical staff   25

4. Supervises a section of very large numbers of hourly rated employees and/or groups of staff including some of professional level   33

5. Directs the work of a large department including senior professional staff   41

6. Directs the work of a division or a major functional department of the company   50

FACTOR 4.   DECISIONS: WEIGHTING 10 PER CENT

Consider the responsibility of the job holder for taking decisions which affect company operations, whether by recommending action, making operating decisions in accordance with established plans and standards, or making operating decisions in new situations.

Importance   *Points*

1. Minor decisions   7

2. Frequent decisions in accordance with established policy   14

3. Frequent recommendations or decisions not clearly covered by established policy or previous decisions   21

4. Occasional decisions leading to a moderate change in company operation   29

5. Frequent decisions leading to a moderate change in company operations   36

6. Occasional decisions leading to an important change in company operations   43

7. Frequent decisions leading to an important change in company operations   50

FACTOR 5.   SUPERVISION RECEIVED: WEIGHTING 6 PER CENT

Consider the degree and frequency of direction or supervision which the job holder receives.

Degree   *Points*

1. Receives regular and routine assignments of work which is performed under constant supervision; work and performance is regularly checked   6

2. Works in accordance with standard practice under occasional supervision, referring queries to supervisor; work receives some check — 12

3. Employee plans and arranges own work after direction and main work programme outlined; refers to his superior non-routine complex problems only, and policy decisions — 18

4. Employee carries out work within broad policy guide; receives occasional direction only; refers to superior only for interpretation of policy, work requires ability to think and original approach to problems, may have to make decisions within policy guide lines — 24

5. Policy-making role, without supervision and under infrequent direction only sets own standards of output and quality of work — 30

FACTOR 6. WORK COMPLEXITY AND ADAPTABILITY: WEIGHTING 8 PER CENT.

Consider the complexity of the work and the degree of adaptability required from the job holder.

Degree		Points
1.	Simple routine work with limited variety	8
2.	A range of routine activities, not involving sudden changes of work	16
3.	A range of activities, with periodic spells of sudden changes of work, or work requiring a wide range of skills but not involving sudden changes	24
4.	Work requiring a wide range of skills and the ability to make sudden changes to meet demands	32
5.	Work requiring a wide range of skills, and involving continual changes from one activity to another	40

FACTOR 7. RESPONSIBILITY FOR ASSETS AND MATERIALS: WEIGHTING 9 PER CENT

Consider the responsibility of the job holder for the safe keeping of equipment, stock, materials, cash, etc., to ensure that loss, or damage beyond normal wear or obsolescence does not occur. Where variation in value is substantial, the value used to calculate points should be the average level.

Degree		Points	Degree		Points
1.	Up to £1,000	4	6.	£25,000–£50,000	27
2.	£1,001–£2,500	9	7.	£50,000–£100,000	31
3.	£2,501–£5,000	13	8	£100,000–£250,000	36
4.	£5,001–£10,000	18	9.	£250,000–£500,000	40
5.	£10,000–£25,000	22	10.	£500,000–£1,000,000	45

FACTOR 8. CONTACTS: WEIGHTING 8 PER CENT

Examine the frequency and importance of the job holder's contacts, both internally and externally.

		Points
1.	Few contacts apart from immediate associates	8
2.	Routine contacts with people up to own level in other sections or departments *or* in outside organizations to obtain or provide information	16
3.	Contacts with more senior people both internally and externally to obtain or provide information	24
4.	Contacts with more senior people within the company to advise or to obtain decisions *or* external contacts with senior people where it is necessary to put over company views, or to influence decisions	32
5.	Important contacts at all levels to advise or to obtain decisions or agreements for the company	40

FACTOR 9. RESPONSIBILITY FOR RECORDS AND REPORTS: WEIGHTING 6 PER CENT

What responsibility is involved for the maintenance and preparation of records and reports?

Degree		Points
1.	Maintains a simple filing system involving only the selection and replacement in files; sorting of mail and simple copying of material	5
2.	Maintains routine records and prepares simple statements	10
3.	Maintains a number of routine records, and prepares a few statements *and/or* maintains more complex records *and/or* prepares an occasional simple routine report	15
4.	Maintains a variety of records, and prepares several different kinds of statements *and/or* maintains a number of complex records *and/or* prepares a number of simple reports *and/or* occasional complex reports	20
5.	Maintains complex records and prepares periodic complex reports	25
6.	Prepares a wide range of complex reports on non-routine subjects	30

FACTOR 10. RESPONSIBILITY FOR CONFIDENTIAL INFORMATION: WEIGHTING 6 PER CENT

Evaluate the job holder's responsibility for handling confidential matters and material.

1.	Little or no access to confidential material	7
2.	Access to confidential material such as employees' salaries, records, etc.	15
3.	Occasional access to major confidential material disclosure of which could cause embarrassment or loss to company	22
4.	Constant access to highly confidential material disclosure of which could severely affect the company	30

FACTOR 11. PHYSICAL SKILL: WEIGHTING 5 PER CENT

Consider the extent to which some physical skill is required on the work.

Degree		Points
1.	Low degree, such as is found in most clerical posts	5
2.	Moderate degree, used for some part of the working day, such as typing skill required 50 per cent of her time by a Clerk Typist	10
3.	Moderate degree, used throughout the working day: Typist, Accounting Machine Operator, Draughtsman	15
4.	High degree of skill, used for part of the working day	20
5.	High degree of skill, used throughout the working day: Commercial Artist, etc.	25

FACTOR 12*. WORKING CONDITIONS: WEIGHTING 4 PER CENT

Consider the working conditions which the job holder is exposed to:

1.	Normal office/factory conditions	5
2.	Above average fumes, or noise, or heat, etc.	10
3.	Excessive amount of fumes, noise or heat	15
4.	Dangerous working conditions requiring special care at all times	20

---

*This factor should not normally influence the grading of a post but some special payment may be made to cover certain conditions (especially items 3 and 4).

systems also involve the use of a series of factors against which the requirements of individual jobs are assessed. The number of factors varies in individual plans from three up to sixty or more, with an average of about twelve.

Each factor is assigned a weighting according to its considered importance. The various levels or degrees within the factor are then defined and values given to these levels. These values may be in the form of an arithmetic or geometric progression, or some less orderly sequence. However, the defined steps between levels are unlikely to be in even units. In operation, the range of steps actually used within the various factors often varies so much that the simplest analysis will show how the carefully calculated factor weightings have no great validity in operation. This is the real problem with points systems—that it is difficult, if not impossible, to develop a set of scales and values which can bear even the shallowest study.

However, this type of evaluation may suit the requirements of some companies, and there is no reason why, accepting the limitations, it should not be used. Reasonable scales of points which produce a logical picture when applied to a wide variety of jobs should produce an acceptable pattern across the entire company. But the proof of the results is to be found by checking against a *ranking of bench-mark jobs*.

This system has the advantage in certain circumstances that unskilled line participation can to some extent be reduced and people with limited training can be used to collect and evaluate job information. Periodic reviews of factor weightings are essential to incorporate changes in relative market values of different job families.

One of the better schemes in use in this country is described in Fig. 6.8.

Points to grades

Figure 6.8 covers a full set of factors in a points evaluation system. Each job is 'processed' through these factors, scoring points according to the requirements of the job against each one. The total number of points accumulated for each job is then used to determine the grade, each of which has a points range which is separate and non-overlapping. These phases are des-

Factor	(1) Weighting %	(2) Maximum points (weighting x 5)	(3) Number of degrees	(4) Points intervals— Maximum points Number of degrees
1. Education	12	60	7	8–9
2. Experience requirement	16	80	8	10
3. Supervisory responsibility	10	50	6	8–9
4. Decisions	10	50	7	7–8
5. Supervision received	6	30	5	6
6. Work complexity	8	40	5	8
7. Responsibility for assets	9	45	10	4–5
8. Contacts	8	40	5	8
9. Responsibility for records	6	30	6	5
10. Responsibility for confidential information	6	30	4	7–8
11. Physical skill	5	25	5	5
12. Working conditions	4	20	4	5
Totals:	100	500		

Figure 6.9   Evolution of points value

cribed in detail in Fig. 6.8. However, initially, there are the preliminaries of selecting factors to be used and the allocation of weighting.

We believe that the selection of factors is essentially a personal thing, and certainly the choice will be peculiar to the individual organization, conforming to its traditions and methods. We would only advise a critical examination of the selected list to ensure a reasonable balance and wide coverage of the various aspects of job content. It is easy to slip into the fault of covering one principal factor under half a dozen 'different' headings.

Once the factors have been selected, the next step is to allocate weightings. This is again an individual and arbitrary operation. So wide is the potential range of factors and variation in weightings that we can only advise a critical appraisal of the relationships between the factors and weightings to ensure that they are logical.

A sensible approach is to think in terms of 100 units to be divided up in weightings. These can always be expanded subsequently in order to achieve the selected magnitude of points, for example, multiplied by five to extend the points range to 500.

The total points for each factor should then be divided by the number of degrees in the factor in order to produce an arithmetic points progression through the factor range.

The stages for the system described in Fig. 6.8 can be tabulated as set out in Fig. 6.9.

Evaluation procedure

The procedure that is generally followed for evaluating jobs using a points system is based on the following principles.

Job descriptions and job specifications (see Figs. 2.1 and 2.2) are obtained for the jobs under study. These are carefully studied together with organization charts which show the reporting relationships between all the positions. Each job is evaluated factor by factor and the appropriate degree of each factor is recorded in a factor analysis sheet (Fig. 6.10). Some Job Analysts record brief notes to account for their factor ratings.

The points value of the degree assigned in each case is recorded on the evaluation schedule—the values are normally printed

Date: ....   Job number:...............

Factor	Degree	Points
1. Education:		
2. Experience:		
3. Supervisory responsibility:		
4. Decisions:		
5. Supervision received:		
6. Work complexity:		
7. Responsibility for assets:		
8. Contacts:		
9. Responsibility for records:		
10. Confidential:		
11. Physical:		
12. Working conditions:		
Total:		

*Intangible rating   High ....

                         Med. ....

                         Low ....

*Note: This factor covers such requirements as personality, dealing with person-
        nel problems, security, etc., not fully covered by other factors.

Figure 6.10   Factor analysis sheet

alongside each degree. The points scored against all the factors are totalled for each job and the total points rating recorded at the bottom of the factor rating sheet.

After all the jobs in the study have been evaluated and, if that has been done by a group of evaluators, after the final points ratings have been determined, a check is made on the validity of the ratings by recording all the ratings on a factor comparison sheet (see Fig. 6.11). Jobs can either be grouped by section and departments, or alternatively by job families, e.g. with all the finance jobs or all the engineering jobs on one sheet. A cross-check is made both on the ratings horizontally as well as vertically. By this it is meant that the ratings are compared with each job, job by job, particularly to see that there is a logical relationship in the ratings between similar jobs as well as jobs differing in seniority in the chain of command. For example, if it is found that a number of factors have been rated higher for one job than for the job immediately above it in seniority, both the jobs should be checked and if necessary re-evaluated in case some of the factor ratings have been inaccurate.

Similarly, if the ratings are studied factor by factor disparities in evaluation can easily be noted and checked. This sheet also provides a basis for all subsequent additions to the list of posts, which can then be ranked under each factor against previous decisions. After this verification, the next stage will depend on whether it is a follow-up check on an existing classification system with an existing grading structure.

Proving an initial study

Taking the case of an initial study, once the selected jobs have been 'processed', it will be necessary to decide how many grades are required to cover the jobs under review. This in turn is associated with the type of salary ranges and amount of overlap between each range which is required (see Chapter 8 on Salary Structure).

Assume that we require eight grades of jobs to keep the example very simple and that we have arbitrarily selected a range of 500 points.

We require, say, a logical arithmetic progression of points ranges through the eight grades, and this will be provided with-

Job number	Job title	Factor ratings												Total points	Intangible rating	Job grade	
		Education 1	Experience 2	Supervisory responsibility 3	Decisions 4	Supervision received 5	Work complexity 6	Responsibility for assets 7	Contacts 8	Responsibility for records 9	Confidential 10	Physical 11	Working conditions 12			Present	Evald.

Figure 6.11 Factor comparison form

in the 500 total points, i.e. 120, 175, 230, 285, 340, 395, 450, 500.

These figures become the maxima of the points ranges, so that we have the following table :

Grade	Points range	Grade	Points range
C	83–120	G	286–340
D	121–175	H	341–395
E	176–230	I	396–450
F	231–285	J	451–500

The points ranges might have been calculated using a geometric progression, if similar progressions had been used for the points spread for each factor.

Some modification may prove necessary, either to factors, factor intervals, weightings or points ranges, after trial runs with bench-mark jobs. However, this summary explains a method of arriving at a complete operational points system of evaluation. An excellent aid to this stage is a list of all posts in descending order of points values, see Fig. 6.12.

Points spreads which have been calculated for each job grade are marked off on the descending order of points list and the jobs thus allocated to each grade are studied to see that they do indeed 'fit' at this level in relation to other jobs in the grade. Border-line job ratings and allocations to grades should be examined with particular care to ensure they are slotted into the appropriate grade.

From this graded list, job classification schedules, as shown in Fig. 6.13, can now be drawn up for presentation to management.

New jobs should be evaluated in the same manner and fitted into the points lists as a check to ensure that these fit with the other jobs at the revaluated grade level. Equally, when the grading of a job which has already been evaluated is challenged it should be re-evaluated, preferably by different evaluators, and ranked against jobs with similar points values.

Job number	Job title	Points total	Grade	Remarks
2.00	Sales Manager	456	J	
3.00	Chief Engineer	454	J	
4.00	Chief Accountant	442	I	
5.00	Production Superintendent	420	I	
6.01	Senior Personnel Officer	390	H	
3.05	Senior Engineer	382	H	
3.11	Group Leader (Design)	378	H	
3.12	Group Leader (Development)	378	H	
2.11	Senior Sales Officer	350	H	—Borderline case, may be grade 'G'
4.11	Accountant—General	334	G	
3.24	Engineer—Design	320	G	
2.23	Publicity Officer	315	G	
5.21	General Foreman	308	G	
4.23	Internal Audit Officer	300	G	
6.27	Personnel Officer	295	G	
5.25	Foreman—Assembly	282	F	—Technical graduate— market rate may dictate grading.
2.26	Salesman	275	F	
5.33	Buyer	260	F	
5.27	Foreman—Shop	258	F	
3.34	Assistant Engineer	245	F	
5.28	Foreman—Process	240	F	
6.34	Personnel Assistant	238	F	
5.31	Chargehand	226	E	
4.36	Audit Clerk	218	E	
3.42	Technical Assistant	204	E	
2.43	Customer Service Clerk	188	E	
6.43	Secretary	180	E	
5.42	Progress Chaser	168	D	
3.44	Technical Clerk	159	D	—Title misleading— mainly clerical work
5.43	Assistant Buyer	158	D	
4.44	Accounts Clerk	144	D	
2.46	Statement Typist	125	D	
6.44	Personnel Records Clerk	123	D	
5.44	Shop Clerk	115	C	
4.46	Copy Typist	110	C	

Figure 6.12   List of jobs in descending order of points value

	Grade J	Grade I	Grade H	Grade G	Grade F	Grade E	Grade D	Grade C
Finance:		Chief Accountant		Accountant. Internal Audit Officer		Audit Clerk	Accounts Clerk	Copy Typist
Production:		Production Superintendent		General Foreman	Foreman. Buyer	Chargehand	Asst. Buyer. Progress Chaser	Shop Clerk
Marketing:	Sales Manager		Senior Sales Officer	Publicity Officer	Salesman	Customer Service Clerk	Statement Typist	
Engineering:	Chief Engineer		Senior Engineer. Group Ldr.	Engineer	Assistant Engineer	Technical Assistant	Technical Clerk	
Personnel:			Senior Personnel Officer	Personnel Officer	Personnel Assistant	Secretary	Personnel Records Clerk	Copy Typist
Points spread for each grade	451–500	396–450	341–395	286–340	231–285	176–230	121–175	83–120

Figure 6.13 Job classification schedule

Follow-up study

When an existing job classification structure has become invalid
due to many changes in the job structure, or through lack of
maintenance, a different procedure is usually carried out.

The jobs are evaluated in the same manner as explained above
and points ratings determined. These ratings can be plotted on a
scattergraph against the existing grades (see Fig. 6.14). A line

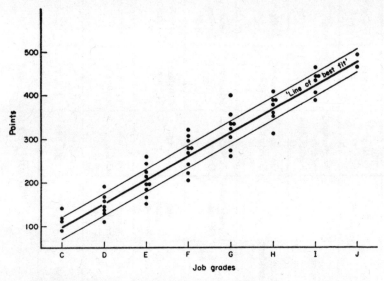

*Figure 6.14   Scattergraph of points ratings
plotted against grades, showing 'line of
best fit'*

of 'best fit' is drawn visually through the scatter plots and minimum and maximum lines drawn to show the points spreads for
the different grades. Using this technique, jobs falling above and
below their appropriate points spreads can be identified visually
if each plot is numbered and reassigned to evaluations and
review.

The technique of preparing a descending order of points list
can again be used equally successfully, but many evaluators

prefer the use of a scattergraph as a visual aid when discussing ratings with management.

In either method, points spreads are established and the gradings of new or changed jobs are established subsequently against these ranges. More complex analyses of points relationships can be carried out, including calculation of the line of best fit by the method of least squares. However, for our purpose this is rather overdoing things, and visual lines of best fit save a lot of time and are just as meaningful.

Operating notes—points systems

Some snags which many practitioners of points evaluation encounter are as follows. In evaluating jobs with a high personality factor, such as Salesmen, Personnel posts and Public Relations Officers, the use of routine factors only can lead to very low gradings. This is because the personality factor is not fully covered. One practical answer is to include an extra factor for such an 'intangible' and to apply it as an extra weighting for jobs of this kind—as one of the adjustments needed to make points evaluation work.

The local market rate of each job is really the main criterion of where it should be graded. Evaluators must be guided by this simple economic law and should not attempt to grade jobs purely academically, based on the actual points ratings. For example, the job of Comptometer Operator may fall very low in the grading structure on its theoretical points score, but it is far wiser to employ a grading which guarantees a salary high enough to retain people performing this job. This salary level would recognize the high demand related to small supply.

The evaluation of jobs by the 'points' method requires some basic training in this technique. There are so many traps inherent in this type of evaluation that the uninitiated will inevitably spring one or two of them. The most dangerous trap is, incidentally, a calm feeling of confidence that the system, being quantitative, is arithmetically foolproof, and that therefore that it is impossible to go wrong. Nothing could be further from the truth! It is essential to review the factors and weighting regularly.

If trained evaluators are not available the second-best alternative is to appoint a high-calibre member of the personnel organization to be responsible for the whole operation, and for this person to seek advice from people in other companies who are always happy to talk about their schemes .

Operating notes—general

The following notes still apply to points systems principally, but are more general in content.

If the study is very large there will inevitably be a need for further staff to obtain job information and to evaluate jobs. Whoever the people selected may be, they should come under the control and direction of the person responsible for the study. At all costs the temptation to form 'committees of experts' drawn from all departments should be avoided. If anything is guaranteed to snarl up the entire operation permanently, it is the committee approach. The simple reason for this appears to be partisan jealousies and personality clashes, and the more senior the members of the committee, the tougher the problem. Setting time limits for the evaluation of each job is no answer to this problem, for one or more committee members may refuse to accept the other members' ratings of jobs in their own department. The only solution in practice is to have completely impartial evaluators.

Before the main evaluation study is undertaken it is wise for all the evaluators to carry out a sample evaluation run on a small number of varied jobs to check the correlation of rating results. Quite often one of the raters may have a strong but possibly unconscious bias in favour of one or more factors, or one department's jobs. If this is discovered before the main evaluation a decision can be taken as to whether the rater should be changed, or whether the bias can be corrected. Some people tend initially to rate consistently high or low, and if they are unable to remedy this attitude it is definitely preferable for them to drop out of the evaluation phase of the study at least.

It is axiomatic that any job classification study must be carefully planned in advance, and then carried out as fast as humanly possible to avoid large collections of job data and evaluation becoming outdated due to organization changes. This is easy to write but much more difficult to ensure in practice.

The individual or team carrying out the study will have to contend at some time with open hostility, inter-office politics, strong-man pressure treatment and downright apathy and lack of interest. Having said that, and painted the blacker side of the picture, it can only be recommended that these occurrences be looked on merely as interesting and challenging problems (as indeed they are), but they can waste an awful lot of time. This, again, merely highlights the need to plan and programme every phase of the study, and to maintain the time-table at all costs.

When the main study is completed, it is a helpful move to return copies of completed job descriptions and specifications to department managers and to persuade them of the need to keep the job information up to date by notifying the study leader of any organization or job changes. A procedure should be planned and introduced for maintaining the job classification structure accurate and up to date, otherwise all the value of the original study will be lost. This may consist of nothing more elaborate than an annual check with each department to pick up any job changes, and this will probably suffice. However, at best the changes in classification, and the initial classification of new jobs, should be dealt with at the time they occur.

Profile method of job evaluation

An evaluation technique which has been in use in the USA for a considerable time and which is now finding increased favour in the United Kingdom is generally known as the Profile System of job evaluation. It is used mainly for evaluating high-level staff and management jobs.

Basically it is a 'points' system but is distinguished by the apparently small number of factors employed, often only three. These factors, however, are multi-dimensional in that having made a decision on, say the amount of knowledge a job calls for (shown on a vertical scale, see Fig. 6.15), the experience rating for the job (shown on a horizontal scale), then has to be read off. Where the degrees of the two factors meet, a points score for that overall factor then has to be read off. This is often way up in the hundreds due to the weighting system employed.

As in many other evaluation systems, if this approach helps

the person concerned to think about the job and to analyse it in relation to other jobs, thus arriving at an appropriate grade or salary range, then it has achieved its objective—to grade and price the job in relation to other company jobs under study. The system is just as subjective as any other and has no particular

Knowledge \\ Experienc e	1–2 yrs	2–4 yrs	4–8 yrs	8–12 yrs	Over 12 yrs
1. Good basic education without specialization.	10	20	40	80	160
2. Proficiency in a technical subject without a professional qualification.	20	40	80	160	320
3. Professional qualification in a single science or business field.	40	80	160	320	640
4. Higher professional qualification. Expert recognized knowledge in one or more scientific or specialized managerial fields.	80	160	320	640	1280
5. Complete professional knowledge of scientific and/or management function. Recognized authority on his subjects.	160	320	640	1280	2560

Figure 6.15 Profile method of know-how

magic. Probably the Business Criteria approach described earlier is more objective and meaningful to top business executives.

Time span

The time-span concept was evolved by Dr Elliot Jaques in the course of his work on the Glacier Project. He found an interesting relationship between the time which is allocated by a supervisor or manager to a subordinate for the completion of assignments, and the pay level which the individual instinctively considered fair for the work he was doing.

Scepticism at the apparent simplicity of the concept plus the considerable difficulty of assessing time-spans in most industrial organizations had held back general acceptance, particularly from those working in this field. Accurate measurement of time-span is fundamental if the concept is to be used.

As with other forms of evaluation, time-span is measured by examining each job in detail, initially with the immediate supervisor and subsequently with the job holder and with the manager two levels above. The longest time allowed for any single assignment within the job is identified and registered as the time-span of the post. Where the job consists of a series of individual assignments allocated singly, the measurement is slightly different, being the longest period from assignment of a task to the point where the results are reviewed.

The influence of a single factor which appears to be only a small part of the total job may determine the time-span: for example, training a senior subordinate may be assigned 18 months while no other assignment is allowed over 12 months.

Job classification schedules

The results of any job evaluation exercise, regardless of the methods used to carry out the study, must ultimately be presented in an easy to read and use form which can be distributed to appropriate managers and personnel staff. The most common form of presentation is the Job Classification Schedule.

These overall schedules of job grades are developed as the master documents in salary administration, and show, on a large chart, a grid with job grades on one axis and organizational units on the other, on which all graded posts are officially recorded. Fig. 6.13 shows a typical job classification schedule, as used by a major company.

These schedules are 'published' to appropriate members of management. The complete picture is prepared in a brochure for top management and, for middle and junior management staff, extracts covering the relevant parts of the organization for which they are responsible.

Personnel staff, such as Recruitment Officers, normally have access to these schedules for the range of jobs they administer, but in industry these would exclude levels more senior than their own, and invariably exclude their own department also. Within the personnel department, only the Chief Personnel Executive and the Salary Administrator would normally have copies of the complete set of schedules.

Participation in evaluation

The major factors determining which method of evaluation should be used in an organization are dependent on the often prior decisions of allowable cost, on how quickly the exercise is to be completed and who is to participate in the study. A group of two or three specialists with a minimum of line management aid are unlikely to be able to get through 5000 staff positions in a year using points evaluation, but points evaluation might be the choice for a group of untrained evaluators who are to use a 'scientific' approach through a whole series of evaluating committees, and need to achieve common standards.

Let us examine the possible participants and the parts they may play.

The *Consultant* often plays a part in introducing a new scheme, particularly in smaller organizations which cannot justify the employment of a full-time Salary Administrator, or even a Personnel Officer, of their own. Consultants rarely have a permanent interest in a company and are concerned with selling a 'packeted' salary administration plan done up as glossily as the company purse will stand. While many excellent schemes have been developed and introduced by consultancy firms, many others have been gimmicky, thoughtless plans which reflect lack of appreciation of the subject, or any understanding and training (say where a scheme is developed and introduced by a Recuitment Specialist), or even sheer lack of interest beyond obtaining the contract.

If consultants are used it is advisable to make sure that the individual consultant concerned has some relevant knowledge and experience, and it is recommended that a senior member of the organization buying the scheme should be assigned to participate as fully as possible in its development and introduction, ultimately taking it over when it is fully implemented, thus ensuring continuity and an adequate understanding of the structure, its operation and periodic updating.

Effective training for the individual selected should be arranged and incorporated into any contract signed. It may also be worth while adding a 'maintenance' contract for three or five years as a form of guarantee in the event of difficulties arising in operation.

The *Specialist Salary Administrator* is now to be expected in any organization with 1000 or more salaried staff.

The specialist will usually be an individual with varied personnel, and possibly other, experience in addition to having at least five years' experience covering all aspects of salary administration in organizations with sound, modern salary policies. At the time of writing, such organizations are still in a minority in the United Kingdom and are often predominantly companies with strong American links. It follows that experienced Salary Administrators are also rare. Limited experience in a small organization or in an organization with poor policies or uninterested management is not a sound background for developing new schemes.

The Salary Administrator is a company man, part of the personnel organization, and reports direct to the top Personnel Executive. In a subsidiary organization, the Salary Administration Officer would probably report to the Local Personnel Manager.

His responsibility would minimally cover the development of salary administration policy, on a company or local basis, the development of job and salary structures, the training of managers and supervisors in the administrative policies and procedures, and the audit and control of salary changes within the policy. The various aspects of this responsibility are fully covered in this book and there is no need to expand here beyond commenting that the right person in this position should have the confidence and respect of management in planning individual salaries. Otherwise, the function would be reduced almost to a clerical level.

The *Job Analyst* is a form of trainee Salary Administrator, concerned almost wholly with one part of the total picture.

Often a man of high intelligence but limited experience, he is frequently learning the rudiments of job structure as a preliminary to moving into the wider aspects of the personnel function, either in salary administration or elsewhere.

The real responsibility for salary administration lies not with the specialists but with *Management*. The manager may be advised, and may even have his limits set for him, but he must make his own decisions regarding the individuals for whom he is responsible. In other words, he must manage!

The manager's responsibility clearly goes beyond the administration of his staff's salaries. The immediately associated activities of planning the evolution of the organizations which are his responsibility, and the development of employees to fill the positions which are created or fall vacant, lead on to planning the progress of each individual's salary. In all this, the decisions on the shape and size of the structure, the people to fill it and the individual salaries to be paid are the manager's responsibility.

At a lower level, the *Supervisor* and other middle management staff have similar, but obviously lesser, responsibilities.

The *Individual Staff Employee* does not play a major part in the administration of his own salary. He will be expected from time to time to provide detailed information on the make up of his job to help management ensure that they are paying him a realistic salary for the basic position he fills. He may also participate by raising a query concerning his pay level—by pointing out to his supervisor or manager that he would be paid a higher figure by company 'X'; or that he considers that the relationship between his own salary and the salaries of 'certain other people doing the same job' is unreasonable. By these queries, the individual employee may draw attention to those suspected or unnoticed minor anomalies which develop for a multitude of reasons in all organizations and can be easily checked and corrected before they get out of hand.

The part that *Trade 'Unions* should play in evaluation has changed rapidly in recent years. The role they wish to play, and are increasingly playing in industry as well as in national and local government and the nationalized industries, is set out in the earlier chapter on salary administration and the trade unions.

As we get further into the era of greater participation, the trade union role as representatives of staff who are participating in the activity of evaluating their own jobs is bound to lead to changes in the approach to evaluation. After all, participation involves taking into account the other party's views on how the evaluation should be done and the factors and weightings which they consider to be relevant.

This situation may create its own problems, for unsophisticated involvement may lead first and foremost to a system of classification and evaluation which is simple, clearly defined and acceptable to the representatives. These considerations throw heavy limitations on any evaluation scheme and sometimes result in the use of inadequate plans to meet the essential criteria. For example, much of the Civil Service grading gives undue emphasis to academic qualifications, years of experience and service, and tends to provide man grades rather than job grades. This sort of inflexibility may lead to very wide divergencies in the real weight of work which identically graded individuals with similar basic qualifications may do.

Summarizing the above, *Top Management* play the role of policy makers, determining with the aid of their advisers which type of evaluation is most suited to the specific requirements of their own organization. The quality of the advice, and most particularly the breadth of understanding and experience behind the advice given at the initial stage, and at all subsequent times when the scheme is reviewed, will substantially influence the success or failure of the plan.

The extent of participation by other parties is dependent on the requirements of the overall plan, and within these requirements the willingness to participate of all other individuals concerned depends to a great extent on their handling by the Administrators controlling the plan.

National grading structure

The variation in approach and style of Salary Administration in different companies and industries presents the major problem for any attempt to achieve national salary equity. It is theoretically possible, as well as socially desirable, to create some national framework in the form of national grading structures for specific families of jobs which cross industry and company boundaries.

Some countries have already established such structures, and have made them work well. Any country, sophisticated or emergent, which adopts a philosophy of equitable remuneration practices, may create and use a national grading structure.

There are two alternative structural forms. In a free economy, series of structures for individual job families are essential, while in a more controlled environment an integrated 'one-hundred-grade' structure is feasible.

However, we do not consider this book to be the place to set out the detailed procedures which we have developed for the creation and implementation of such structures.

Chapter 7

Job Market Families

All jobs fall naturally into groupings of 'like jobs' known as
'families'. These families have a special significance for Salary
Administrators as the patterns of job market values are aligned
to job families. The fact that values change within one family
is largely irrelevant to values of other job groups, for the value
changes are likely to reflect changes in demand or supply in that
family, and individuals with different ranges of skills will not be
affected.

Job family theory

The basis of the job family theory is that jobs with a number of
common factors group naturally and logically together and, as
they tend to become associated, to form a job family. The
common factors which bind them together are usually related
primarily with background educational and training requirements, but the associated ease of interchangeability of personnel
from job to job within a group is also significant. Examples of
typical job families are :

1   Typing and secretarial posts.
2   Mechanical engineers.
3   Accountants.
    E

Within such families as these are ranges of separate jobs which require similar standards of basic training, any of which might be undertaken by people with similar job-training experience. Each family includes a range of jobs which extends through the whole hierarchical pyramid of associated jobs.

While individuals may move from one job family to another, this movement is very limited when compared with that taking place between jobs within a family. For example, an employer does not lightly employ a Tram Driver as an Architect, particularly where qualified and experienced Architects are available. An important result of this situation is that while shortages of specific types of staff tend to become general within a particular family in a specific locality, this shortage is not easily offset by transfer of people from other, even associated, job families. Salary trends resulting from these shortages also tend to be restricted to the affected job family. Compensatory staff movement to offset rising salary levels will take place only slowly, as new people are attracted to acquire the basic training and skills required. Readjustment of salary patterns may take place over a number of years, particularly if a growth in demand is added to a shortage of suitably trained people.

The overall result of this situation is that movements in market values tend to take place separately for each job family, rather than throughout all types of jobs identically at any one time. Fluctuations, which admittedly are normally of a minor nature, constantly vary the relationships between the current local market values for the various families. Awareness of this local movement is important, as a sharp local rise in a market rate which is unobserved may lead to an equally sharp rise in staff turnover within the particular job family.

Where movement is more drastic, as in cases where the demand far outstrips the supply (in recent years for Typists in Central London, or for computer staff nationally) the results of these movements can be extremely serious if the current position is not kept under constant survey. However, the categories of jobs concerned are clearly definable in job family terms.

Some companies have taken note of the close job family/salary relationships to the point where they have broken their salary structure into a series of independent structures based directly on a set of significant job families. These smaller salary structures can be adjusted easily and at limited cost to keep them closely in line with current market levels. It is possible to amend such structures, as any change on market rate movement occurs, with a minimum of survey work.

Market values

It is important to recognize the role which market values play in determining the shape and level of salary structures—and indeed grading.

Economic law of supply and demand operates here. As we have seen with secretaries in the London area, and computer staff nationally, the salary levels we pay to types of staff who are in short supply may escalate faster than inflation of salary levels generally, or where rising living costs alone provide the pressure.

In fact, all salary levels are influenced by the supply of and demand for the relevant types of employee. If the supply is excessive, the rate of rise in values will be slow (unless there is a trade union to provide artificial pressure). Where supply is exceeded by demand, rates will rise whether or not they are stimulated by union or other activity. As a general comment, a 'free' market situation operates for most staff jobs, but becomes distorted where supply is adequate and a strong union exists.

There is not, in our view, an absolute set of value relationships between jobs, so that the changing pattern of market values is a fundamental which must be constantly studied and adapted to.

Personal values at top management

As an extreme example of changing market values for a staff category, it is important to be aware of the soaring salary, and indeed total remuneration levels, for really high calibre managers. Their value has escalated considerably over the last few years as the demand for 'professionalism' increases.

Due to heavy taxation, these valuable people may often expect, and attract, offers of a 50 per cent increase in basic salary for a move to a company where their profit-making talents and know-how will be fully used. An interesting question to ask in defence of such startling salary movement is 'what is the market value of a manager who can turn a loss situation into a high return on capital in a couple of years?'

Clearly, the answer is provided by the top management of thrusting companies who are prepared to pay exceptionally high salaries and benefits to people whom they recognize as profit-makers. These executives are 'risk takers', whatever they may call themselves, in that they have the courage to take decisions based on proven judgment and a sound analysis of a situation.

This concept holds equally good for high calibre functional advisers, and for the broader based line executives. The value of people with the vision and know-how to obtain the optimum profitability from a company's assets—that is, its manpower, plant and machinery—is measurable only, perhaps, as a share of the profit they create.

It is now common knowledge, through the disclosure of remuneration resulting from the 1967 Companies Act, that this concept of remuneration by share of profit does operate in the UK. For example, several chief executives, leading the rapid growth of their companies, have received incomes in excess of £100,000 by such formulae.

Coming back to 'market values', the small number of exceptionally competent top people are in such demand that individual package deals must be negotiated, which take into account the job opportunity and scope, as well as the potential financial reward. The economics of supply and demand cannot be measured in so small and personalized a sample.

Job families and coding

In a few countries, national job classification structures exist and official publications contain standard job descriptions linked to job titles, or describe jobs and recommend normal titles. In this country, there is at the time of writing, little common acceptance of titling standards, so that an individual title, taken without reference to job content or organization background, may be largely meaningless. Even within an organization, titles may not fall into any clear pattern and may be misinterpreted by people in different parts of the same organization. This problem can be so great, particularly in a large company, that it becomes desirable to establish a uniform degree of standardization internally. In fact, the advantages of doing this can be appreciated in even relatively small organizations.

The particular association with salary administration comes from the fact that job titles must be used on job classification material, as an abbreviation of the much fuller supporting descriptions of each job. If significant variation occurs in interpretation of any single job title's meaning, it is likely that the types of salary anomalies which result from having no salary structure will still occur; and their effect may even be exaggerated by the support of an apparently effective job classification structure to justify the anomaly.

From this, one must conclude that nomenclature used in any job classification material must be supported by adequate, published and definitive material. To achieve this a certain amount of analysis of existing titling is necessary, followed by a series of policy decisions on titling form and style, and subsequently by the clear definition and acceptance of a range of titles. These basis stages are described below.

A case study

The first step is to obtain full details of the present titling position. What is the full range of job titles used in the organization? And, from job analysis information, what is the actual job covered by each title?

As it is highly probable that widely differing jobs will be found under any title in use, it is advisable to examine each individual job in this study. This will not normally involve the acquisition of more job information than has been obtained for basic salary administration purposes, but the requirement to examine job titling should be borne in mind at the time the initial job analysis programme is planned.

If the number of descriptions does not exceed, say, around

one hundred, it is possible to move directly to a final grouping of identical jobs. However, above this number and certainly where large studies are involved it is necessary to go through one or more intermediate stages.

Classifying a large number of individual jobs begins with a preliminary breakdown into broad family groupings. Ideally, some reference book would provide an immediate list of possible families, but no such book yet exists for all occupations in the UK. The possible degree of breakdown is very much open to discussion and different authorities tend to split up jobs into different basic categories. Let us examine an example.

One of the major families covers all clerical occupations. This clerical job family may incorporate the sub-groups of office machine operators, typing, secretarial staff, and so on—sub-groups which have separate identities but very close ties with the ordinary Clerk.

There are, for example, a large number of Clerks who type and Typists who carry out some clerical work; many Payroll and other Accounts Clerks are adept at using comptometers and other calculating machines. The girls who type a stencil may also operate the duplicating machine.

This overlap between substantial sub-groups with major job families sets a number of problems. In the initial stages of a study it encourages the use of definitions covering a small number of very large, but independent, families.

Although the major families tend to be independent of each other, there is still plenty of scope for 'border disputes' (as with most other aspects of salary administration and association functions). For example, on the fringe between the clerical job family and production job family one finds Progress Chasers and Progress Supervisors. The work done by these people may be substantially clerical, but the association with the production operation is very strong. Examining individual posts one finds that some Progress Chasers spend a higher proportion of their time on the shop floor, genuinely progressing production operations, or out visiting suppliers progressing company purchases. For others, the nature of their work requires them to spend most of their time working off progress schedules, checking clerically that the programme is on time and only occasionally investigating deviations from schedules. Perhaps the titles should differ, but the line between the two categories could not easily be drawn. The further decision on whether the appropriate job family should be 'clerical' or 'production' would prove equally difficult, and would indeed be arbitrary. We suggest that the point where the line is drawn is less important than achieving a company-wide understanding of the boundary!

We have used these examples to show the difficulties that one faces in determining the breakpoints during the initial analysis of a large group of jobs. As a starting-point for a future exercise the following simple breakdown is offered as a basis for dis-cussions :

Finance
Development and design, including research
Manufacturing and processing, including
    manufacturing services
Marketing
Personnel
Distribution
Processing
Legal
Public Relations
Patents
General Management and administration
Clerical, including Secretaries and office
    machine operation

Longer definitions of these basic families are unnecessary as the titles are self-explanatory, and we have no doubt that they will be adopted and amended, altered and split, to meet the indivi-dual circumstances to which they may be applied.

However, in order to demonstrate in detail further stages in an exercise of the type under discussion, we propose to make use of extracts from a major study in an engineering company. In this study, the major families used were as follows:

1   Finance
2   Technical development

3 Technical services
4 Manufacturing
5 Marketing
6 Installation and commissioning
7 Personnel
8 Clerical
9 Miscellaneous administrative

In arriving at this breakdown for all actual jobs, difficulties were experienced in a number of areas. For example, technical staff concerned with development of products specific to customers' requirements could fit into either 'marketing' or 'technical'; and the staff in a chemical services laboratory with a wide range of applications to production, development and customers' problems offered a similar query. However, these difficulties were relatively minor, and each borderline group of jobs came under scrutiny in the next and subsequent stages.

The next part of this major study required a breakdown into some seventy-five significant sub-groups which were sketched out before the stage began.

Perhaps the biggest difficulty was in sorting the descriptions into these sub-families. No ideal sub-family groupings were considered to exist, so the series of groupings that were developed did no more than break up the jobs within the company into what appeared to be logical categories. Each of the initial definitions was amended and developed as the study progressed and the family groupings became more apparent.

Thus the marketing job family became subdivided into:

1 Marketing and sales administration, covering the management of the function.
2 Home marketing services.
3 Export marketing services.
4 Publicity, advertising and sales promotion.
5 Market research and product planning.
6 Technical sales, and applications services; and sales engineers.
7 Sales representatives.
8 Customer service, order progress and liaison.

The largest number of subdivisions was found in the production job family, although some of the groups were small and subsequently contained less than ten individual job titles.

It was considered that the clerical job family split most naturally into sub-families closely linked to the other major families, for example, finance clerical and marketing clerical. There was also a general clerical category for the rather low-level non-specialized Clerks found in all functions, and separate categories to cover typing and secretarial staff, and office machine operators.

Individual jobs within families

This stage was started with a series of piles of job descriptions, each pile containing the groups of similar jobs in the sub-families selected above. Each of these piles had to be split up into smaller groups containing complete batches of exactly identical jobs. This final breakdown was reasonably coarse to avoid hairline decisions and excessive interpretation difficulty, and covered approximately six hundred categories.

This stage can only be completed successfully by the most careful examination of each job description and constant matching up with other individual descriptions. In the course of this detailed analytical review an impression of each job category crystallizes and can be recorded briefly in, say, twenty or thirty words, for future reference and expanded definitions.

In the course of the analysis, some jobs in each category will inevitably stand out as anomalies, to be thrown aside at this stage. It is usually worth adding a pencilled note or comment in each of these cases indicating the initial grouping and the reason for rejection. These cases, if dealt with fully on the first run, tend to slow down progress out of all proportion to their importance. Dealt with as a miscellaneous group at the end of the main study, a fresh look, based on the job-grouping experience gained, will often result in the job being immediately slotted into the appropriate category.

A look at one or two examples from this final analysis is worth while :

The Department of Employment *Classification of Occupations and Directory of Occupational Titles (CODOT)*, first published in 1972, is a valuable addition to the material available on job coding for analysis purposes. However it is on a scale which might limit its value to most individual companies and may not incorporate all the sub-divisions of activity that a company may wish to identify.

Job titles in the clerical/manufacturing sub-family:

Progress Clerk
Scheduling Clerk
Change-note Clerk

Basic function
To direct and co-ordinate the manufacture of all products in accordance with divisional objectives. To direct and plan use of production space; determine the location of various production lines; advise on requirements for additional production capacity. To co-ordinate the various functional parts of manufacturing, including purchasing.

Reports to: General Manager

Duties and responsibilities:
Develops a production programme and budget based on the marketing forecast, and on present and future manufacturing facilities.

Ensures that production control is effective; that short term production targets are constantly re-appraised and all aspects of the production activity are kept in step with current plans.

Co-ordinates and directs the purchasing and stock control function to reduce costs by bulk purchase and by minimum inventory, by arranging staggered delivery of orders in parallel with manufacture and sale.

Plans and directs the allocation of individual products to the various factories and shops.

Co-ordinates and directs the various manufacturing services, including layout and equipment planning, methods planning and work study to ensure that best methods and equipment available are used.

Co-ordinates and directs a quality assurance plan by ensuring adequate checks at all stages of material supply and manufacture.

Maintains a constant check on cost levels to ensure that all production is achieved within established budgets.

Figure 7.1　Short job description of a Production Manager)

Ordering Clerk
Specification Clerk
Stock Clerk
Stock Analysis Clerk
Stock Control Clerk
Stock Records Clerk
Shipping Clerk

Job titles in the personnel/training sub-family:

Training Manager
Senior Training Officer
Training Officer
Senior Training Instructor
Training Instructor
Graduate Training Supervisor
Training Courses Planning Assistant
. . . and so on.

Establishing the results (job definition and description)

Successful completion of a study of this type does not mean that
the results will be automatically absorbed and put into use. It
will not, immediately and without further effort, become part
of company usage. It must be explained, 'sold', published, and
generally announced with 'fanfares of trumpets' so that all
interested parties and particularly users of titles are fully acquainted and appreciative of the policy and philosophy evolved
from the study.

In plain day-to-day operating language, this means: that the
results of the work must be clearly explained to all managers and
personnel staff, and that some *permanent reference work* must

be prepared to ensure that the results do not degenerate into impressions, gradually becoming obsolescent.

Of these two tasks, the former is the easier of the two. An analysis of the changes which have been made to the previous titling position can be prepared for each part of the organization. This analysis provides the basis for discussions and final negotiation covering all jobs in the company and the re-establishment of all job titles.

In the course of these discussions, a variety of minor disputes occur which require the use of all the diplomacy the negotiator can apply. Sometimes the status of individuals known personally to a senior manager appears to be diminished by a proposed retitling. This is particularly the case where long-service employees have 'acquired' supervisory or managerial status on a loyal service basis rather than on job responsibility. Individual company decisions must be made to determine that flexibility will, or will not, be exercised in respect of titles of long-established staff. But it should be recalled that there will be little good resulting from a study in which recommendations are rejected in favour of a range of 'personal anomalies'. In the long term, such cases should inevitably decrease, although it is unlikely that they will ever die out completely.

This post requires a knowledge of the operation and application of the company's products, ability in written communication techniques and in the processing and production procedures of publication. It requires a mastery of technical vocabulary.

The job holder reviews copy for technical accuracy and clarity, writes and re-writes copy to improve readability and general clarity, using his own judgement.

The Technical Editor consults with Authors and makes recommendations and decisions on the handling of technical matters in publications and training material.

Figure 7.2   Short job description of a Technical Editor

A further element of disagreement which will cause no great difficulty, however, is that certain titles have strong one-industry associations which may not be fully appreciated by a small specialist team. Concessions should always be made to local, knowledgeable management where they can show that the title is in use nationally. Bottlewashers in the marble bearing industry are called Cleaning Supervisors. Inside Sales Engineer is often used to cover a Technical Sales Clerk taking orders by telephone in a small sales office. The term 'technician' has been found to have substantially different meanings in different localities.

The second part of the establishing process is the publication of job title definitions. If we recognize the title Accounts Supervisor, how shall we be sure that it means the same to all users? The best way is to define each job as simply and clearly as possible and then make the definitions freely available to all staff who need to know.

In a large organization, which may have produced between 500 and 1000 position titles, resolving that number of standard descriptions is no light task, and the result is no small volume; but this task should be tackled.

With little supervision, types statistical and other complex material. Uses own initiative in determining layout of material into final form, including the building up of separate data into a single schedule.

Duties may include use of shorthand to take dictation of technical reports and schedules, and preparation of stencils or other masters for production of large numbers of copies.

Figure 7.3 Short job description of a Statistical Typist

The job descriptions produced should be as brief as possible, and must be absolutely clear. A hundred words of meaningless waffle can be utterly infuriating in their uselessness. These descriptions have to be written by experienced people who make each word contribute something to the description.

The precise form and length of these descriptions is again a matter of individual choice, but Figs. 7.1–7.3 are useful guides, and others have been given in Chapter 5.

We notice that the number of organizations in the UK which have manuals of job descriptions is still relatively few, and that most of the pioneers have strong American associations. It is interesting to note that such manuals are normal in North America, where their value is much appreciated, and where the degree of title inflation is substantially less, and under control.

The United States Department of Labor publishes a dictionary of occupational titles which provides a degree of governmental interest and support.

Chapter 8

Salary Structure

The diversity of salary structure types in use in this country and in other countries as well is as wide as the variety of job evaluation methods.

Salary structures consist of related series of salary rates, levels or ranges applicable to individual jobs or groups of jobs. They vary a great deal between different organizations, the various forms being associated with widely divergent points of view on the philosophy of salary planning.

Each of the main types of structure likely to be found operating in the UK, and the philosophies behind them, are discussed below. The types of structure examined range from the most rigid through to the most flexible :

Rate for the job or flat rate.
Rate for age scales, or time progressor scale.
Incremental salary scales.
Flexible incremental scales.
Merit salary scales.
Salary guidelines and maturity curves.

Rate for the job, or flat rate

The use of a pattern or structure of single rates for individual jobs is very rare for staff posts, but is not uncommon for groups of hourly-rated or manual occupations, although even hourly-rated posts now have some form of merit range or wage spread more often than not.

A single rate presupposes a low basic level of performance of a simple task and anticipates little effective variation in performance above or below this level; variation is either unlikely or impossible.

This excludes virtually all normal staff posts from using this type of structure, for the normal range of effectiveness in many types of posts is 2.5 : 1. Where a single rate or narrow bracket is used, there is no incentive for better people to give of their best. Staff posts which may be covered in this way are likely to be of a manual nature and are probably classified as staff jobs due to some local tradition, or as a 'reward' for long service on the part of the job holders.

Salary adjustments for people in these posts are limited to national or other negotiated awards primarily to reflect significant changes in the cost of living. The better-than-normal performers in these jobs may achieve higher salaries only by promotion to higher-graded posts.

Individual rates covering jobs in this category should directly reflect the immediate local supply and demand situation and be strictly related to the local market rate in the truest sense of that phrase.

Rate for age scales (or time progression scale)

The use of a single rate linked to each age, for a post or for a group of employees at an early, and identical, stage in training, is not unusual. Normally, an arrangement of this sort would be applied to a group, or groups, with basically similar educational backgrounds engaged on identical, or parallel and equivalent, training courses, at too early a stage in their training for supervisors to recognize potential differences in performance or probable future contribution. This type of scale is particularly used to cover groups of staff such as trainee junior clerical and technical staff, and other trainee categories up to the age of about 21.

Outside industry, scales of this type are very much more widely used within the public sector—the Civil Service and Local Government, etc—directly linked to age up to varying points which sometimes extend beyond age 30.

This direct link to age is replaced by years of service at the relevant grade level for most posts filled by promotion rather than direct entry, and this extension of age scales to incremental scales is covered separately. Age scales may be constructed on the basis of a series of fixed single rates at each age level, or alternatively, a spread of money of limited merit range at each age may be defined.

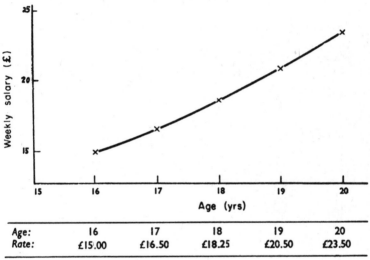

Age:	16	17	18	19	20
Rate:	£15.00	£16.50	£18.25	£20.50	£23.50

Figure 8.1   Rate for age scale – single rate (junior staff)

The use of a single rate requires considerable care. It is important that each figure should be based on local 'going' rates and on precise measurement of the local market, and possibly an appropriate adjustment to ensure that the level is adequate to hold good performers may be desirable. That the single rate should be able to withstand competitive pressure is vital, as there is no room to manœuvre. Variation and movement in local levels needs to be reflected quickly in scales of this sort, unless the rates are set deliberately high to take account of this danger.

Where the single-rate approach is used, separate scales of rates at each age for a variety of occupations or groups of jobs will normally be required, for example :

Scale 1—may cover absolute first-level trainee clerical staff and the operators of simple office machines such as duplicating machines.

Scale 2—might cover routine clerical staff and junior typists.

Scale 3—covering the next level of clerks, the majority of typists and junior shorthand typists and so on.

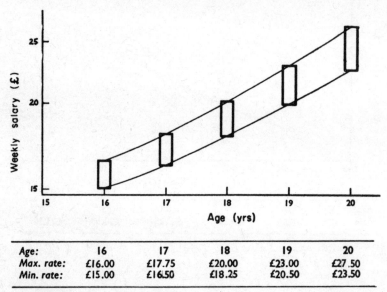

Age:	16	17	18	19	20
Max. rate:	£16.00	£17.75	£20.00	£23.00	£27.50
Min. rate:	£15.00	£16.50	£18.25	£20.50	£23.50

Figure 8.2   Rate for age scale – with merit range (junior staff)

Each of these groupings of jobs would be associated with the local pattern of market values and would have its own appropriate scale which would vary with market changes. Figure 8.1 shows a typical structure of the single-rate type of age scale.

It is more usual among major companies to make use of small merit scale ranges at each age. The philosophy here is based on one of the fundamental concepts of good salary administration, that it pays to reward the better performers, irrespective of age, in order to provide incentive to work at maximum effect. This can be achieved even among the youngest trainee employees, is advisable in all circumstances, and is invariably effective in use.

The same factors apply in respect of structure form and up-keep as in the single-rate structure, in that scales are necessary for several levels or groupings of jobs unless very wide 'money bands' are to be used. Also, the local market value picture must be watched, although the effect of minor fluctuations is less critical.

Figure 8.2 shows a structure in which a short merit range is used for each age in each grade, and can be compared directly with the example showing single rates.

Where merit-range, rate-for-age scales are used normal practice tends for the majority of individual salaries to follow either the minimum line or the midpoints of the ranges at each age, with only very minor variation, while a relatively small proportion of outstanding performers are granted larger increments (within the scale limits) and tend to follow the maximum line. However, in those organizations which have a highly sophisticated appreciation of salary administration at management level, a scatter of salaries will build up around the middle of the salary range for each age with the salaries of poorer performers dropping towards the minimum and those of outstanding people rising towards the maximum line, as they should in any merit salary range. There is generally a high turnover rate among junior staff, particularly under the age of 21, and it is sensible to make full use of the merit principle as a means of rewarding them for good work and encouraging them to stay with the organization.

In this context, and as an additional incentive factor to variation of salary in line with individual performance, it is becoming usual to give young people under the age of 18 salary increases twice a year—on their birthdays and 'half-birthdays', i.e. precisely midway between the two birthdays. These more frequent 'injections' of incentive keep up interest and morale at little additional cost.

At 18, young people are faced with full adult National Insurance contributions and, particularly in the London area, with a substantial increase in travelling costs as they cease to benefit from concessions as young persons. It is usual to take these factors into account in developing rate-for-age scales and to make provision for larger than usual steps in the scale at the time of an eighteenth birthday.

Rate-for-age scales up to age 21, with the inference of treatment as 'juniors', sometimes lead to difficulties for female staff, in particular among employees who are able to do a full adult job from about 18. It is important to take this potential ability into account in developing the shape of a scale. It may be advisable to provide only minimum salaries from age 18 to 21 for birthday salary adjustments, and leave the maximum permitted salary at each age quite undefined so that the normal adult salary can be applied where appropriate. This, clearly, is a highly flexible approach, within which the Personnel Officer may be called to advise on individual salary treatment in the majority of cases in order to achieve common standards.

Where employees are ready to match up to the requirements of a full adult job and find that a scale holds them back to a rigid junior salary, the more competent individuals amongst each group of staff treated in this way will tend to leave for higher-paid posts in organizations with less rigid salary structures. Rate-for-age scales for junior staff should be looked upon as a 'flight of steps' up which the junior employee climbs to adult status and the adult salary range for the occupation in question, and the step-ladder should be adjustable to the individual.

Where rate-for-age scales go beyond the age of 21 rather different factors apply as discussed under the next heading.

Incremental salary scales

Incremental salary scales are basically an extension of the rate-for-age concept to adult staff. These are widely used in the public sector, for salary administration in the Civil Service, Local Authorities and in nationalized industries.

Where incremental scales are in use, the age criterion is gradually being overridden, from the mid 20s or early 30s, by date of an appointment to a particular post and subsequently years of service in that post. Incremental scales are rarely found in industry, where they are normally considered to be much too rigid in application, and inadequate when it comes to setting individual reward. However, they do provide, within the areas in which they are used, less difficulty in negotiation with the various unions and Staff Associations which are often associated in their development. It is to be regretted that these bodies tend to reject individual reward on merit in favour of a policy of 'equal rights for all'. Incremental scales usually result in the better people carrying the poorer, or lazier, at each grade level without additional reward.

It is often stated that scales of this type assume a uniform middle level of performance, distinctly attractive to poor-calibre employees, but with salary-range maxima generally unattractive to outstanding people. Certainly, where a system of this sort is operated rigidly, poor performers invariably have their salaries subsidized at the expense of the best performers. The only way in which outstanding performers can be rewarded within a system of this sort is by promotion to a higher grade, to the higher salaries which obviously go with the higher levels. Classification under such a system tends to give heavier weight to the individual rather than to the job (which is more proper), and this makes it incompatible with modern salary administration philosophy.

Figure 8.3 shows pictorially part of a Civil Service type of incremental salary structure.

Flexible incremental scales

Over recent years, there has been a trend away from the rigidity of public sector application of normal incremental scales. Some of the nationalized industries have been prime movers in this trend, taking their original salary philosophies from the Civil Service and then attempting to move closer to industrial practice.

The usual way in which this is achieved is either by varying the periods between the award of increments, or by making it possible to give a double increment or to withhold an increment on the service anniversary. In this way, the outstanding performer and poor performer can move up to the scale maximum in widely different periods of time, and may never attain the full maximum in some cases.

Systems of this sort have begun to find some favour in

industry, particularly in one or two very large organizations where, for simplicity of operation (unfortunately associated with a reduction in managerial responsibility), the salary scale and

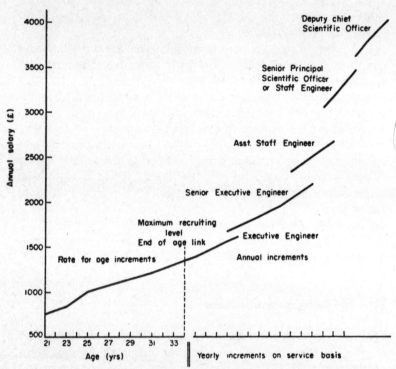

Figure 8.3   Diagram of Civil Service type technical staff pay structure

the period of time which an individual is expected to take to reach the maximum are rigidly allied and defined. Within these clearly defined limits, the manager is then asked, not what salary recommendations he wishes to make for his staff, but whether each individual is a 'five-year man', a 'seven-year man', or a 'ten-year man'—these being the normal periods of time permitted for travelling to maximum salary at defined performance levels. Within these time limits the differences between the starting-point salary and job-maximum salary is divided into equal annual increments. An example of this type of structure is shown in Fig. 8.4.

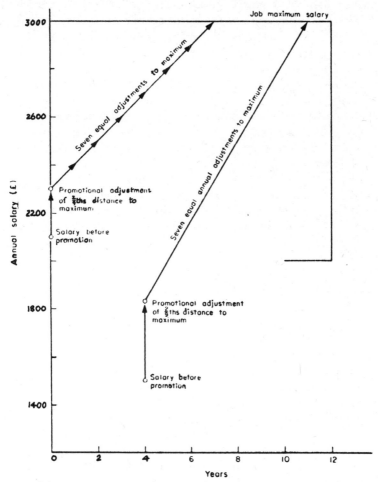

Figure 8.4 Graph of job maxima reached by equal annual increments

Merit salary scales

The great majority of organizations in industry use merit salary scales. The most usual procedure in industry is for these salary ranges to be established for each level or grade. Within each salary range there will be little or no 'internal structure' or restriction in the form of standard increments or steps, qualification basis, or other impediments to completely free salary movement on the basis of individual merit within these ranges. Thus, managers can determine individual salary levels and plan individual salary progress on the merit basis. While age, long service, time-keeping and sundry other irrelevant factors are sometimes allowed to interfere in minor ways with the actual operation, the most substantial and influential factors affecting salaries are the employee's level of performance in his job and his future potential for promotion.

Merit salary structures normally consist of a series of overlapping salary ranges, corresponding to grades in the organization's job grading structure. The spread allows for a number of periodic salary adjustments which will reflect the increased value of an employee to the company as his experience and ability grows.

The salary range for grade 1 might be from £x to £y, and the range for grade 2 begin midway between £x and £y and extend from this point to a maximum at some distance above £y. Some typical structures and common variations are explained below. As in all pay structures their precise form in any situation is based on normal practice, and on survey information of actual salaries and salary ranges used by comparable organizations for equivalent staff who also have their salaries progressed on a merit basis.

Figure 8.5 shows an example of the most common form of merit salary structures. The relationships between the individual grade salary ranges usually follow a fixed percentage progression between the mid-points of a sequence of grade salary ranges. It is usual in major British companies for the amount of this percentage progression to be of the order of from 15 to 20 per cent, i.e. the mid-point of one grade salary range will be 15 to

20 per cent higher than the comparable figure of the salary range for the grade below. This progression is reflected in the minimum and maximum figures, subject to variation in salary range spread.

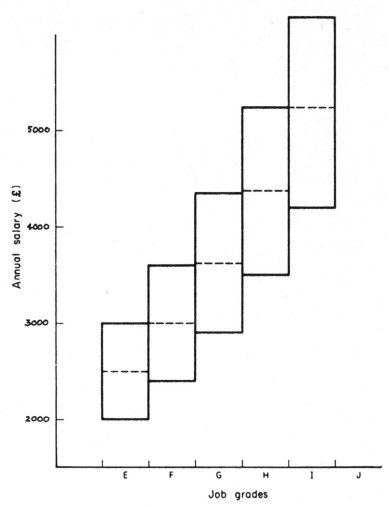

Figure 8.5 Standard merit salary structure of 50 per cent with half-overlap

The spread of the actual salary ranges, that is the difference between the minimum and maximum salary, is usually greater for career staff than for clerical and the lower-level technical staff. As a general guide the spread used by major British companies is on the following lines.

1 Maximum figures of salary ranges covering senior or career staff are usually between 40 and 50 per cent above the minimum.

2 For clerical staff and junior technical staff the percentage range is reduced and may be as little as 20 to 25 per cent.

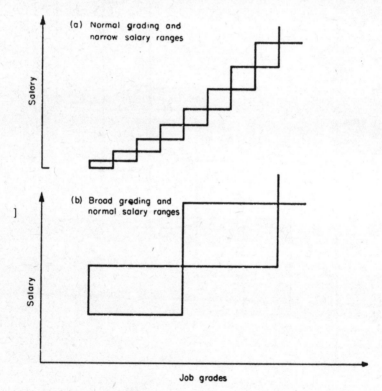

Figure 8.6 Merit salary structures – non-overlapping ranges

Although the figures quoted in the preceding paragraphs are widely used by many British companies, they are by no means universally accepted; in fact, there are three principal variants of merit salary structures and these are illustrated in Figs. 8.5, 8.6 and 8.7.

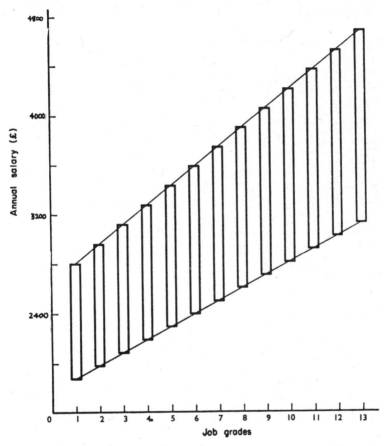

Figure 8.7 Merit salary structure − fine grading and with many salary brackets overlapping

In Figs. 8.6a and 8.6b, it can be seen that the individual salary ranges do not overlap, so that employees who are in different grades cannot possibly earn identical salaries, no matter how great the variation in their performance levels. Structures of this type may be built up by using very much narrower salary ranges, perhaps of the order of only 10 per cent, see Fig. 8.6a. Alternatively, one may have a much coarser grade structure as shown in Fig. 8.6b.

Either of these alternatives is likely to result in a salary structure which will be out of line with the competitive salary market at a number of points. This may be owing to a too-coarse structure resulting in the salary ranges being too high or too low near the divisions between grades, or result from the salary brackets being too restricted to allow normal salary movement. This latter type of structure finds some favour with certain organizations in North America, but is usually also associated with above-average salary levels.

Figure 8.7 shows the results of having a very 'fine' grading structure following which, in order to have fully competitive salary ranges for the posts in each grade, it is necessary to have widely overlapping salary ranges. In a structure of this sort, it becomes possible for identical salaries to be attained in a great number of different grades, thus reducing the value of differentiation between jobs.

A structure of this sort should always be scrutinized carefully to ensure that it cannot be immediately improved. For example, can the number of grades be justified? Is the volume of disputes over grading in borderline cases becoming excessive owing to the narrow and difficult-to-define groupings. If the number of grades is proved to be necessary, which is unlikely, is it also essential to have such wide salary ranges? The combination of grades with overlapping ranges will tend to discount any value the structure has, for an individual can be paid an identical salary in any one of a large number of grades.

As a general comment on this type of structure, it normally indicates troublesome and ineffective administration and is often a sign that salary administration in the organization needs an overhaul and tightening up.

The most usual type of merit salary structure is that shown in Fig. 8.5. In that structure the combination of number of many grades and width of salary ranges is such that each range over-laps the next highest range by approximately half.

The reasonably good performer with wide experience of a post at one grade level can be given the same salary as, or a rather higher salary than, a young untrained man in a post in the next highest grade. The scope for people in different grades to be on the same salary is limited, normally spanning only two grades at any one time.

	GRADE............		
	Average	Above Average	Excellent
Lower half of range	£120	£180	£240
Upper half of range	£80	£120	£160
On maximum salary—(continued good performance—bonus payment)	£100	£140	£200
Salary range	£2,400–£3,600		

	GRADE............		
	Average	Above Average	Excellent
Lower half of range	£140	£200	£280
Upper half of range	£100	£140	£200
On maximum salary—(continued good performance—bonus payment)	£120	£180	£240
Salary range	£2,800–£4,200		

Figure 8.8   Table of merit increase 'norms'

As shown in Fig. 8.7, where this situation occurs over a large number of grades the value of the structure tends to be signifi-cantly reduced. An important further aspect is that the incentive to take on more responsibility and complex work is also reduced by an excess of grades as salary scope resulting from promotion to higher grades is not significantly better.

Some unusually large organizations adapt the merit system in various ways. Some build up series of *merit increase tables* giving guide salaries at ages and/or average or normal merit increases for different levels of assessed job performance.

Figure 8.8 provides an illustration of a table of this sort.

In operation, this approach is inclined towards the same degree of rigidity as is found in Civil Service type of incremental salary scale. A large degree of initiative is taken away from managers and the tendency to lose interest and follow the 'automatic' scale is likely to be strong in any organization where the top management adopts an approach of this type. In fact, this practice tends to be a means by which managers contract

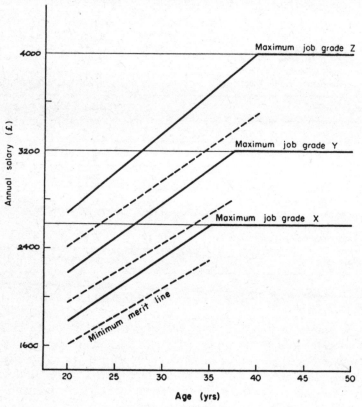

Figure 8.9   Diagram of salary channels for merit increases

out of the vital management responsibility of individual salary planning. This responsibility is discussed fully in Chapter 12.

An alternative to tables of increase 'norms' and a slightly more flexible form of approach which avoids the publication, however restricted, of actual tables of figures, is to plot the equivalent graphically. The resultant picture is shown on a graph, see Fig. 8.9.

Basically, this approach makes full use of a salary range, but it places restrictions on the salary movement of younger staff in the grade and often sets higher minima for older staff. A pattern of below the normal minimum salaries is proposed for young people, who are considered unlikely to have reached the requisite minimum standards. Even for those who may have reached these standards, top limits considerably below the salary range maximum are imposed, with a restricted progress rate towards the maximum and a minimum age at which it can be attained, which may be around the 40-year mark for some senior grades. The 30-year-old 'ball of fire' is virtually forced out of any organization which chooses to operate such a system.

This particular difficulty is inevitable when any degree of flexibility is lost. The outstanding performer, with high potential, is restricted to limits well below the grade maximum, and possibly below his personal market value, pending opportunities for promotion which may be slow in materializing. As always in situations of this sort, the exceptional people move on to places where salary scope is less restrictive.

In-grade rates

Most companies make full use of merit salary structures inevitably find that a number of jobs are not ideally covered by the main structure. In these cases they normally develop 'ingrade' rates or ranges. These are shorter salary ranges or individual rates, divorced from the main structure, which are appropriate and competitive for the type of job which they cover and which fall normally but not essentially within the appropriate grade salary range. Figure 8.10 shows this pictorially.

There are a number of staff jobs which for salary determination purposes are progressed in special scales of this sort. Such

scales often fall partway between the simple concept of a flat
rate for the job and the merit salary scale concept. Examples of
jobs normally covered in this way are Chauffeurs, Messengers
and similar uniformed staff; the group of senior skilled manual
workers who are occasionally granted staff status, such as certain
types of Inspectors; most of the first level of production supervision who may be either Chargehands or Junior Foremen; and

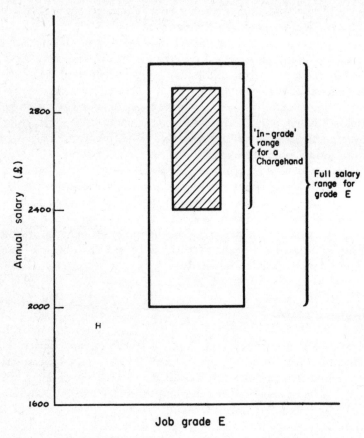

Figure 8.10 Diagram of 'In-grade' range

also non-manual groups whose salaries are linked closely with recommendations made by their Staff Associations or Trade Unions.

The basis for progressing salaries within these narrow salary ranges may in some cases be on an age or service basis with only limited account being taken of performance variation.

The individuals concerned will sometimes object to anything more than the most narrow of differences between salaries within the group, which may result in a tendency to grant all members of the group non-identical 'merit' salary adjustments at the same time. Even the better performers are sometimes found to prefer to conform to the accepted rate at certain points in their careers, before they break away into higher-grade work.

Basic salary and salary ranges for most of these people are influenced by national wage awards or local negotiated changes. Outside this their prospect of salary advancement must be at the best restricted, if not extremely limited.

Salary guide lines and maturity curves

In recent years, a great deal of study and research has been devoted to the evolution and evaluation of salary guide lines and maturity curves—and a great deal of nonsense has been included in the material written about these concepts.

These lines may be decided by one of two concepts. The first concept is based primarily on actual percentile distribution curve obtained from analyses of large numbers of salaries of individuals with similar basic training or employed on similar types of work, for example professional engineers, clerical staff, office machine operators. Figure 8.11 shows percentiles based on a scatter of engineering salaries.

Alternatively, a more empirical method uses guide curves developed from the observation of a number of individual career salary graphs. Such guide lines are also called salary maturity curves.

These guide lines are used as a sample substitute for conventional job grading and salary range by some of their supporters. Appropriate salaries are read off the curve according to the age and level of potential of the individual. The major difficulty in

F

application is to determine with any degree of precision the 'ultimate level of potential', as the amount of guidance available for calculating this appears to be extremely vague. Alternatively, previous salary progress within normal merit plans is assumed to provide guidance on potential progress for the balance of a career.

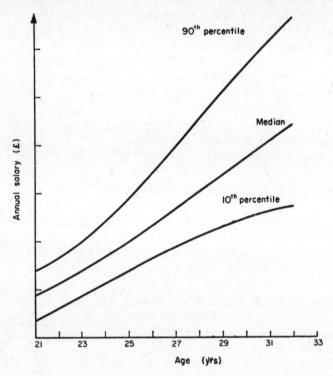

Figure 8.11 Percentile distribution of salaries paid to graduate engineers in the electronics industry

There are few if any rules for salary levels in this philosophy, at least for people with good performance and potential. The only problem is that there are often fewer job opportunities than high-potential staff and it is easily possible to finish up paying extremely uneconomic salaries to staff performing jobs much below their calculated capabilities. There is some merit perhaps in that the high salaries may tend to retain good staff who might otherwise leave, but psychologists suggest than an underemployed individual will be dissatisfied however well he is paid and wish to leave anyway!

Chapter 9

Salary and Benefit Surveys

The purpose of salary and benefit surveys is to obtain current, competitive remuneration data across the whole job spectrum so as to establish a basis for the maintenance of a pay and benefits position relative to that of comparable organizations.

It is necessary to do this to ensure against the probability that a company's pay and benefits 'package' will drift out of line with those of competitive organizations. The result of this drift might be an increasing loss of better-calibre staff as they leave to obtain higher salaries and more favourable conditions. Alternatively, an organization's salary levels may move above market levels to uneconomically high levels. It does not follow automatically that high salaries lead to higher productivity, and this is always true where the high pay is unplanned and illogical.

Surveys provide the basic information to enable an organization to avoid this situation.

A survey is an investigation of a current position. Assume for a moment that the survey is to investigate current salary levels for a certain category of staff. The investigation should cover the job content and grading of these staff within the company, and the actual salary and salary range picture of equivalent staff in comparable organizations. An analysis of this sort should provide a basis for a clear decision on a course of action.

Surveys range from large-scale studies covering all types and level of jobs and the full range of benefits when setting up remuneration structures initially for an organization, to quick telephone checks on current salary levels for a single job, or a single aspect of a benefit. They can vary through all points between these extremes to meet the requirements of a specific problem, for surveys should always be designed to provide an answer to a specific query. However, some variation from this model approach may be needed on occasions, to add to the interest of the resulting analysis for participating organizations.

Major surveys, to provide a complete check on an organization's salary and benefit situation, should not be necessary more often than once every two years and probably even less frequently, but they should be planned at regular intervals. It is possible to get a multitude of intermediate checks from minor surveys and from the reports of other people's surveys to which you contribute.

Smaller surveys in a great variety of forms should be undertaken at any time throughout the year as the need for such a study arises. A rise in the turnover of a particular category of staff, for example, is the warning light which should spark off an investigation including a market survey.

Scope of the survey

The first decision to be taken when planning any survey is the scope of the study. If it is to be a salary survey, how extensive should it be? If a small group of jobs is under particular study, they may be closely related to a number of similar posts. For example, Computer Logic Designers are often closely linked with Technical Programmers, and a survey to indicate salary movement may show much more if both categories are covered.

The study may be undertaken to check the whole of a salary structure. If this is the case, consider which are the key areas or positions that will most clearly indicate movement with a minimum of 'Survey Contributor' effort. And what type of information will most clearly reveal the story? If the position at one point in time is already defined, for example, information on subsequent salary movement may be more conclusive than a great deal of individual salary data.

The survey may be planned to cover a review of a benefit, or some aspect of a benefit. This might be into the normality and definition of a 'Widows and Orphans Clause' in a pension plan. Such a study may cover schemes with and without clauses of this sort and compare variations in contributions or funding to cover the cost of the additional benefit.

The limitations to be placed on a survey are likely to be established, at least in part, after a detailed internal study of the problems under review. Determination of possible weaknesses in existing company practice provides clues to questions which should be answered.

Whom to survey (the 'range' of a survey)

Once the scope of the survey has been decided, the next step is to decide on the best sources of the information which is required.

Occasionally, one of the professional institutes or bodies, such as the Institute of Personnel Management, various employers' organizations, the Institute of Production Engineers, Institute of Chartered Patent Agents, and so on, may be able to provide some guidance on the study. The British Institute of Management, Industrial Society and Institute of Personnel Management are useful in regard to benefit studies but, in general, information from these organizations tends to be limited by their resources. Keeping in touch with current salary information over a vast range of jobs would be extremely difficult and these bodies simply do not have the facilities to do this. The Institute of Office Management provides a service of this sort for clerical workers.

This means that one falls back on other industrial organizations. Within these, it is possible to prepare a series of lists of 'organizations to contact' for use in different circumstances and studies.

The obvious one is 'other organizations of similar size in the same industry'. This is probably the most difficult group, but the group one comes to know most about.

The next list is of organizations in close proximity to one's own plants or locations, with whom you compete directly on a day-to-day basis for clerical and junior technical staff.

Further lists cover organizations with which you compete for senior staff at longer range; organizations which set the pace on salary or benefit matters and need to be watched in respect of future trends; and organizations which occasionally take action of some form which has an indirect bearing on your own policy or practice. An example of this last situation might be of a company on the fringe of an industry, which is weak in negotiations with trade unions and may be used to set off a round of salary adjustments or a costly benefits improvement.

The range of a particular survey will be determined largely by the scope. The type of information required will determine in advance which group or groups of organizations are to be approached.

Willingness to participate

This seems an appropriate place to comment on the hotly disputed question of how willing organizations are to participate in surveys.

It is quite impossible to generalize and say categorically that organizations will co-operate if they are approached properly. This is just not true. In all industries, and for all sizes of organizations, the majority of companies will co-operate willingly with you in carrying out a survey while a definite minority will reject all advances. Some companies in this minority are members of small tight cliques which will not look outside, while others reject the basic idea that they have anything to gain or learn. A very few appear to remain isolated, clutching the creations of their personnel departments tightly to their bosoms, not daring to let the outside world see how bad things really are!

In the experience of the authors, the personal approach is the best in all circumstances when launching a survey. If the man on the other end of the telephone has met you face to face, he feels he knows you and acts rather differently than he might towards an unknown shape which relates only to a pestering voice.

A 'contact' is built up gradually, and becomes in many cases a personal friendship which is a basis for all future business. We have always tried to meet all the people we include in our surveys—tried to meet them over lunch so that the conversation spreads over the philosophy of our subject and on into more personal subjects, and the relationships evolve beyond that of a purely business nature.

On the basis of this friendship, we would reckon always to 'phone a contact' to ask personally for support on any major survey, and also many minor ones, before writing. This completely avoids the cold opening of a letter arriving unheralded on his desk, bringing an unexpected and unwelcome increase in work.

Naturally, one must be always ready to contribute to surveys in return—willingly, fully, and giving some priority to requests, however inconvenient may be the timing. In this way, mutual appreciation and trust are established.

Who are the contacts?

Over the past five years the authors, for various reasons, have had contact with over three hundred organizations of all sizes in most industries on salary and benefit surveys. The larger organizations have Salary Administrators, or Personnel Research Managers, or Staff Managers who sometimes spend a significant amount of time on the activity. In other companies a Personnel Manager with rather more general interests usually includes survey work as one of his activities. Small organizations almost always have someone who is responsible for personnel or staff matters—a Director or the Secretary or sometimes a part-time Consultant—who will take part in an occasional survey. It is a small organization indeed which does not have an allocated responsibility for personnel work and is totally outside the survey area.

The survey approach

The survey will be launched by a series of telephone calls to personal contacts in prospective participating companies, to clear in general terms that they are interested and able to contribute. Details of subsequent stages follow later.

However, there may be an organization that you would like to include but with which you have not previously had contact. If you can make contact with the Personnel Manager on the telephone, you might say something like :

'Good morning, Mr Jones, my name is John Smith, in the Personnel department of the Excelsior Electronics Company.

'We are making a study of salaries being paid to Goal

Designers and I should be very interested to compare notes with you.

'Before you comment on this, could I first give you a full account of our own position and the reason for the study, and the form we want the study to take . . .'

Or if he is at the other end of the UK or never available when you telephone, you might, as a last resort, write as follows :

'Dear Mr Jones,

'From time to time we undertake surveys of the salaries paid to certain categories of staff—surveys which are of general interest to the group of companies which contribute as they all receive summaries of the information collected.

'We are currently carrying out a study of salaries paid to Computer Programmers for both technical and commercial applications. Over a dozen major companies, including both manufacturers and users, have agreed to take part, and we should welcome participation by your company.

'I enclose a set of brief job descriptions covering various levels of Programmer. We should like to receive information on actual salaries and salary ranges for these categories, together with other information which is relevant in respect of your salary policy, such as rates for age. (At Excelsior we make no use of age scales for adult staff.)

'We hope to publish an analysis of the results before mid-May. Individual companies will not, of course, be identified in the summary with the exception of our own company.

'While writing to you. I should like you to know that we are always prepared to exchange salary and other information in this way if you should wish.

'Yours sincerely . . .'

The basis of the study

If the scope of the study is limited to salaries paid for one job or to a single aspect of a benefit policy, a telephone conversation or letter will be quite adequate for defining the terms of reference and asking the questions.

In any study having greater scope, the next stage is to lay the

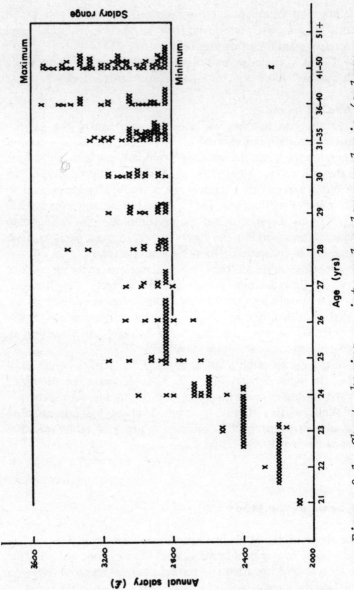

Figure 9.1 Chart showing an internal salary analysis (salary scatter by age) for a bench-mark post (design-draughtsman)

groundwork for comparisons. Assuming the study to be a salary survey, the organizing company would prepare basic data which could be sent to participating companies to show precisely the posts which formed the bench marks on the survey.

This data would take the form of a brief job description and a simplified organization chart to show the bench-mark post clearly in relation to surrounding posts. Figures 5.3 and 5.5 showed a selection of typical job descriptions which might be used for surveys.

Data should also be obtained at this stage of the salaries paid by the surveying company to all holders of the posts selected. This should be as detailed as possible for *internal* use, showing— probably in scattergraph form—the age, salary, performance and potential pattern of all holders of each post in relation to its current salary range (see Fig. 9.1).

Separately, a 'digested' short form should be prepared for handout, showing the salary range, median salary and number of staff covered. Where appropriate, some additional note to explain a peculiar salary position should always be given; for example, a median salary of £3900 in a range of £3200 to £4000 should be explained by a simple statement such as: 'Four of the five current job holders are in the age range 57–63'.

The detailed job information on the bench-mark jobs should be sent by mail to the participating companies. This package would probably exclude the salary data at this stage to avoid introducing an early bias—it is regrettably easy to fall into rating a surveyed job solely by what the other organization pays. ('They pay £3825; what have we got in that department around the same level?') While this selection may turn out to be a good match salary-wise, it is much less likely to be a good job match than one resulting from a proper examination of the job information itself.

The purpose of this advance handout is to enable the participating organizations to look closely at each of the jobs you wish to study, and prepare appropriate information on posts in their own organizations as a preliminary to discussion.

If the study is to cover a benefit or benefits rather than salaries, or is to cover benefits in addition, the same basic approach should be used.

SALARY AND BENEFITS SURVEY

Part 2: SUMMARY OF MAJOR BENEFITS FOR STAFF

Bonus/Profit sharing: Which staff participate in any bonus profit sharing scheme? Please give a brief summary of these payments.	
Overtime payment: What is the top limit for overtime payment? Is there any compensation above this limit?	
Hours: What are the basic hours for office staff? Works staff?	
Holidays: Which staff get 3 weeks' annual vacation? ...4 weeks' annual vacation? Do you give more than 6 statutory days' holiday?	
Meal subsidies: Do you provide luncheon vouchers? Do you provide subsidized meals in canteens?	
Pension: What (if any) are the pension contributions of the employee? ...the Company?	% of salary. % of salary.
Sickness absence: Please give brief details of your Sickness Absence Scheme.	
Other benefits? (Such as subsidized goods, etc.)	**(Please describe benefits)**

Figure 9.2 Short-form questionnaire designed aid survey discussion

It may be sensible to ask for general statements of policy and procedure, which are usually available to cover things like a pension plan, or it may be preferable, in a different situation, to write down briefly a series of questions or headings to indicate the slant of your interest, as a basis for discussion (see Fig. 9.2).

The purpose of all this preliminary paper work is to give participating companies an opportunity to brief themselves before meeting you. Do not forget to send two or three copies of these forms for use as working copies.

Mail survey

You may wish to make the survey entirely, or primarily, by mail. This may be for several reasons, when organizations are very widespread or when an unusually large number of companies have to be contacted.

If this is the case, the information sent out should be rather more precise and detailed and the questionnaire very carefully worded. On a salary survey, the questionnaire should ask additionally for details of variations on matched jobs, such as differences in reporting lines, grouping of responsibilities, numbers of staff supervised, and so on, as well as salary details. Figure 9.3 is a simple format of this type. Your requirements should be made clear, either in a brief set of instructions preceding the survey material, or in a covering letter.

Whether the survey is to be by mail or by discussion, if the information provided is to be at all substantial the whole set of material should be put into a neat, attractive cover for despatch to participants. Presentation is important in any field and the specialized personnel field is no exception. This attention to detail in addition to professionally sound survey material gives a favourable image of your organization and of your own competence. The cost of the extra effort will be found to be neglible compared with a costing of the executive and other time that has been devoted to the study.

SALARY SURVEY: MALE FACTORY SUPERVISION

	GRADE 4		GRADE 5		GRADE 6	
(Examples)	*Junior Chargehand* (In charge of a group of semi-skilled employees, allocating work to others and working with them.)		*Chargehand* (In charge of a group of skilled employees, allocating work and giving advice, also carries out some product work himself.) *Assistant Foreman* (In charge of a large group of semi-skilled employees, normally including chargehands. Engaged full time in supervision.)		*Foreman* (Supervises several groups of semi-skilled employees, including chargehands, or a large group of skilled employees, normally including chargehands. Decides order and allocation of work.)	
Age	Minima	Maxima	Minima	Maxima	Minima	Maxima
15......						
16......						
17......						
18						
19......						
20......						
21						
22......						
23......						
24......						
25						
Maximum salary payable						

Figure 9.3 Questionnaire form for a survey conducted by mail

What salary information to ask for

Unless it is intended to carry out very sophisticated statistical analyses of the survey data, which would normally be done with the aid of a computer or punched-card equipment, it is necessary to ask only for a minimum of salary information. This might be the salary range, or the actual highest and lowest salaries and the median or average salary for each position.

Some organizations ask for upper and lower quartiles, but such requests are not popular and may lead to loss of support from the participating company or even false information.

Depending on the scope of the survey, it may be reasonable to exchange notes—or full details—of the form and shape of salary structures, and where the bench-mark jobs fit. Or a survey of junior rates may require an exchange of the complete rate-for-age scales or similar detail covering the salaries for junior staff.

In salary exchanges with public bodies using incremental scales, organizations using more flexible methods of individual salary determination will find that there is sometimes an advantage in taking a series of individual cases, precisely defined, and establishing salary levels for these in each structure as the most accurate means of comparison.

To sum up these notes, it is clear that the requirements of each survey are distinctive. Whether or not those requirements can be attained must be assessed, and a realistic target set, before the survey is commenced.

The meeting

In any major survey and certainly those concerned with middle and senior management positions—covering either salaries or benefits or both—it is advisable for representatives of participating companies to meet to clear up any queries regarding the actual identity and value of jobs, so that they can pin-point equivalent positions in their own organizations. At these meetings, the discussion often reveals pairs of actually matching jobs outside the strict limits of the survey which provide a much better guide to the relationship between salaries in the two organizations than the bench-mark posts selected. It is always worth while making notes of jobs which are an exact match, as well as those which you rate half a grade or a complete grade higher or lower. From these notes, it is possible to make adjustments after the salary data is obtained to allow for differences in job values.

From the previous paragraph it can be seen that although these meetings may start the discussions round the selected bench-mark jobs they may subsequently range over a selection of associated jobs, examining these to widen understanding of organizational relationships which must have been established for this degree of frankness to be achieved without initial waste of time in excessive 'sparring'.

On Directors' remuneration, there is a strange reluctance on the part of many companies to discuss salary and benefit levels. However, a great deal of information on remuneration at top levels is published in annual accounts, although it is usually best to discuss such matters as well. We find that once mutual trust has been established between the senior personnel people of different organizations, they will discuss salaries at all levels. Clearly, this is essential in the modern business world and it is good to see so many of the old-fashioned conventions and taboos disappearing.

If anyone has doubts about the advisability of divulging this information to another organization, his reservations represent doubts about the entire survey procedure, for knowledge of the competitive position is equally important to all levels. Usually, reservations are linked with concern about potential 'body-snatching', which is surely less likely if salaries are properly arrived at—but, without surveys, how can one be sure?

Naturally, the strictest confidence and discretion must be maintained in such matters, but at least they can, like sex, now be discussed without embarrassment.

Analysis and interpretation of data

When all the survey data have been received—and this may necessitate one or two gentle reminder letters—the next step is to analyse the information. The positions which were described and used as examples for the survey should be assigned grades in line with the company's own job classification structure, taking into account all the known variations in job content which justify half-grade or grade variations from the bench-mark levels.

Accumulated salary data can be analysed in a variety of ways. A variety of data does not open the way to easy use of statistical analysis, but it can give a reasonably clear picture of market salary levels.

As an initial and fairly simple run, take a large sheet of graph

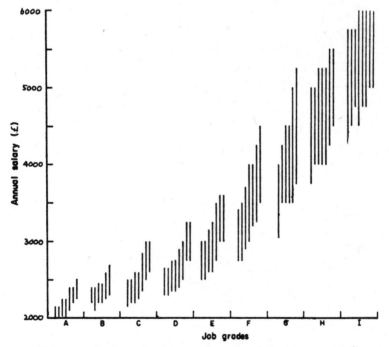

Figure 9.4   First rough plot of all data accumulated in a salary survey

paper. Draw on it salary intervals down the vertical axis, and a grade scale on the horizontal axis with the grades at regular intervals.

Then plot the accumulated salary data for each of the benchmark jobs against the appropriate grade. Place dots for each actual salary plot, and bars to indicate salary ranges, possibly using colour to indicate the different job families or contribution companies. As this is prepared, a rough pattern becomes immediately apparent (see Fig. 9.4).

Initially, freehand lines can be drawn through the average salary levels, and through the average level of maximum or highest actual salaries as well as through the minimum or lowest actual salaries. This pattern of lines indicates reasonable salary limits for each job level or grade, and the salary progress between grades (see Fig. 9.5).

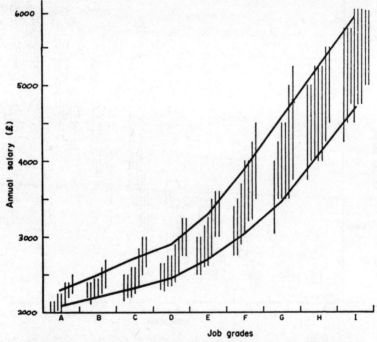

Figure 9.5 The salary range data of Figure 9.4 with maximum and minimum lines overlaid

From the minimum, mid-point and maximum salary curves drawn on the graph, we can read off points on each curve against each grade, as a basis for determining salary limits for each grade. This approach is extremely simple, and may be particularly suitable for the smaller company where the Personnel Manager has inadequate time for more involved statistics.

It is possible, by use of coloured symbols on the chart, to see which companies set higher or lower salary limits, and from this information to draw the conclusion that salary levels, say, 5 per cent below the survey average levels would be adequate in one's own company, or at whatever competitive position is considered appropriate.

Statistical analysis

The method described above is clearly the simplest way of analysing the data obtained at such length. However, while it may be difficult to apply highly sophisticated statistical techniques to the analysis, it is well worth while making a rather more thorough analysis on the following lines.

An average salary, or some other measure of central tendency, should be calculated from the accumulated data, separately for each grade in the job classification structure. This measure should be based on one or more of the forms of data collected, such as the mid-points of the salary ranges, medians of salary scatters, or average salaries. From these figures, each of which is a form of determining a middle level of salary for the job concerned, a salary mid-point can be determined.

Reference to any basic textbook on statistics or to a Statistician should help to determine the best method of analysing the forms of information obtained, and in assessing weightings to be given to individual pieces of data.

From the grade mid-points obtained, a line of best fit can be calculated by using the statistical technique of least squares. If this is done, a Statistician's aid may be desirable. Alternatively, a simpler approach is to draw a visual line of best fit, freehand. Plotted on a graph a statistical line of best fit will look like Fig. 9.6.

A weakness of this procedure for the uninitiated (and indeed

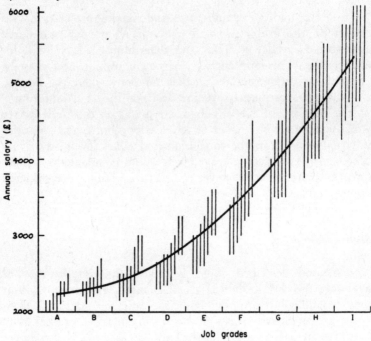

Figure 9.6 The salary range data of Figure 9.4 with the 'line of best fit' calculated by the method of least squares

of the technique of least squares) unless corrective action is taken, is that a small sample at the extremities of the structure may significantly alter the curve. Such a sample can be identified visually by drawing up the simple scatter shown in example 6.4. Separate colours for each company will indicate any which stands clear of the general trend. Unless these samples can be proved reliable, it is much safer to discard them before beginning calculations.

Out of these calculations comes an average competitive salary curve, and from this you can determine whether your existing salary ranges need amending in any way.

Analysis of benefits information

Any survey of benefits provides a series of answers against a series of questions or headings. The first stage in any analysis

Benefit	COMPANY A Excelsior Electronics	COMPANY B	COMPANY C	COMPANY D
5. Holiday entitlement Which staff receive 3 weeks' holiday?	Weekly staff with less than 2 years' service	Staff on salaries below £2,000	Staff below age 21	
Which staff receive 4 weeks' holiday	All other staff	Staff on salaries below £3,500	All adult staff, except—	
Which staff receive 5 weeks' holiday?	Nil	Staff on salaries of £7,500 and above	General management (approximately, those on salaries above £8,000)	
What additional days do you give?	6 statutory holidays	7 statutory holidays, (Includes New Year's Day)	6 statutory holidays, plus 2 Christmas shopping days each year	

Figure 9.7 Extract from an analysis of fringe benefits

must be to list the questions and rank all the answers, company by company, on a large sheet of paper. Figure 9.7 shows an extract from a shedule of this sort.

After this point, analysis is not usually possible in the same sense as with salary data. It is necessary to appraise the information systematically and determine firstly where the surveying company stands in relation to the general picture and, secondly, where the company would like to be.

Finally, the survey will provide details of normal practice at the approximate level selected by the company. Basic determination of benefit levels is relatively straightforward. Not so easy is the detailed operational procedure within which the benefit will function.

Developing a company salary structure

Once the point is reached at which the full salary data are available and the competitive salary curve has been calculated, it is possible to develop the Company Salary Structure. The actual positioning of this structure in relation to the competitive salary curve represents a company policy decision of major importance.

The obvious and most straightforward course is to build the structure immediately around the competitive line but, for various reasons, some adjustment from this line may be considered appropriate.

The survey may have a bias towards a high salary area—say London or some other major centre—while the company's sites are more provincial in location. (This situation is quite likely to occur if the survey has a heavy weighting of one industry.)

Studies of recruiting and 'asking' rates may indicate that a certain differential from the survey average is reasonable, perhaps a uniform 5 per cent below the average level, or a variation from 10 per cent at lower levels and nil at senior levels to conform to the recruiting picture. All these known factors should be taken into account by calculating an amended line which becomes *the company curve*—the basis of the Company Salary Structure.

A further possibility is that the company may wish to 'pace-set', i.e. to set its salary levels at higher levels than its competitors.

To do this it may decide to set its structure deliberately 10 per cent above average levels shown by the survey, and again a company curve should be calculated.

The next step towards the establishment of a Company Salary Structure is the determination of the required width of salary brackets. Major company practice, with some variation, is for maximum salaries to be 50 per cent above the minimum salaries in each grade, which allows substantial scope for individual salary variation on merit. Some companies and industries tend to use much tighter bands of 30, 35, or 40 per cent ranges, and a few have longer spreads.

Assuming that a 50 per cent spread is to be adopted, the maximum and minimum salaries can be calculated speedily as follows:

$$Y = \frac{100X}{200+X}$$

Y is spread from midpt to max %
X is spread from min to max %

Take the salary at the grade point on the Company Salary
Curve—   = Mid-point of the salary range (125)
Mid-point *less* one-fifth   = Minimum salary (100)
Mid-point *plus* one-fifth = Maximum salary (150)

As cross checks on the calculated figures, a rough graph will show up any figure out of line, and a 'Pascal's triangle calculation' will confirm the smooth relationships.

The full salary data provide an adequate guide to normal practice amongst competitive organizations. There may be some variation on salary range spread at different grade levels, with the spread for clerical and junior posts in particular tending to be significantly more narrow than those for career staff. This picture should generally be reflected on your own structure, unless you have good reason for being different.

Not every company is establishing a new salary structure, of course, but may be revising an existing structure. Adjustments to an existing structure will take into account the differences between the old and new competitive salary curves and developments in company policy. It will also consider to a lesser extent the internal pressure on the structure, and the known pattern of recruiting rates over previous months.

Adjustments to individual salaries following the establishment of or adjustment to salary scales are discussed in Chapter 12, 'Salary Planning'.

Presentation to management

In order to put over to management recommendations regarding your salary structure, it is necessary to present the results of the survey.

One way of presenting the accumulated, analysed data for management is to show it in the form of a series of box graphs. These may be a series of separate graphs, one for each grade showing the competitive picture and with recommended salary ranges drawn in alongside (see Fig. 9.8) or it may cover the whole structure on a large sheet, with the calculated lines of best

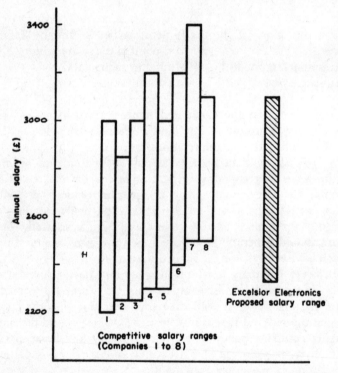

Figure 9.8 Chart showing competitive salary ranges, covering one grade, with proposed salary range for 'home' company shown alongside

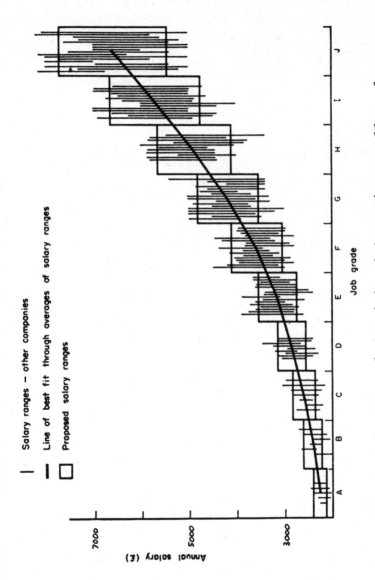

Figure 9.9 *Large chart giving information on all grades*

fit superimposed to show the average curves for competitive minima, mid-points and maxima (see Fig. 9.9).

Alternative presentations could be in a variety of forms, including the simple chart showing the proposed company salary

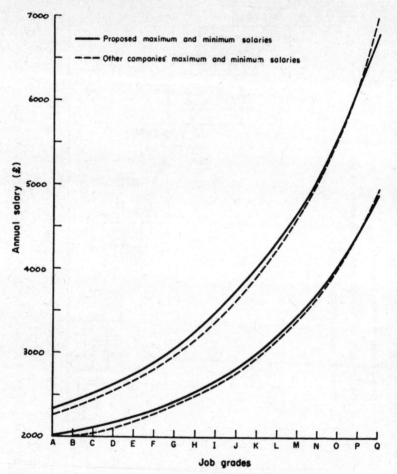

Figure 9.10 Graph showing the maximum and minimum salaries for all grades ('home' company and others)

curve, plotted against the competitive curve of the average values (Fig. 9.10).

The actual form of presentation selected should always take into account the known interests and preferences of the management to whom it is to be submitted. This should cover things like size, use of colour, content of presentation, specific company data, etc.

Presentation to participating organizations

A complete summary of all competitive salary and benefit data should also be prepared for all participating companies, and sent to them as soon as possible after a survey has been completed and the results analysed.

The summary of salary data could take one of several forms :

1   A series of tables showing lowest, average and highest salaries for each job for each company. Notes on job differences and possible reasons for salary variations usually support this type of summary (see Fig. 9.11).

2   A series of graphs showing salaries for groups of jobs by company sales turnover blocks (see Fig. 9.12).

3   A series of box graphs showing each company's salary range for each position under study (see Fig. 9.13).

Similar summaries can be prepared to show the results of benefit surveys (see Fig. 9.14).

Great care must be taken in these summaries to modify any distinctive attached notes and comments in order to avoid revealing company identities. The exception to this is, of course, that information covering the organizing company should always be clearly marked. In presenting information, it is reasonable to use code numbers to identify information from each participant —numbers which can be quoted individually to the companies concerned to enable them to check back on their contribution if they should wish.

Once again, we stress the importance of taking trouble with the presentation of this material, to ensure that it is passed out in as effective and clear a manner as is possible. This attitude inevitably pays off every time, in winning recognition of an

SENIOR DESIGNER

Works under the supervision of Chief Designer.

Guides approximately six design draughtsmen, in developing designs of minor to main assemblies and components to obtain efficient product operation and production economy, by devising original construction specifications or suggesting modifications based on investigations of construction and test performance.

Desired qualifications: Degree or equivalent in Mechanical Engineering plus a minimum of five years' practical training and experience in this or related work.

Number of companies: 10			Median rate: £4,727					
Co. code	Salary range (£)			Actual salaries (£)			Total remuneration (including bonus) (£)		
	Min.	Max.	Mid-point	Low	High	Average	Low or Min.	High or Max.	Average or Mid-point
1				4,600	4,900	4,750	4,600	4,900	4,750
2	4,226	4,643	4,434	4,260	4,505	4,435	4,380	4,755	4,640
3	4,350	5,000	4,675				4,350	5,000	4,675
4*	4,345	4,830	4,587				4,345	4,830	4,587
5	3,780	5,200	4,490				3,780	5,200	4,490
6	4,428	5,142	4,785	4,250	4,750	4,550	4,562	5,187	4,937
7	4,440	4,920	4,680	4,560	4,800	4,644	4,560	4,800	4,644
8	4,450	4,900	4,675			4,650	4,450	4,900	4,650
9	4,300	5,000	4,650				4,365	5,100	4,733
10	4,600	5,250	4,925				4,600	5,250	4,925
Average	4,310	4,931	4,621	4,418	4,739	4,606	4,427	5,106	4,727
Excelsior	4,380	5,060	4,725	4,417	4,672	4,567	4,380	5,060	4,725

*Matched position. No equivalent.

Figure 9.11 Survey information for management – table of data obtained for each bench-mark job

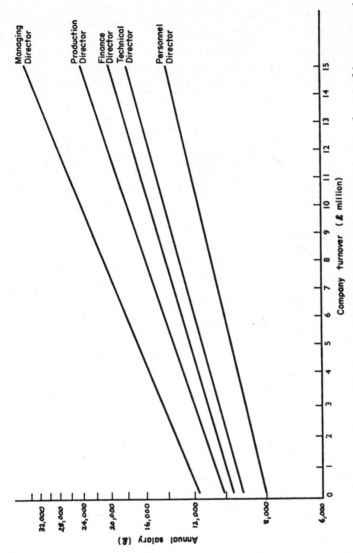

Figure 9.12 Survey information for management – graph of directors' salaries against company turnover

efficient and effective study, and in indicating professional competence.

Other people's surveys

You will inevitably be asked to participate in many surveys by other organizations, at one time or another. As we have said before, it pays to help others, and usually results in reciprocal aid when you want it.

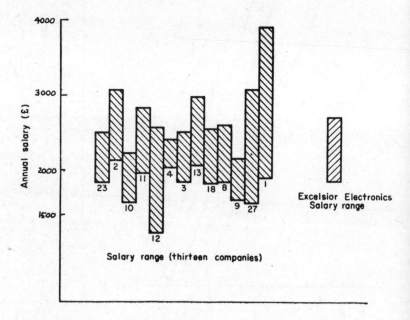

Salary range data:	
Highest maximum	£3880
Average maximum	£2630
Average mid-point	£2178
Average minimum	£1726
Lowest minimum	£1340

Figure 9.13 Survey information for management – block chart for a bench-mark job (Cost Accountant)

HOLIDAY ENTITLEMENT

Four weeks' entitlement

All staff employees of the companies taking part in the survey were able to
qualify for 4 weeks' annual holiday at some stage of their employment.

Eight companies (47 per cent) granted 4 weeks' holiday to all staff either on
joining or after 1 year's service.

Nine companies had status or salary levels at which staff became eligible for 4
weeks' holiday without service qualifications, e.g., monthly staff in most of
these nine companies became eligible for 4 weeks' holiday after periods of
service of a year or less.

Five (29 per cent of the total) of the companies in the second group granted 4
weeks' holiday to the balance of weekly staff after periods of service ranging
from 3 to 15 years.

Four companies (24 per cent) granted 4 weeks' holiday to all our staff on attainment of a stated salary level, generally in the region of £1,000 a year, e.g.
(a) £1,140 for male and £955 for female; (b) £1,000.

Five weeks' entitlement

Eleven companies (65 per cent) granted 5 weeks' holiday to some staff, predominantly to 'Senior Management' only.

Six of these companies granted 5 weeks to 'Senior Management' automatically.
In the other five, service qualifications, sometimes as long as 20 years, applied

Two of these companies extended 5 weeks' holiday to all staff after periods of
service: 10 years in one case, 25 years in the other.

*Figure 9.14 Survey information for management –
extract from a brief report on a benefit survey*

However, you will probably have to make a decision sooner or later, whether you wish to participate in a survey carried out by consultants, or in a particularly massive and time-consuming study to be undertaken by one of your contacts.

It is sensible to weigh up quite coldly what value you will get out of any survey, taking into account potential future aid on your own surveys. You should participate only if it appears to be a competently prepared study from which some useful information will emerge in summary form. You should also look for a large proportion of positions which you can match, or where you have some particular interest in the results.

Surveys which appear to be incompetently or poorly prepared, or will involve unreasonably massive effort and cost, or have little potential pay off, should be avoided politely.

In the long run, your own surveys will be outstandingly the most useful and much of your contribution to other studies represents only payment for reciprocal participation. However, other surveys by competent Salary Administrators which result in well summarized analyses can be extremely useful.

Research studies by non-industrial organizations, the results of which may be regrettably widely quoted, are usually too vague to have any practical value. In a different class, national statistics and regular studies by employers' organizations have the value of bench-marks for trend purposes.

Chapter 10

Position Guides and Objectives

A considerable amount of effort can be devoted to producing descriptions of jobs and responsibilities which may be of little or no value. It is important to identify all immediate and probable future applications of the information to be assembled and presented, and to determine the valid life of this data.

Applications of position guides

Job information may be collected as part of an organization study or it may be applied to a salary grading exercise. It may be required to explain to an employee details of his position— or clarify the objectives he is expected to meet. It could be a recruitment specification. It may define the extent of a manager's authority.

It is relevant to comment that many exercises are carried out for one purpose, but that the information, once collected, is applied to a variety of other requirements for which it may not always be suitable.

Ask for 'job information' or a job description and your request will mean different things to different people. Before we ask what information is required, consider the various applications and their information requirements.

Remuneration

As this book is about remuneration, we have considered already the information we need for salary determination.

G

Performance

As a basis for assessing a manager's performance of his job, the primary need is for a clear statement of his objectives, incorporating as much measurable content as is feasible. This is largely straightforward with line management positions, but is less easy with the advisory content of staff positions.

Apart from basic *job* objectives, it is also necessary to cover special objectives such as those related to improving personal relationships and staff development. These, of course, are highly personal objectives, but are attached to criteria to be used for performance review of a current incumbent.

The 'good housekeeping' aspects of a job will probably not be covered by objectives. These maintenance activities are continuous and rarely contain specific tasks which would be measured in a performance review—except where some aspect had gone seriously off-track.

The problem in setting objectives, either as a comprehensive guide to a manager as to what is expected of him, or as a complete basis for performance assessment, is that one of the key aspects is the manager's reaction to and treatment of the unforeseen. Even where objectives are set for just one year ahead in a sophisticated planning environment, it is probable that some of the assumptions built into the plan will prove wrong and the situations facing an individual manager will have some different slant from those anticipated. The variations may be minor, but reaction to the unforeseen is an important aspect of assessment.

This last point is not something one can build into the set of objectives, but is a factor to bear in mind in wording original objectives, and in evaluating results.

Appointments

For recruitment, internal placement, succession plans—all situations where the requirements of a job are to be matched against people—job information must also be translated into a man specification.

The process involves the translation of objectives, and difficulties to be faced in achieving these, into the actual work to be done and skills required. From this may be built up a model of the individual likely to be successful in the role. Some adaptation of this ideal may be necessary in order to fit the individual into the existing team—to allow for existing strengths or weaknesses, and to allow for style of management, personalities, etc.

A man specification to be used for any selection purpose would include data on :

1   *Knowledge*—the education, training and experience required.
2   *Abilities*—the intellectual qualities and application abilities.
3   *Personal motivation*—the drive; the self-starting ability; etc.
4   *Physical*—age, if relevant; sex, if relevant.
5   *Personal choice*—job satisfaction factor; environment.

Job understanding

Where a job is significantly altered, or where a new man is appointed, we may need to provide the individual with a complete picture of the job as a starting-point. For this application, a broad outline of the purpose of the job, plus current objectives, may need to be supplemented with detailed information on the more routine but essential 'good housekeeping' activities.

This type of information may be required from time to time in a flexible growth organization, to re-establish the form of job or obtain agreement between a manager and his superior, following a period of job development. Factors such as resources, authority, and relationships may need to be covered in particular detail.

Organization analysis and planning

Where an organization structure is to be analysed, a detailed picture of the existing content of all jobs within the area under review will be required to tell the full story of the current structure.

The way people actually spend their time is particularly significant, and tells a great deal about the actual as opposed to the intended structure, which may be set out in the form of objectives, resources, authority, and relationships.

The type of questionnaire described earlier for salary purposes is also valuable for organization analysis. It will immediately highlight all conflict in reporting relationships, and the section covering utilization of time will draw out a clear picture of how the organization is working at present. Which are the key roles and people? Where is there duplication and conflict? Where are the strengths and vulnerabilities of the present style of operation?

Where a formal organization plan is prepared following a study, the basic purpose and broad objectives of each post will be outlined as well as those of the total activity. Man specifications may also be appropriate where personnel changes are envisaged, and it may be appropriate to adjust the specifications of some roles to the personal skills available.

Details of jobs at this stage are likely to be less precise than any current picture, but the main outlines should be clear enough for practical man specifications to be prepared as a guide for management planning and the company's training and development programmes.

Content of a management position guide

While the content of any individual guide will be influenced by its intended applications, and few guides need to be fully comprehensive, it is worth outlining the full picture as a basis.

Identification

The first step is to identify the post and its place in the organization. This hardly needs comment, but the essential minimum information is :
1   Title of the post described.
2   Title of the position to which the incumbent reports.
3   Titles of all positions directly supervised.
4   Functional relationships if these exist.

Basic purpose of the job

Why does the job exist? What is its primary function? This is also fundamental, but surprisingly often the answers are not clearly stated. In general, I find that the basic purpose of any post should be capable of being stated in a couple of simple sentences. Where this is not readily done, an immediate close look at the organization structure (or the job incumbent) is frequently justified.

As an example, the purpose of a General Sales Manager's job might be :

> 'To organize and lead a field sales team to achieve or exceed planned volume of sales of . . . without exceeding the budgeted expense or resources.' (This statement is clearly expanded by reference to the sales forecasts, budgets, and any stated objectives.) A second sentence might qualify some aspect of this purpose.

Current objectives

The most important part of a full position guide will be the statement of current objectives assigned to the incumbent. These are obviously likely to change in content over a period of time, but at each point in time will influence the whole character of the job. As we discussed separately, objectives and operating environment jointly provide the basis for the required man specification.

As mentioned earlier in this chapter, objectives have to be as specific as possible, and be capable of measurement where possible. The development of meaningful objectives is discussed in detail later in this chapter.

Linked to objectives should be an assessment of potential difficulties in achieving these—the environment factors—for it is this combination which will be used to provide the man specification, and by this route an evaluation of the current market value for effective performance of the job.

Performance standards

Directly related to objectives, a position guide should contain a summary which begins with a phrase on the lines :

> 'Performance will be considered satisfactory when . . .'

Objectives are not always set out with great precision. Where they require, for example, achievement of the 'best possible results', further statement of the standard which will be considered adequate will be of great value to the job holder. There can be enormous differences between objectives set as 'ideal aiming points' (which frequently happens) and the more specific statement of what will be considered acceptable. Even tidily stated, quantified and timed objectives may leave much to interpretation which can be clarified by defining performance standards.

As with objectives, the production and selection of meaningful standards takes time. As with objectives, that time is almost invariably felt to be well spent. Once a manager has used a position guide incorporating standards, he is not likely to be satisfied with anything less.

Resources and authority

A position guide which does not show the resources made available to the incumbent to enable him to carry out his tasks will be inadequate.

The financial budget for his activity presents these resources in one form, but this needs to be backed up by clear statements in other language. For example, the total budgeted pay-roll cost should be backed by a list of the manpower or manpower types and levels on which the figures are based, for any manpower budget should have arisen from an assessment of the work which will need to be done and the skills required for achievement.

Similarly, production or technical resources available should be stated 'in clear' rather than only the financial translation.

Given resources, what freedom will the manager have to use them? As the degree of freedom delegated to him to use these resources is variable, a statement of authority will be required.

Specifically, freedom to authorize actual expenditure as opposed to recommending for someone else's signature is something which a manager must know. Also, can he recruit and vary the salaries of his subordinates without reference, or alter his staff size or mix?

We need to set out the limitations clearly so that he is able to get on with his job without having to worry whether he is exceeding his authority—or finding that his authority is variable!

Accountability

As authority is delegated from above, the manager must know to whom he is accountable for his actions in exercising his authority. It is a curious phenomenon that some managers have dual or multiple upward reporting relationships, and it is conceivable that they may receive conflicting instructions from their various superiors. In such a case, a manager may feel acutely vulnerable—a situation easily avoided by defining accountability to a single superior.

Authority is delegated from above. It is delegated by the individual holding the post which carries the authority to be delegated. This individual is entitled to retain some control over the delegated power, and to withdraw it if necessary. In view of this relationship, the subordinate may not, logically, be accountable to anyone else.

The incumbent of a staff position is equally accountable for his actions for he may also have direct authority delegated to him.

The authority which a staff man may exercise over an individual who is 'functionally responsible' to him is quite different. He may have responsibility without direct authority. He achieves his results by lobbying and persuasion, with the knowledge that he can use the heavy authority of his chief if necessary. This recognizes that staff functions are essentially part of a chief executive's office, assisting with the development and implementation of corporate policies. The real authority of any staff appointment is linked to his standing in the chief executive's office—which can be personal and not definable for a subsequent incumbent.

Defining the actual authority of any staff appointment is difficult. It will depend on the competence, effectiveness and personality of the incumbent in relation to the line management team. Perhaps it is often best left to be worked out in practice!

Position: General Sales Manager

Reports to: Managing Director—Excelsior Engineering Co. Ltd.

Reporting to him: Home Sales Manager
                            Export Sales Manager
                            Marketing Manager

Functional relationship with Group Marketing Director.

Purpose or Function: To organize and lead field sales operations to achieve or exceed the sales targets set out in the company's business plan, without exceeding budgeted expense or resources. To organize and lead necessary marketing activities, and develop field sales strategies for all products.

Specific objectives for the year 19xx (abbreviated form)

1. To achieve the sales growth of 14% to £6.300,000, as set out in detail in the sales budget (reference PX 13, dated 00/00/00); these sales to be achieved within the expense budget shown.

2. To complete preparations for the launching of product X by 1st April.

3. To test market product Y in N.E. England during August-September and recommend further action by 1st October.

4. To ensure that forward market analyses are carried out covering the Z product range and possible developments for that range; report to the product development committee by 1st July, recommending lines for R & D effort on this range.

5. Improve the speed of order analysis to achieve daily order summaries by product group, as soon as possible. Develop follow-up procedures to investigate variation in intake by product group.

6. Draw up organization and manning proposals by October, to separate the sales organization of Z product range by July next year. Determine the effect on the remainder of the sales organization—draw up and implement individual training and development plans for staff affected.

Note: The detailed performance standards for the General Sales Manager have not been shown.

Resources:

Personnel: Field force of Field Sales Managers—
                              4 Area Managers
                              18 Sales Engineers.

                Internal force of Marketing Manager—
                              Sales Office Manager
                              2 Contracts Engineers
                              5 Office Staff.

Financial: See budgets for detail.

Equipment: 26 cars; various product samples. See budgets for detail.

Figure 10.1 Position guide

Authority:

Full authority to act within operating budgets and objectives.

Approval required for

1. Establishment of operating budgets and objectives.

2. Special orders likely to have a material effect on forecasts or which carry any special risk.

3. Capital expenditure in excess of budget.

4. Appointment and remuneration of managerial staff.

5. Changes in commission schemes.

6. Activity outside defined geographical and product areas.

Accountability

To Managing Director

Frequent informal meetings on all aspects of sales and marketing activities of the business for general reporting and information.
Prepare monthly report covering activities of department.
Prepare daily order reports.
Prepare *ad hoc* reports as required.

To Group Marketing Director

Informal meetings from time to time on aspects of marketing policy and strategy.
Prepare monthly report covering market developments.
Obtain agreement (with Managing Director) to marketing organization and staffing changes.
Prepare regular market analyses and P.R. expense summaries.

Relationship:

Production Control Manager: daily liaison on variations from scheduled production likely to affect deliveries; weekly meeting to ensure that production meets sales requirements.

Technical Manager: liaison as required on special customer requirements; monthly product development committee meeting to review future product requirements and progress on existing development projects towards availability for sale.

Good Housekeeping Factors:

Ensure effective reporting from and control of field staff.
Ensure that field reports are properly analysed and action taken where required.
Ensure that staff are properly utilized, and potential abilities are developed.

for a General Sales Manager

Relationships

Where an organization is complex, it may be relevant to specify the important cross relationships, which may be essential to the effective working of the structure. For example, a purchasing or inventory control function may be linked to an accounting department rather than to manufacturing; in which case, liaison with the production control activity will need to be very close if stock investment is to be minimized but production is to run smoothly.

'Good housekeeping'—the continuing job

Where the current objectives indicate the major immediate priorities and the basic purpose provides a back-cloth, most positions contain a volume of regular or minor activities which are essential to the job. For example, the straightforward administration of a department, the welfare and development of subordinates, the continuing eye on systems, the required participation in committee work, are all essential activities which absorb time and may be delegated only in part. These 'good housekeeping' activities require to be stated where a full statement of the requirements from an incumbent are set out.

This part of the position guide may appear very detailed and long-winded, but for the man who is newly appointed it can be an enormous help in getting to grips with the full job.

Figure 10.1 shows a full position guide prepared in reasonably abbreviated form.

Notes on style

Language

At a seminar some time ago, a speaker summarized language for some purpose under the headings 'imperative'—'indicative'—'decorative'. The last thing one wants in a position guide is decorative language—padding.

One manager I know refuses to read anything over one quarto side. At best, he will read the front page of a larger document. Recognizing that managers generally are busy people with far too much to read, position guides need to be crisp and concise—if necessary, in staccato part sentences which convey meaning without wasting words.

Long-winded presentation is indicative of muddle or indecisive thinking.

'Discrepancies'

When information is collected, variation in understanding of the content of a job between manager and subordinate is sometimes revealed, particularly in companies with 'permissive' styles of management. If job information is to be of any real value, it is essential that discrepancies be resolved speedily between the parties concerned—or through appeal to some higher authority.

Organizations can exist, and be effective, where there is overlap of responsibilities between departments, where individuals have multiple reporting relationships, even where supervisor and subordinates have differing views about the subordinate's job. But these things all add to the difficulties of any operating situation and are to be discouraged, quite apart from the confusion they add to any job analysis!

Maintenance

As jobs and organizations are dynamic rather than static, I make no use of previously prepared information until it has been reviewed and updated, regardless of how recently it may have been prepared. Opinions and views can change remarkably quickly on occasion—perhaps as a wider scene becomes apparent—and it is essential to work on current material.

Objectives

Pricing of jobs needs to be linked to some form of statement of the job and the standards of performance required. This is likely to be arrived at by defining the objectives which an incumbent will be expected to achieve, the difficulties he is expected to overcome, the resources he will have at his disposal and his freedom to use these.

From this data we may arrive at a specification of the individual likely to be most successful in the situation. The price we should have to pay for such an individual in the free market is the central fact in pricing the job.

While the basic purpose of any job is likely to be reasonably constant, and should be clear enough for it to be stated in a couple of brief sentences, the *objectives* of a job are likely to be changing constantly.

Consider the case of a Sales Manager of a new product division. His purpose is to achieve maximum sales of the new product range, subject to remaining profitable within defined limits. This purpose may remain virtually unchanged for ten years or more.

In the first year, his objectives are related to market research and test markets, to creating a small sales force at minimum expense, possibly on a 'commission only' basis, to evaluating each step on a 'go/no go' basis. (The man specification probably includes the phrase 'must have an entrepreneurial flair'.)

A couple of years later, the product is established, highly successful and profitable; there are no serious competitors yet in the field. Objectives are concerned less with marketing, and emphasize a requirement for a rapid build-up of the field sales team, recruiting the right personnel, training them, developing supervisors; evolving better incentive plans; very little emphasis on controls of any sort.

By the fifth year, the competitors are thick on the ground and are beginning to be felt. Profit margins are still high, but have been trimmed a lot, and promotional expenses are rising. The order-taker salesmen are proving less effective. The Sales Manager's job has altered in scale in terms of the number of subordinates. His objectives are switching back to evaluating the competition and acting to hold sales growth.

A year later, objectives require a build-up of market research, development of sales promotion support, emphasis on identifying product development requirements, re-training or re-staffing of the field force. (Somebody has suggested changing the title of the job in line with the changing man specification—and they are wondering if the original entrepreneur is likely to grasp enough of what his bright new marketing people are producing.)

Within ten years, the job has broadened further. Objectives

include preparing for and launching new and additional products as well as strategic planning to get the best out of the earlier range. The span of skills required by the man who is now entitled 'marketing director' is very different from the original enterpreneur, but the post is still that of top sales appointment in the division.

Perhaps few jobs change at this pace. My belief is that very many are changing even faster, and that the rate of change is one of the fundamental problems of man management today.

With change of objectives comes change of man specification, and pressure on training and development programmes—and of obsolescence, redundancy and precise recruitment.

The implication for remuneration is that as any commercial situation changes and new objectives are set, the evolving man specification must be continually re-priced. For the individual who survives with change against a toughening man specification rises steeply. For the individual in a start-up position with a declining man specification, our problem is transfer to better utilization and replacement with less expensive material.

Executive manpower utilization is closely linked with motivation—with retaining high-level job satisfaction in a rapidly changing world. The remuneration aspect provides an alternate means of measuring present utilization. A £7000 man in a job revalued at £5000 after a two-year revitalizing stint will feel under-employed and apply pressure for job growth when promotion is not forthcoming.

But let us get back to objectives.

The company's objectives

All objectives assigned to a job stem directly from the commercial objectives of the group or company or division. The tasks which the commercial unit sets out to achieve require certain work to be done. Most work has some functional link (to accounting, or production, etc.), so that the total volume breaks down into a series of tidy parcels. The head of each function is assigned his parcel—effective achievement, on time, is essential if the total objectives of the unit are to be fulfilled.

The parcel for each function is likely to be broken down into a series of subsidiary parcels for the next line of managers; and to be further allocated until we reach the level of staff whose assignments tend to be wholly of a shorter-term nature.

The total pattern of objectives will be closely linked and inter-dependent. Failure to complete quite a minor objective on schedule in one area may throw out a whole series of other plans across the whole organization.

If we are to establish objectives, we must know first of all the overall business intention. If this is not reasonably defined, then the limitations on the precision and value of any objectives set for individual managers are likely to be substantial, for there is an insufficient foundation on which to build.

Where there is lack of precision in overall commercial objectives, I find that, while objectives for managers may be stated in apparently precise form, they lack measurables. Thus on very subjective grounds a manager may 'succeed' or 'fail', for the basis for evaluation cannot be adequately measured.

The discipline of defining standards as a basis for the review of performance is clearly worthwhile in such a situation. The whole basis of objectives setting is analytical, and to stop short of specific conclusions can suggest only that the analysis has been incomplete or that the executive team is not competent to draw conclusions.

Objectives setting implies planning. It implies that a management team has made a comprehensive assessment of its environment and of potential change; has reached certain specific conclusions as to what it may reasonably expect to accomplish in the reasonably short- to medium-term future; has stated these and the problems it expects to overcome in acceptably precise terms; and is setting out to achieve its plans.

If the team has done things thoroughly, and it is likely to have done so if it has produced quantified answers, it will have incorporated assessments of every aspect of its business in each of its conclusions. This obviously includes personnel factors.

Objectives for the General Manager

The objectives of the chief executive of any organizational unit are quite simply the successful achievement of the commercial objectives as a whole, qualified by longer-term factors.

Where the General Manager identifies the key objectives or

purpose of his job, and sets against these (for agreement with his chief) the standards of performance which he believes are achievable and acceptable during the immediate year, he will be able to understand the appraisal made of his performance.

One serious problem in objectives setting can arise where a chief executive deliberately puts aside all long-term factors in order to achieve or beat the profit target for the current year, on the grounds that he is striving for bigger things and may not be around in three years' time! Proper supervision from his chairman or other immediate superior is the only practical means of ensuring that this does not happen.

Objectives for a top functional manager

The executive in charge of a line activity such as a manufacturing, sales or technical department, is likely to have objectives which are quite specific. To start with, he will be required to produce or sell a stated volume of goods of a stated mix of types, to stated tolerances, to stated costs, and programmed to stated dates. At least monthly, and probably more frequently, he will be able to see clearly whether his primary objectives are being achieved, to assess the causes of variations, and to take corrective action if he is off course.

The objectives of a sales manager may be to expand sales as much as possible, with defined minimum volume figures quoted. Within this dynamic objective, we can state that performance is acceptable when the sales volume reaches defined figures, linked to other factors of product mix and sales expense.

'To achieve an overall volume increase in sales for the region of 15 per cent over the 1974 figures during 1975.'

In planning implementation, subsidiary standards set might be :
'To maintain all existing major accounts as customers of the company, the only losses to be where a business is closed' and

'To identify by June 1975 all major accounts with an expected growth potential for the year in excess of $7\frac{1}{2}$ per cent, to ensure that the company's share of this growth exceeds $7\frac{1}{2}$ per cent during the period July–December 1975.'

The manager may well have a variety of secondary objectives, but any assessment of his performance will give very substantial weighting to the primary activities. However, standards can still be set :

'To draw up procedures for the use of technical support by . . .' (date)
—or on market information :

'To ensure that all new and improved products being marketed by competitors; competitors' critical price policies and efforts to win our accounts; are reported by sales representatives immediately.'

Objectives for a subordinate manager

The objectives of a subordinate manager will vary substantially in line with his type of activity. The man leading a straightforward operating activity will have simple and precise objectives : to produce or sell or otherwise process specific quantities of products, paper, etc.; to control his department in order to meet scheduled production targets within quality and cost standards, and within his expenditure budget.

In service activities, targets will be less precise, but are likely to be measurable within reason.

Objectives: staff role

The senior staff man may be given no authority, and is therefore unable to take any operating decisions. His objectives are necessarily in a different form (and assessing his achievements is more complex).

He will have been appointed for some purpose which can be defined. If the purpose is known, what factors or measures will enable us to assess what has been achieved? The question should also be asked : 'Who were the individuals able to influence achievement or failure apart from the staff man?'

Objectives are likely to be stated in the form :

'To influence attitudes of management at large to the acceptability of transferring from piece work to high day rates. To ensure that there is an adequate understanding of the problems involved, particularly the need to develop supervisory strengths, and to encourage action to move towards a high day rate structure by . . .' (date)

We may not be able to measure attitudes, but in a year's time we should be able to assess whether there has been advance in acceptability of the idea—and in three years, whether we have achieved the intention through the action of others.

Standards are less easy to set in staff areas than in line, for the line manager has concrete targets which he is expected to reach, while the staff man can make few decisions and the extent of his influence is not measurable in simple terms. We might use :

'The programme of adoption of (management by objectives—say) is not held up as a result of lack of understanding of the methods and procedures, as revealed by questioning any manager who is so delayed.' Or

'The quality of . . . is not found to be below standard as a result of lack of advice . . .'

Environmental factors—impact on man specification

A man specification is likely to be substantially influenced by the environment in which the job holder will be expected to operate. Where two jobs are basically identical, one may exist in a situation where all external factors are favourable and the incumbent will be able to succeed easily, while the other may be hedged in with difficulties.

Two export sales managers in the same industry, and with similar targets in export markets in identical countries, may need very different skills. Mr A has a well-established product of high quality, competitively priced and with no real competition in an expanding market. His problem, if he has one, is to explain the delivery delays due to the heavy order book. The current man specification is similarly undemanding. Mr B has a new product which has been rushed out and has some initial 'bugs'. The price is rather high in relation to the strong competition, and the market is close to saturation. If he is to be successful, the incumbent will need to bring a wide range of skills to bear, quite apart from the supporting resources he will need. The man specification is tough.

Commercial difficulties represent the major part of environmental factors. It is reasonable to assess the difficulty of achieving each of the objectives defined. How are they to be achieved? What are the factors which may restrict success? How may these be overcome?

If these appear straightforward, then the man specification will be related directly to the requirements imposed by the job itself. But if there are particular difficulties, the additional skills necessary to overcome these will upgrade both the man specification and the job.

Resources available for achievement are equally important. Where the support is substantial, problems diminish in relative size. But where tough objectives are set and the resources available are barely sufficient to cover the work to be done, the skills required from a manager to ensure success are correspondingly wider.

Freedom to deploy resources may become a factor in some organizations. While adequacy is one aspect, tight control on utilization from some higher level may restrict freedom to operate and add difficulties which must be offset by higher man specification.

Political environment is less easily defined and qualified. The level of political activity in any organization is always difficult to measure and is rarely constant. Yet the level of political difficulty confronting any job at a specific point in time is a factor in determining the man specification.

For example, a new staff appointment in a traditionally functional structure has a pathfinding job. His skills in selling his abilities to cynical managers may influence his success or failure, yet this is not an obvious skill identifiable from his job description and objectives.

Finally, *performance standards* are associated with existing company attitudes, and this is as important an environmental factor as any. If you wish to change the pace of a company, or in any way alter the existing attitudes, the personality factors you will need to build into your man specification will be very high. In fact, these skills of overcoming inertia (which are more than extrovert enthusiasm) are of high market value and are unlikely to be acquired by accident.

Chapter 11

Appraisal

Let us take ten Clerks in a department—any department, and any ten Clerks doing identical jobs—and examine how well they are doing their jobs.

The first Clerk is painstaking, slow and accurate. A second is very fast, but his speed is more than offset by a high degree of error and irregularity in his work. A third is 'coasting along', the job under control but output moderate owing to his lack of interest. He could cope with a much bigger job and is actively looking for one! Each of the Clerks has some facet of his performance and personality that makes him quite different from the others. The measurable output varies substantially, as does the accuracy of the work and the amount of subsequent checking required.

Is it fair and proper to pay each of these employees an identical basic salary? And, if not, in what way and for what reasons should their pay vary? The answers to these two questions are fundamental to any modern concept of salary administration—yet answers are not clear cut and standard.

Unionized staff generally support the view that there should be no differences in pay for performance, beyond minor ones. 'If some individuals are able and willing to do their jobs better than others, it is not the fault of the individual that he is less productive than his fellows.'

At career staff levels, the opposite view is generally held, that individual performance and ability should be linked to wide salary variation.

It is increasingly possible for differences in performance to be assessed analytically, unemotionally and accurately. It is increasingly in the interest of managers to respond to better-than-average performance and reward competent staff accordingly.

The conflict between these opposing views is extremely difficult to solve in the practical situation. Defence of a situation where appraisal is applied to salary administration is only possible where the appraisal system can be shown to be objective and fair. The continued use of personality-based appraisal systems which are so open to emotional bias cannot be defended. However, it is very much easier to tick a few boxes on the typical personality trait format, the managements continue to invite inevitable trouble by use of outdated systems. If appraisal is to be used, let us accept that it takes time and thought to do properly, and that the value of the exercise amply justifies the effort.

Assessment of performance can be approached in a variety of ways, the more common of which we shall discuss, particularly emphasizing their relevance and application to salary administration.

Performance appraisal methods

It is clearly essential to make some attempt at accurate measurement of performance if the appraisal is to be taken seriously into account as a factor which will influence salaries.

A moment's thought confirms that performance cannot be easily measured on a scale, and that, even supposing it could, the performance of an Engineer and that of a Clerk necessarily could not be measured on a scale using the same factors.

It is vital that factors which are applicable to the job held, and which are important to the organization, should be determined and defined. It is also important that the individual making the appraisal should have a sufficient knowledge of the job held by the employee on whom he is reporting.

The usual procedure is for one of the various types of appraisal forms to be completed by the employee's supervisor and manager, one and two levels above him. Some authorities are critical of reports by immediate supervisors who may know the employee too well. More than two levels above, the individual is unlikely to be known well enough.

It is interesting to note that most forms or methods in use are changed at relatively short intervals by the organizations using them, as being or becoming ineffective in various ways. There are various reasons for this, of course, but it does not occur in companies whose managements are performance appraisal orientated, and who accept the values of assessment systems. But in a less enlightened atmosphere, where managers tend to be distrustful of appraisal, the constant change is often a vain attempt to keep one jump ahead of 'bending the system' by reporters!

The summary which follows examines some of the main systems of appraisal in use, describes their operation and considers their relative merits and deficiencies.

There is no single system of performance reporting which has achieved general acceptance. The basic types of formal assessment in use can be listed as follows.

1   Simple verbal appraisal.
2   Ranking method of appraisal.
3   Forced distribution/forced choice method.
4   'Tick box' schemes—the linear scale method.
5   Whole-job appraisal—strong/weak points.
6   Appraisal against pre-set objectives defined in position guides.

Simple verbal appraisal

The simplest of all appraisal methods is embodied in the often-asked question, 'Is he any good?'. 'Yes' or 'No' answers give a minimum of help—a 'Yes, but . . .' answer tells a little more.

Stage two is to ask if he is 'Poor—Adequate—Good—Very Good or Outstanding'. The answers to this five-point-scale question collect around 'Good' and 'Very Good', but there is a better chance of highlighting the man of unusually good or bad performance by the use of unusual ratings.

From these quick and frequently used verbal appraisals, we proceed to the various types of more formal rating.

Ranking method of appraisal

One of the most effective of the simpler forms of performance, or potential, appraisal consists of asking supervisors to place employees in a rank order on the basis of their relative performance. The simplest ranking plans restrict the exercise to employees doing similar tasks at one time or in one ranking, and also make no attempt to predetermine the factors to be considered.

The rankings produced by this method identify the outstanding performers and the poor performers with reasonable accuracy, and probably indicate that the middle group are sufficiently similar in value to the organization for further differentiation to be of little value. This method has the basic disadvantage that supervisors may rate individuals unrealistically for a variety of reasons, such as personal likes and dislikes.

A development of the ranking system is the definition of factors to be considered and general advice and guidance on how the exercise is to be carried out. An experienced supervisor in charge of a typing pool will not find difficulty in preparing a simple ranking of her staff in respect of speed, accuracy, and perhaps in layout and other factors. A Chief Draughtsman or Clerical Supervisor would be similarly competent in respect of their staff. At more senior levels, the manager might rank his supervisors on supervisory ability, or on judgment and other factors which require clear definition, if any sort of standard is to be achieved.

These limitations lead quickly to attempts to define all the factors to be used, and immediately to a realization that the factors themselves will be incomplete, even in relation to a simple job, unless the appraisal requirements are impossibly large.

Forced distribution/paired comparison method

A variation of simple ranking, in which supervisors seem invariably to group employees of similar aptitudes together rather than to try to differentiate between them, is found in forced distribution and paired comparison systems.

Supervisors may be given a series of pairs of employees and asked to say who is the better of the two. Comparisons between each member and each other member of a group enable an overall ranking to be built-up, although the peculiar phenomenon of circular triads, in which *A* is better than *B* who is better than *C* who is better than *A* may lead to a certain amount of grouping.

Forced distribution usually applies to larger groups of employees. The aim is to identify, on the basis of whole performance, the best 10 per cent and the worst 10 per cent, and then the next best 20 per cent and next worst 20 per cent, leaving a residue of 40 per cent as the block of average performers.

These relatively simple methods have the advantage of being reasonably fast, and, if more than one rater is used, of being acceptably accurate.

'Tick box' schemes—linear scale methods

The use of a linear scale to 'measure' level of performance may be considered equivalent to the use of points evaluation for measuring jobs. Performance cannot be measured specifically. There are too many factors to take into account, too many variables, for any scale to be defensible.

Schemes using linear scales, or performance measurement, may be concerned with one type of job, or all jobs in an organization. They may attempt no more than a single overall assessment of performance, or they may require a series of reviews under a number of factors or traits. They may use a short line marked 'good' at one end and 'bad' at the other, with no defined intervals or guides to intermediate values, or they may attempt to state clearly an interpretation in words for each of a large number of points along separate scales for each trait.

Within this wide diversity of linear scale systems, most of the schemes in use in the UK have muddled along during the past decade, all too often in the hands of people with an inadequate understanding of the purpose of appraisal or the meaning of the results obtained. However, this does not mean that all these schemes are useless by any means, and some of the better ones have served their purpose well. In practice, there is a great deal to be said in favour of linear scale schemes, particularly as a means of establishing the appraisal concept in a relatively unsophisticated company.

As these schemes vary so much, we have examined each of the four main types below, and discussed the merits of each variation.

1 Overall rating of performance on a simple scale The best example of a procedure of this type would require an overall appraisal of performance for all types of employee in an organization using a scale of from 1 to 5, with no guidance beyond an indication that a rating of 1 is very poor while 5 is exceptionally good. The results of such a scheme invariably show a grouping of ticks into levels '3' and '4' of well over 90 per cent of the total appraisals! The 1 or 2 per cent of staff marked in the lower ratings and the 5 per cent in the top rating identify *probable* outstandingly bad and good performers, but this rating is certainly not conclusive without further evidence.

Such a plan invariably requires some additional questions or space for a brief written report in support of the basic appraisal, and this obviously reduces its value both as a speedily completed exercise and for easy reference.

It is important to note that additional reports on each individual by other supervisors and managers sometimes show alarming variations in appraisal level and also in the additional notes, possibly due to the lack of serious thought devoted to an apparently simple exercise. As with all appraisal reporting systems, only extensive training and guidance, in this case out of proportion to the simplicity of the plan, can improve this position.

Our conclusion is that it is unlikely that a plan on these lines will prove very satisfactory.

2 Appraisal within groups of similar staff Where groups of staff are engaged on similar work, such as Accounts Clerks or Draughtsmen, a more elaborate form may be used for each individual category, defining a series of appropriate traits in each case. Within each trait, levels of performance or attainment can be indicated and a reliable performance ranking can be achieved.

The factors selected for each category should be based on the more important facets of the job content, such as 'accuracy' for Statisticians (but not for Receptionists), and defined performance levels on scales can be established in line with job requirements.

FACTORS:

Output	(1)	(2)
Does he produce the volume of work you would normally expect from the employee on this post?	Exceptionally high output	Output above standard
Knowledge		
Does he have a full understanding of all aspects of his job?	Exceptionally wide knowledge of his subject	Full understanding of job requirements
Accuracy		
Is he accurate?	Very accurate and reliable	Accurate—rarely makes a mistake
Initiative		
Does he make proper use of his initiative within the limits of his job?	Exceptionally sound— reliable over the full range of his job	Makes sensible decision at all times
Attitude		
Is he co-operative?	Extremely co-operative	Works very well with others
Adaptability		
Does he learn quickly and adapt to new situations?	Exceptionally well able to cope with new situations	Learns quickly and adapts to change

Notes and comments:

Supervisor   Date   Manager

Figure 11.1   Simple 'tick-box' appraisal

RATING FORM (CLERICAL)

cation of employee)

(3)	(4)	(5)
Meets the required standards	Tends to be rather slow	Needs constant prodding
Satisfactory—able to cope with all-round situations	Fair degree of knowledge, but requires some help	Needs a lot of help
Normally accurate	Inclined to make mistakes—work must be checked	Unreliable—inclined to repeat errors
Satisfactory	Inclined to keep to the rules—slow to use initiative	Keeps rigidly to the rules
A willing member of the team	Not always helpful	Awkward
Learns readily	Slow to adjust	Does not adjust—suitable for repetitive work only

Date	*Personnel Department*	*Date*

form to cover clerical staff

MERIT RATING REPORT

Name: .... *Age:* ....

Job Title: .... *Service:* ....

FACTORS:

In each case, consider the requirements of the job, and how well the employee matches up to the requirement.

Consider whether he has sufficient training and experience to carry out his work satisfactorily:

Consider whether he completes a satisfactory volume of work:

Consider the quality of his work; is it up to the standard required?

Consider his reactions to changing conditions and requirements:

What is his attitude to his job—his willingness to work as a member of the team?

Is his timekeeping satisfactory?

Notes:

Figure 11.2 General

(MALE STAFF)

.... *Division:* ....

.... *Section:* ....

REPORTS

Limited knowledge and experience	Good standard of training and experience	High standard of training and experience	Exceptionally high standard
Exceptionally high output	Output above the average for similar staff	Volume satisfactory	Volume not adequate (Comment in notes below)
Quality and accuracy always very high	Quality and accuracy generally good	Quality always acceptable	All work requires checking
Slow to adjust to change	Adapts to change satisfactorily	Adapts to change and copes with new work quickly	Exceptionally adaptable
Exceptionally co-operative	Works very well with others	A good team member	Awkward
Regularly late	Late on a few occasions each month	Rarely late	Extremely punctual

	Prepared by:
	Approved by:

linear appraisal form

This approach provides the basis for cross-comparison of performance between groups employed on similar work in different departments. Comparison can be carried out by simple cross-reference factor by factor. In a very large organization, values may be set on factors and scales evolved to enable rough overall scores to be calculated and a company-wide rank order produced.

It is important that common understanding of all wording is achieved, both through the use of clear-cut simple language, and by training sessions in which deviations of interpretation are identified. Comparison of scores produced by different raters should be examined critically, and no comparison whatsoever should be made between scores obtained on different groups of forms covering separate occupational groups. Figure 11.1 shows a form of this type developed to cover clerical staff.

Within the obvious limitations, the approach discussed above provides a reasonably accurate guide to variations in levels of performance between staff on similar work. However, it ignores completely the problem of trying to establish a standard measure of performance for *all* employees, particularly in a large organization.

3 Linear appraisal form designed to cover all types of staff The comprehensive plan, developed for the appraisal of all staff employees in a company, is forced to move away from the precise factors which may apply specifically to a small group of like jobs, and attempts to find general factors common to most types of activity. The inevitable effect, which is clear from all examples of forms of this type, is that the traits become less clearly defined to allow for interpretation in different types of activity, and personality factors tend to be used in place of job factors.

Figures 11.2 and 11.3 are typical of the better forms of this type, and give a useful indication of the range of factors, such as Job Knowledge, Work Quality, Output, Initiative, Adaptability, and so on, which could be adapted in any new scheme. The selection of factors for every new or revised scheme of this type would take into account considerations similar to those influencing the choice of job evaluation factors.

Operationally, the manager who is faced with assessing

Work Quality

Consider the neatness, thoroughness, accuracy of the work done in relation to basic standards required.

1	2	3	4	5	6	7	8	9	10

Unsatisfactory in all respects	Work requires close check and generally falls short of requirement	Satisfactory quality, subject to normal check	Good quality work with few errors	Constant high standard with no errors

Dependability

Consider the extent of supervision required, and the willingness of the employee to get on with his work without constant watch

1	2	3	4	5	6	7	8	9	10

Requires constant supervision	Needs encouragement to get on with work	Gets on with his work under normal supervision	Requires a minimum of supervision	Completely dependable and reliable at all times

Initiative

Consider his ability to use his initiative to deal with problems, and his willingness to accept the responsibility of so doing

1	2	3	4	5	6	7	8	9	10

Follows the rules and refers all queries to his supervisor	Requires assistance with most queries	Requires some assistance when queries arise	Self-reliant and competent	Exceptionally successful in his actions

Output

Consider his productivity against the normal requirement of his post

1	2	3	4	5	6	7	8	9	10

Output inadequate	His output is less than expected	Produces an acceptable volume of work	Produces more than is normally expected	Produces an exceptionally high volume

Figure 11.3 Part of a tick-box appraisal form

Supervisory Ability for an employee who has never had supervisory responsibility, or some similar problem, may feel uneasily that the resulting appraisal is not going to reflect the real value of the individual in his present post. He may leave the space blank, but in some plans this would mean that the employee's total score would be low owing to a 'nil' against the non-relevant factor.

A compromise in this circumstance might be the addition of a minimum or mid-point score for the omitted trait, or inflation of the employee's total score excluding trait 'X' by a percentage factor based on the weighting of the omitted trait. However, it would be preferable simply to indicate that the score excluded a mark for one factor.

If as many as 20 per cent of traits are not relevant to an extent where no attempt to rate the employee on those factors is possible, some amendment to the plan is clearly indicated.

It is inevitable that most schemes of this sort are subjected to attempts to convert the results into an arithmetical score. The arguments which are covered in the discussion of points systems of job evaluation apply equally here. However carefully factors are selected, some will inevitably be inadequate for some groups of jobs, if not all; weightings applied are arbitrary, and scales within weightings are attempts to create semi-scientific measures where none can be proven, and perhaps none exists.

Statistical analyses of results obtained over large samples can provide some help in checking for inadequacies. The initial stage required the selection of factors, the definitions of the factors, and the overall weightings chosen to be accepted by the company's management. Subsequently examination of the distribution of appraisals against each factor can provide a basis for review, and suggest the need for variations in definitions, values assigned to points on the scales, and possibly other changes to ensure a reasonably normal curve of distribution of both appraisals and scores. Calculation of the standard deviation* of actual scores for each factor, using the number of ticks in each box, provides an exact picture of the real weightings, as the relationship between the standard deviations for each factor

* A good textbook of statistics will explain normal distribution and standard deviation, show the calculations, and supply formulae; e.g. Moroney's *Facts from Figures* (London: Penguin Books).

reflects the actual relative weightings. For example, a high standard deviation indicates use of the whole range while a low standard deviation indicates a cluster of ticks and use of a limited part of the range, which reduces the effective weighting.

The linear scale or 'tick-box' type of performance appraisal scheme can provide a valuable guide to performance levels if intelligently used. By this, we mean simply that the obvious limitations of the system should be recognized and taken into account in all interpretations of results. As an example, comparisons of results covering staff in different types of jobs should not be considered as a precise guide to relative performance levels.

4 Company-wide linear scale method—theoretical perfection For the addict of the points system of job evaluation, optimum results may appear to be obtainable by linking the points system of job evaluation directly with a system of apprasisal. In such a scheme the factors used in the job evaluation plan would be duplicated in the appraisal plan; the weighting of factors in the appraisal plan would be varied job by job, precisely in line with the job evaluation scores for each post, so that each individual would appear to be measured solely against the evaluated requirements of his job.

This sounds an ideal plan, until one recalls the unscientific basis of both job evaluation and appraisal, or investigates its administrative complexity. Such a plan is systematic, and is feasible but would it be worth the time and effort when compared with some of the simpler and more effective plans discussed next?

Whole-job appraisal—strong and weak points

The chapter on job evaluation methods (Chapter 6) concluded with the statement that whole-job ranking is basically the best system as it recognizes the limitations of the evaluation process and works within these limitations. Similarly, in 'whole-job appraisal' we recognize the limitations of the appraisal process and adopt flexibility, to provide the best possible result within these limits.

H

EMPLOYEE APPRAISAL FORM

Employee:............................ Job Title:................... Dept./Div.................

Appraiser:... Date:.....................................

A. What are the employee's strong points?

B. What are the employee's weak points?

C. What is the effect of his weak points on his job?

D. What is being done to remedy weak points?

E. What action do you intend to take to broaden or promote this employee during the next twelve months?

Figure 11.4 Simple 'whole-job' appraisal form with strongest/weakest point questions

In this system we reject any attempt to convert performance appraisal into mathematical formulae and set about the serious, practical problem of how each individual's performance can be improved and how he can best be employed. The system asks about his strong and weak points, or its questions are directed specifically to relate to performance within the job's requirements.

Figure 11.4 is one of the simpler type, asking general questions about overall performance, strengths and weaknesses. It is a form which provides a sound basic appraisal of an individual in a job; it gives help to a supervisor counselling his staff on their performance, or recommending salary action, but provides little help for determining the better of two closely matched performers. Perhaps this does not matter.

Figure 11.5 is of a more sophisticated form, introduced in a company with a long background of detailed appraisal and with an interested and enlightened management. This form requires a greater than usual allocation of time. It is devoted primarily to improving performance and secondly to determining the approximate area of the salary range appropriate to performance. It requires a series of discussions (a better word than interview in the circumstances), between the supervisor and employee, initially to define and agree the various aspects of his job; next a counselling based on the supervisor's estimate of the employee's performance against each of these aspects, on which appeal to higher authority is permissible in the event of disagreement; and finally a formal signing of the agreed assessment by the two parties.

As a means of appraising and improving performance, it is unlikely that the 'whole-job appraisal' procedure can be beaten, even in its simpler form. In application to salary reviews, the shortcomings of each individual and his improvements over the year, it can provide guidance on appropriate salary levels and pace of salary progress through a salary range. It emphasizes the individual nature of salary planning, and shies away from the procedure-before-flexibility type of administration which tends to be encouraged by scored appraisal methods.

Staff Appraisal of..

Job Title:	Department:	Division:

Firstly	Secondly
On this side of the form, list out brief statements of the DUTIES and RESPONSIBILITIES, listing them in descending order of importance.	On this side of the form, comment on the employees' performance against each of the duties and responsibilities of the job. Where appropriate, quote examples in support of your comments, covering specific important incidents.

Figure 11.5 'Whole-job' appraisal form of open-discussion type

Appraisal against objectives

A further variation on 'whole-job appraisal', which is of particular application to senior staff and executives, is concerned with appraisal against pre-set tasks. This procedure, too, recognizes that appraisal has many aspects other than those affecting salary administration, the most important of which is to get the highest level of performance from each employee and involves the associated activity of ensuring optimum employee placement to enable staff to give of their best.

One of the most effective ways of achieving this incentive through appraisal is to examine, critically and informally, the achievement of each employee in relation to tasks set or to demands made on him over a period of time. This approach is best known as *Management by Objectives*. While this approach is used most at executive levels at present, there is no reason why it should not be adopted for more general application, except that it is time consuming.

The operation requires that, at the beginning of a year, or whatever period is selected, an executive be charged with a specific assignment or series of tasks, and will determine, with his superiors, a programme of planned achievements during the coming months. Periodically, and at the end of this period, he will sit down again with his chief to examine critically how the programme has gone, where it is off schedule and why—not so much to see who was responsible or apportion blame, but to examine what might have been done, if anything, to foresee and prevent the events which influenced the programme adversely.

This form of tuition in overcoming high-level management problems—under competent top management—can be highly effective.

In modified form, this approach can be used at any level and for any type of staff. Employees can participate in writing down the key aspects or requirements of their jobs to be completed over the coming months, against which they will be appraised. This may also help to get some employees back on track where their concept of the job differs radically from their supervisor's view.

At the end of a period of time, the same type of review of achievement and constructive study of shortcomings, sympathetically conducted, should lead to high minimum levels of performance.

This approach may be particularly applicable in organizations using salary scales requiring regular incremental progress towards a maximum for a particular type of work. Encouragement to achieve a high basic level of performance coincides with development to a high level of salary, and performance failure should lead to transfer to a more appropriate work level.

Clearly, in a normal merit type of salary administration, improvement in peformance could be geared individually to provide maximum or near maximum salary as comparable levels of job performance were attained.

The appraisers

The ultimate success or failure of any appraisal scheme depends utterly on the supervisors and managers who are responsible for rating the employees under their control. This is not the place for a lecture on the training and preparation of these executives for their task, but a brief comment on the essential nature of these preliminaries to a successful appraisal scheme should be noted.

It is important, first of all, that the raters have confidence in the scheme they will use. This implies that they both understand the basic philosophy of staff appraisal and appreciate the specific purpose of their own company plan. It is also important that they should be given maximum help and guidance in fulfilling their part in the exercise, if possible by some form of short practical training. One way is for a small group of executives to rate a carefully described example employee, and then to discuss, under the guidance of a Training Officer, the reasons and basis for their decisions. Such training helps substantially in developing common purpose and understanding.

Bias by the rater is sometimes evident, perhaps in favour of one individual, or affecting all employees reviewed. The use of second and third raters, particularly where they do not see each other's reports, is an effective method of identifying bias, although cutting it out is far less simple. Bias is not important in flexible reporting schemes once it has been identified but, in a scored system, it is potentially dangerous as it is likely to give seriously wrong ratings. Attempts to apply any form of corrective factor inevitably turn the final answer into an entirely bogus and valueless figure!

Application to salary administration

When all the effort has been expended just how useful is the appraisal result when salaries are being reviewed? The short answer is that it should provide an invaluable guide and reference document to be at the manager's hand, but that any rigid application of an appraisal result to a salary decision should be totally avoided. Schemes which incorporate some form of scoring have an unfortunate façade of accuracy, and there is always a temptation to apply some rigid calculation to the result to determine salary action.

One large engineering company operating a scored merit rating scheme decides which of the weekly staff shall receive salary adjustments by saying:

1   That increases, where awarded, will be about 8 per cent of present individual salary, which gives an average cost of increase of, say, £4 a week.
2   That the company can afford these for 30 per cent of the staff this year.
3   That the 30 per cent of staff with the highest numerical ratings will receive a salary adjustment or a bonus if their salary is high.

This procedure may be slightly better than drawing names out of a hat, but only just, for the pressure on managers to give false ratings in order to get as many as possible of their staff into the top block, the only way of recommending a salary increase, distorts the scheme to the point where the whole procedure is a farce, and all concerned in its operation and associated policy are associated with its disrepute.

Realistic use

Acceptance of the fact that the appraisal rating is an imprecise measure, perhaps to an even greater extent than the assessment of job value, leads naturally to its acceptance as a guide only, when salaries are reviewed.

A careful appraisal can reasonably be assumed to be approximately correct. On this basis, an appraisal provides a guide to the approximate level of salary within a range which is appropriate at the time, within limits established in the company's policy statement. This statement might provide for the top end of a salary range to be associated with outstanding performance, and the middle of the range with a high level, each of which might be quite precisely defined. These points provide the pegging points between the appraisal and appropriate salary.

This approach has been formalized very well in a number of large organizations which have developed better-than-normal appraisal schemes capable of producing a numerical score. They make use of a grid which uses the level of performance and the level of present salary within the salary range to produce a guide percentage for the salary increase. A simple performance × salary adjustment grid of this sort is as follows:

Performance

Top quartile	25%	18%	12%	8%	6%
2nd quartile	15%	12%	8%	6%	4%
3rd quartile	12%	8%	6%	4%	0
Bottom quartile	8%	6%	4%	0	0
Present salary	Below	Bottom	2nd	3rd	Top
(Position in range)	min.	Qtr.	Qtr.	Qtr.	Qtr.

However, some grids are far more complex, using intervals of 10 per cent of the salary range, and of the distribution of appraisal scores to make a 10 × 10 box grid.

With this approach, the assumptions (beyond that the salary ranges and appraisal scores are acceptable) include the overall size of salary increases, the proportion of staff to receive nothing, and the maximum size of increase to be given to really outstanding cases. A competent statistician can produce a grid based on these assumptions.

Flexibility beyond this can be provided by requiring managers to review the end result, and discuss any cases which appear to be unfair.

The whole subject of salarly level determination, of which this is part, is developed in Chapter 12, 'Salary Planning'.

Appraisal of potential

The greater part of this chapter has been concerned with appraisal of the employee's performance of his current job and its influence on his salary. Of no less importance is the appraisal of each employee's potential ability to cope with other posts, particularly at a more senior level.

This appraisal of an employee's potential ability to do a bigger job is an essential part of personnel management, particularly in regard to the staffing function, and success in personnel planning and development.

The procedure consists, quite simply, of assessing what other jobs an employee can be expected to perform competently, how quickly he might attain this level of performance and what training he requires beforehand. To assess these things, the reporting manager is usually guided by the personnel department in the preparation of a brief questionnaire or report, although occasionally a 'tick-box' type of form may be used. Potential reports are often appended to and, as a result, sometimes confused with performance reports.

Figure 11.6 is a basic questionnaire type of report form to be completed only for monthly staff considered to have some potential to go further. The question headings are the basic queries which need to be answered in some form or other about any individual considered to have some potential.

Figure 11.7 shows a much briefer 'initial' appraisal rating system designed to ask little more than whether or not potential ability is present. This example is an extract from a performance report rather than an independent form.

The follow-on from potential reports is first of all the preparation of development and succession plans. Only at this stage can the influence of potential on individual salary planning be considered for, after all, the company with a large stock of potential Managing Directors can hardly afford to pay them all as Managing Directors, particularly those who have little prospect of achieving anything approaching this level!

APPRAISAL OF EMPLOYEE POTENTIAL

Report on:	
Employee's name:	
Position held:	
Position description number:	
Date appointed to position:	
Date of report:	
A. *What are his strong points?*	
B. *What are his weak points?*	
C. *What degree of supervision is necessary?*	
D. *How well does he delegate?*	

E. *How good are his relationships?*
   with (i) More senior personnel
       (ii) Subordinates	

F. *Comment on his judgement and thinking:*
   Accuracy of forecasts
   Attitude to ideas
   Appreciate change
   Foresee problems—and deal with situation
   Does he 'flap'?	

G. *Comment on his immediate future:*
   **Experience required (which posts should
   he hold?)**
   Training required
   What time?	

Report by:	
Appointment:	

(Use the blank other side of this form for additional comments)

Figure 11.6 Appraisal of potential questionnaire

NOTE ON EMPLOYEE POTENTIAL

E	Unlikely to exceed present responsibilities.
D	May be suitable for additional responsibilities. But extent not yet clear.
C	Suitable for additional responsibilities at the same level.
B	Suitable for additional responsibilities immediately/within one year *, at one grade higher.
A	Suitable for additional responsibility immediately/within one year, * at more than one grade higher.

(* Indicate whichever applies.)

IMMEDIATE COMMENT ON THE POTENTIAL RATING

....
Signature—Reporting Authority

COMMENT

....
Signature—Reviewing Authority

Figure 11.7   Brief form of appraisal of potential

In fact, potential alone is not something to reward directly at all. But it is essential that planned career progression towards definitely maturing vacancies should be taken into account in salary progression. Pay competitive salaries for work done, and use staff to their full capacities. The staff you under-employ will leave you anyway—regardless of whether you overpay them for the jobs you permit them to do, or not. The psychological factor, of a requirement to be fully extended in employment, is over-riding. This aspect of salary planning is examined in the next chapter.

Chapter 12

Salary Planning

Your salary administration objectives are likely to include statements such as :

'To pay salaries which are competitive in the industry.'
'To reward good performance and the acceptance of greater responsibility.'
'To pay salaries which recognize the value of each employee's job and his performance in the job.'
'To pay salaries which will attract and retain the calibre of staff required.'

As we have already seen from previous chapters, certain of the above objectives can be realized by the use of a comprehensive job evaluation study to achieve sound classification structures, careful salary surveys which provide the basis for the development of competitive and equitable pay structures, and sound appraisal schemes to assess individual performance.

However, these structures and plans provide only the basic working tools of salary administration. The proper use of these tools for individual salary planning is dependent on the attitudes and understanding of operating supervisors and managers. The training of these people in the involved art of salary planning, and ensuring their attainment of a full appreciation of its concepts, provides the most stimulating challenge in salary administration.

If the aims of an organization include above-average salary levels and larger salary increases to recognize good performance and potential* as shown by better employees, compared with routine salary levels and less frequent increases for routine or mediocre performance by average people, then salary planning is necessary to ensure that an appropriate rate of salary progress is continually reviewed and determined for each employee.

The only times when the effectiveness of salary planning, as an incentive to improve performance, is reduced is in cases of 'across-the-board' increases, negotiated flat salary adjustments, or any other form of automatic salary increase applied equally to groups of employees without regard to the relationship between salary and performance levels. While many categories of staff now accept general or national awards as normal practice and expect them to be provided at regular intervals, they also reject any suggestion that such adjustments are more than a 'right' so that the incentive effect is absolutely nil.

Possibly, a reasonable but lengthy *definition of salary planning* would be that it is the process of matching the salary progress of each employee to his unfolding career. While he has potential to take on more and more responsibility and as his value to the company grows so will his salary increase rapidly in direct relation to his worth, and as he begins to run out of potential and settles down in his final post so his salary growth will slow down until it reaches a terminal, or retirement salary which reflects his ultimate value to the organization.

This sounds relatively simple when written down like this, but in practice, as will be seen, it is an extremely complex process with a high number of variable factors, so that there are many problems in sound salary planning by which the salary of each employee, other than the most junior ones, will follow an entirely different career course.

As immediate examples to illustrate the variability of potential in progress, consider the following cases. The salary progress of staff performing routine clerical jobs, and without much interest or ambition, tends to be a straight-line progress increasing from the minimum of the salary range to the maximum in a restricted number of small salary adjustments, usually limited to about 5 per cent of the basic salary. Once the maxi-

---

* Throughout this chapter 'potential' is used in the sense defined earlier, as the ability to take on greater responsibility.

mum is reached, and for staff in the lower clerical levels this can often be attained soon after age 30 or even earlier, then that may be the end of career salary progress apart from general increases associated with national awards or cost-of-living adjustments.

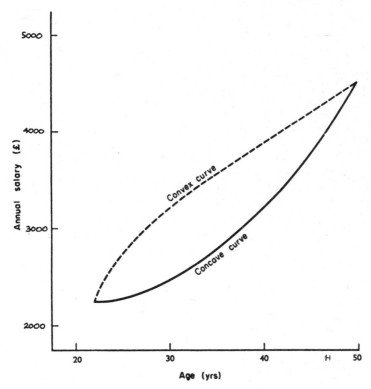

Figure 12.1 Convex and concave salary growth curves

The salary progressions of most middle- and senior-level staff, however, have a very different pattern. Earlier in the century, and even today in some of our long-established and more conservative organizations, their progress used to take the shape of a 'concave salary curve' (see Fig. 12.1). This curve reflected the pattern of clerical staff salary progress through the initial ten or even twenty years and the attitude 'that staff in their early years can't be of much value, as this comes with long service and experience only'. Later salary progress will be steeper for those who 'made the grade' to management posts. However, this represents a thoroughly outmoded concept and is in direct contradiction to our philosophy on salary planning for career staff.

The present trend in enlightened organizations is to employ the 'convex salary curve' approach (see Fig. 12.1) in which individual salaries are varied widely in direct relationship to appraised current and anticipated potential values, so that salaries are adjusted steeply for the better performers with high potential in line with rapidly developing careers until they start to 'run out of gas', while the progressions are slanted significantly less steeply for lesser standards of performance and potential.

The rate of salary progress for these 'career' staff as far as *merit increases alone* are concerned, usually averages 5 or 7 per cent a year, excluding all adjustments owing to inflation. These percentages could be increased by cost-of-living adjustments, and also wage awards, which are sometimes extended to very senior employees. Annual increases for individuals in this 'career' staff category could range between 3 and 15 per cent or even higher, although most usually they would be between 5 and 10 per cent according to individual performance and other outside factors (excluding inflation).

The salaries of top management follow much the same pattern as those of other senior career staff discussed above. However, the frequency of salary increases is reduced and the amounts of individual adjustments are generally steeper, often being between 10 and 20 per cent. In addition, remuneration may be influenced by large supplementary payments in the form of bonus, which may or may not be linked to 'Top Hat Pension' premiums. Bonus at this level can range anywhere between 1 and even 100 per cent at the whim of the organization, but the average, according to our findings in a recent comprehensive survey, is that bonus equates to approximately 20 per cent of annual basic salary for Directors and top-line management in bonus paying companies.

Career salary progress

During his career, each employee's salary progress consists of a number of salary adjustments. These are given for a number of reasons, including merit increases which reflect either improvement in his performance of his current job, or continued good

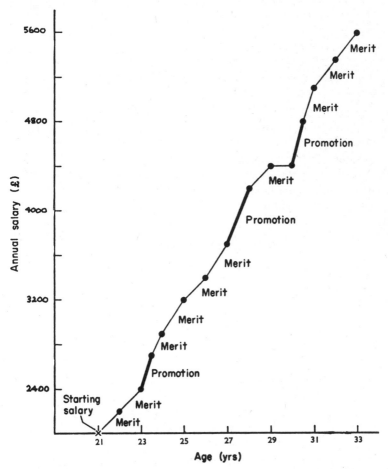

Figure 12.2 Individual career salary curve; detail, showing salary adjustment

service; a few promotional adjustments; as well as an irregular series of inflationary increases, until the employee reaches his terminal or retirement salary. A typical career salary pattern, reflecting this range of types of salary adjustments, might be as illustrated in Fig. 12.2.

Incremental salary scales

The above descriptions and indeed, most of this chapter, are primarily concerned with the type of salary progress found under flexible merit review conditions in industry rather than under incremental salary progress conditions. However, although the means are different, the salary progression of a 'high-potential' scientist in the Civil Service would be remarkably similar. A career salary pattern of this sort would show a series of steps from one grade scale to the next to provide the steep early progress.

The factors influencing salary planning for staff on incremental scales are primarily the same basic factors of career planning. In incremental structures, salary and career progress are tied securely and inflexibly together.

Assembling the components of salary planning

These few words give no indication of the amount of time and effort, or of the number of criteria that enter into salary planning. Each of the main types of salary adjustments, which may be likened to moves in a game of chess, are examined in detail in the sections that follow.

Merit increases (see Fig. 13.3)

This is the basic reason for the greatest number of salary increases, but the term often covers a multitude of dubious classifications, also detailed below, in addition to 'pure' merit.

As their title suggests, these increases are usually given to reward individual merit, and as they tend to be given annually, they are regrettably defined by many companies as 'reward for a good year's service'.

Do these companies pay good salary increases rather than good salaries?

The concept of small annual increments may possibly be appropriate for non-career staff carrying out absolutely routine tasks with little hope of promotion, for whom the receipt of an annual 'nibble at the salary carrot' takes on the comforting aspect of a secure incremental scale. However, it is hardly applicable to career staff where considerable differences in both performance and potential are found. The payment of competitive salaries, at levels in the salary ranges which reflect each employee's value to the company, is much more appropriate and satisfying to senior staff than the receipt of doled-out, routine annual bites at the salary range. The new level of the adjusted salary, rather than the receipt of an increase, will be the significant factor to senior staff of the company's apparent appraisal of the value of their services.

Merit increases should be a means of adjusting salaries to levels which reflect employees' increased values to the company. Such increases should always be significant in size, i.e. rarely less than 3 per cent of basic salary. This is because improvements in performance cannot be assessed with a sufficient degree of accuracy to support a smaller adjustment and, in any case, if the award of a salary increase is to be appreciated, then the amount should always be significant, i.e. large enough for the difference in actual income to be noticeable rather than negligible. In our view, an adjustment of 3 per cent constitutes the *minimum* acceptable size of a merit salary adjustment at any level—once again ignoring the inflation element.

Merit increases should only be given to average or better performers, and not normally to below average or poor performers. For marginal cases, it is appropriate to increase the period between salary increases from the traditional twelve-monthly span, up to twenty-four to thirty-six months, particularly when an employee reaches his final job level in the organization and makes little further performance progress as he nears his terminal salary.

Occasionally, where some internal factor affects individual salary plans, it may be reasonable to stretch out the period between increases for good performers with considerable potential, during periods in which their salaries are high in salary ranges appropriate to jobs they are currently holding, and where there is little immediate possibility of the promotion for which they are clearly suited. It is neither sound sense nor good economics to continue to boost an individual salary in such a situation, other than in exceptional circumstances, as future salary progress would thereby be inevitably mortgaged and the situation is likely to be repeated.

In a situation where a high calibre individual is 'boxed in' at the top of a salary range, it is healthier to release him if he complains rather than attempt to detain him in a state of frustration by continuing salary advances which are economically out of line with the responsibilities assigned. (Pausing a moment for a few brief words on the associated activity of career planning, it is probably possible to hold an individual of this type by giving him some special 'broadening' assignment of appropriate job weight to satisfy him pending his next promotion, but great care should be taken in respect of salary progress.)

The main point to remember for career staff is that each employee will have a different career with an associated individual salary path, and what is suitable treatment for one individual might be entirely wrong for another. In all cases, a serious attempt should be made to forecast career progress over the next few years. In determining the immediate and probable future merit salary progress of each individual, the points to be considered may be set out as follows.

1   When is he likely to grow out of this salary range, i.e. when is he likely to be transferred or promoted? This provides an indication of the possible time span between present salary and some appropriate point high in the salary range, which will be the immediate career aiming point.

2   Which specific appointment is he likely to go to, if he is likely to be ready for promotion within a year or so? This forecast must be linked to availability of a post, or a salary and career problem will develop.

3   How well does he perform his present job and is this level of performance improving significantly? For all staff with limited potential, salary level should be closely associated with performance rating.

Personal gradings

Exceptionally, and we emphasize that word, it may be appropriate to determine a personal grade rather than a job grade for an individual for a specific reason and specific period of time.

This would normally be done for the duration of special assignments which are part of the broadening of a middle manager or a young high-potential employee. The practice would be appropriate during these temporary stages of the employee's career, and would tend to reflect his current, or next probable, grading level in his own field. As an example, the Division Finance Manager being given broadening assignments in other functions may spend periods as Production Controller, Engineering Services Manager, and so on. While these posts might normally carry lower grades, a personal grade would be used to ensure continuing salary progress in line with the individual's overall increasing value to the company pending a planned general management appointment.

Special adjustments

There are, as we mentioned above, a number of associated reasons for increases which tend to be lumped rather uneasily with 'merit'. In down-to-earth salary administration, it is preferable to identify positively the real reason for each adjustment.

For example, the adjustment given to hold an employee in the face of a competitive offer from another company should be identified positively. Such an increase is likely to consist in reality of a number of contributing parts, an element of under-payment and a background of frustration or potentially greater immediate salary or career scope.

Merit salary reviews

Merit salary increases in the industrial scene are normally granted following co-ordinated reviews of all salaries (the annual salary review in many organizations), rather than awarded indiscriminately throughout the year, although there is no reason why this flexibility should not be adopted provided it is reasonably systematized to ensure 'equal opportunity' for all employees.

However these and other relative points on salary review procedure are discussed fully in the next chapter.

Promotion increases

A promotion involves a change of job, from a post in one grade to another which is clearly at a higher level, and carries a higher salary range (see Fig. 12.3).

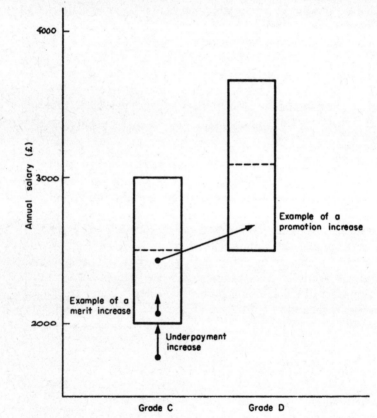

Figure 12.3   Block chart showing a merit increase and a promotion increase

Salary should always be reviewed at the time of promotion, and a promotion increase given which should always be significant and reflect the importance of these milestones in the employee's career. Such increases should be larger than the normal merit increase, say around 10–15 per cent of basic salary in normal circumstances. Occasions do arise, of course, where an individual is already overpaid and a further adjustment to his salary is not warranted.

Where it is considered necessary to have some form of probationary period before confirming a promotion, an increase should normally be given not later than three months after the actual promotion has taken place, if it is to have any effect as an incentive.

Where the promotion has been based on careful appraisal of the employee and on sound selection, it is reasonable to assume that it will be a success. In the circumstances, managers should have faith in their choice and give the salary increases at the actual time the employee is given the new job, for even if the employee should subsequently fall down on the job and need to be replaced, during the period he carries the responsibility he should most certainly be paid for it. Experience shows that the employee who fails to make the grade following a promotion generally appreciates the position and is prepared to accept the realistic readjustment of his salary to its former level in these circumstances. There is nothing more depressing, following an important career step, than having to wait until the following January before receiving a reward for the increased responsibility as is the practice in some organizations.

Promotion under non-merit salary structure

In an incremental salary structure environment, the promotional increase is distinctly more clear-cut. The rigidity of the salary progression system provides for automatic adjustment of salary to the minimum, or appropriate, figure on the incremental scale of the new grade, and the employee has the additional 'boost' of being able to appraise the new set of steps which he will almost inevitably climb.

For those few employees reviewed against maturity curves, promotion may or may not be rewarded significantly. A belated promotion may do no more than bring the weight of work into line with the level of salary already allocated to the individual by plotting his progress along an arbitrary line!

Merit increases and promotion increases are the main types of salary adjustments planned by management. However, there are other types of salary adjustment and these are covered below.

Adjustment to correct low payment

These adjustments are usually to correct individual anomalies where salaries are below the minimum of the salary range (see Fig. 12.3), or exceptionally to adjust salaries which, although within the salary range, are considered to be unacceptably low for individual employees.

These cases tend to come to light following various studies, for example, following a classification or grading review in which a number of posts are revalued and set higher in the structure than previously. In these circumstances, the company may wish to make some immediate adjustment to the individual. Alternatively, depending on the nature of the low pay, it may prefer to defer the adjustment until the next formal salary review, at which time an increase disguised as 'merit' is often granted.

Another form of build up of low payment may occur when an individual on a relatively low salary receives substantial promotion. Normal-sized promotional increases of 10–15 per cent may leave the individual's salary far below the minimum of the new range, and even increases of 25 per cent, a normal maximum limit, may be inadequate. The degree of underpayment which remains may be picked up six months later and a further 'instalment' of money given.

Underpayment increases should only be given to average or better performers, as it is practically never appropriate to increase the salary of a below average or poor performer. Usually, one hopes that such people will leave of their own accord when their performance is not poor enough to justify downgrading or dismissal although, strangely enough, they stick with you whether you give them salary increases or not. They probably know when they are well off!

Salary adjustments to correct low pay should be made as soon as possible, as failure to identify and correct under-payment is one of the main causes of staff turnover and it is primarily the better-calibre staff who leave for this reason.

Increases to correct low payment should not normally exceed 15 per cent if linked to promotion, perhaps 20 per cent, or quite exceptionally, 25 per cent of basic salary at any one time. The amount should always be dependent on the particular circumstances of each case and what the budget will stand, also bearing in mind salary levels and planned salary adjustments for other associated employees.

Probationary increases

Probationary increases are sometimes promised or given on satisfactory completion of a 'proving' period, for service ranging from a few weeks to a year after recruitment or promotion. Unless such increases are compulsory for some reason (they may have been negotiated in principle by a Staff Association), they should be discouraged.

In general if an individual is holding a post, he should be paid at the level for the job and his ability to carry it out. Sound selection procedure and appraisal of the employee's performance and potential provide a proper basis for the determination of initial salaries and all subsequent reviews. The use of probationary periods in these circumstances is almost unforgivable. At best it reflects on the quality of the selection and appraisal methods used, and at worst it indicates an attitude to starting salaries and the granting of salary adjustments with which few Salary Administrators would wish to be associated.

But what of the new recruit about whose future performance there is real doubt? There may, exceptionally, be some justification for reviewing a salary three months after a man joins the company if his ability to do a job is seriously doubted; where he had been the only possible choice at the time. However, even in these circumstances it is preferable to pay the man an appropriate rate for the job he is required to do with the clear understanding that the review after three months will either consolidate his position or lead to his replacement. All too often, weakness in the first respect, of underpaying a man, is followed by weakness when he proves ineffective, and he is permitted to continue in the post.

Birthday increases

Semi-automatic increases are given yearly or half-yearly to junior employees under the age of 21. For staff in this age range, the procedure varies only slightly between those organizations using incremental scales and those operating merit salary structures. However, variation creeps in in the form of size of increments, for these can either be of the standard size for all employees regardless of ability or performance, or can include an element of variation on a merit basis where justified.

The value of merit awards is as significant for these employees as for more senior staff and can be used as a genuine incentive. However, there is a snag in that groups of young people working in close proximity tend to be jealous when there is variation in salary levels, and this may sometimes lead to departures of staff which appear illogical, but still occur. Local practice is probably the best guide in this situation, whether or not this appears the better course on the surface.

At age 18, juniors in the UK are currently faced with increased, adult scale, cost of rail travel and National Insurance payments, and age scales must take this substantial increase in liability fully into account.

Adjustments on transfer

It is normal practice in certain organizations to give an increase in salary to any employee transferred from one location to another—presumably as some form of persuasion or compensation. Such an increase is sometimes disguised as a 'promotion' or 'special merit' increase, whether or not this is warranted.

If the transfer is to a job at the same level there is no call for a salary increase unless it is to a higher cost area, such as would occur in a move to central London from the provinces. More often a one-time, *ex gratia* payment to assist with moving expenses would be more appropriate.

In certain cases, particularly for hard-to-get career staff and management, assistance with the cost of buying and selling accommodation, and with hotel expenses or rented accommodation during the settling-in period should be given. Scales of allowances should be based on the actual costs of the various moves involved and on the degree of company need, as opposed to individual requirement, in each case.

In-grade promotion increases

Where an employee is given a new job which, although in the same grade as his existing one, carries tangibly increased responsibility or traditionally greater status, it is not unusual to recognize this by giving an immediate 'promotional' salary increase which might otherwise be described as an accelerated merit increase. By this it is meant that the immediate increase would cancel any merit increase which might otherwise have been given or was planned for the next salary review.

Such an increase may also be given to recognize gradually increased responsibility in a situation where the employee does not change his existing job but the content is changed or enlarged to a significant degree, although not to the point of justifying a clear-cut change of grade to a higher level.

These increases are looked upon by the employee as a promotion increase, whatever they are called by management, and usually have considerable incentive value.

Incremental salary adjustments

In organizations which use salary structure of incremental scales, salary adjustments 'come up with the rations' for those at appropriate points on the scale, such as at birthdays or anniversaries, with little significant variation associated with performance. If an employee is on an incremental scale, as he completes the further year to the anniversary of his birthday or appointment, he duly receives his official increase, unless he has been quite exceptionally poor or remarkably good, until he reaches his maximum salary.

Clearly such a scheme offers rather little in the form of incentive, which is no doubt why incremental scales are generally avoided in industry, where the influence of Staff Associations is less, thus permitting a more flexible salary approach with greater potential reward for good performance.

This brings us to an interesting point, that where negotiation with Staff Associations is usual, incremental salary scales are favoured. The Staff Association man generally appears to favour equality of salary treatment regardless of variation in effort and performance, which restricts the salary movement of the better performer who, in effect, is expected to subsidize his lazier or less efficient colleagues.

It is unlikely that most of these individuals consider that this is in any way justifiable as being 'fair' or 'moral', and it is certainly not based on sound economic principles. The plain fact is that the two 'sides' involved in establishing the structures are invariably unable to agree on a merit plan acceptable to both parties, and the employers, on the defensive, have been inflexible in their subsequent administration of salaries. The basic lack of trust exhibited by both groups is curious, for while the general 'fairness' of the negotiated scale may be apparent, the blatant unfairness in the treatment of the upper and lower performance fringes is also very clear.

Inflation

There are two main sources of general increases. They may be negotiated, or they may be at the discretion of management. In both cases, they are likely to arise from inflation, and with recent levels of inflation, they can be substantial—possibly more substantial than all other increases !

In the event of negotiated change, the general increase is likely to be closely related to changes in salary ranges for the jobs or grades concerned. They may be specified amounts, or percentages. They are paid with effect from a common date, and do not alter the distribution of salaries within a range, or affect merit adjustments.

It is logical for a company which takes non-negotiated action (perhaps for staff above unionized grades) to follow the same general lines, uplifting the entire structure and salaries within by standard amounts. This action can offset severe inflation, and leave the normal salary planning process clear to continue.

Salary planning

Management tools and techniques

We have now examined the various basic rules which apply to the adjustment of an individual's salary in the salary planning process. Salary planning is not so much a difficult operation as one which becomes involved owing to the large number of inter-related factors. The application of these factors through appropriate procedures is discussed in this section.

Salary planning may involve the planning of one individual's salary progress in the case of a solitary specialist or cover a whole group of salaries at the same time. Whatever the case, the following criteria should be studied.

Job classification: job titles and job grades

It is appropriate, before reviewing salaries, to check that both job title and grade are accurately recorded for each employee and that they represent the current position, accurately evaluated.

Special care should be taken to note and review all personal gradings. These are the special grades assigned temporarily to an individual rather than a job, and may be higher or lower than the actual grade of the job currently being undertaken. The philosophy of the personal grading concept was discussed earlier in this chapter.

Salary range

The Salary Administrator of an organization should always check the competitiveness of salary ranges in advance of a review, and at regular intervals in between reviews. It should be emphasized that, before any salary planning exercise is undertaken, checks should be made to ensure that the current ranges are competitive for the grades, levels and types of staff generally for the work location, at the time of the review. Where in-grade rates are in use, special care is needed to ensure that minor local movement has not upset the rather fine balance which many of these rates have.

The position of each employee's salary within the appropriate salary range is one of the most significant aspects of a review, studied in the light of other salary factors, and this emphasizes the importance of having correct ranges.

Employee appraisals

Appraisal information should be available covering not only the current performance and potential ratings for each employee, but also his previous history, available through earlier reports by different supervisors.

These appraisals should, as was explained in Chapter 11, also indicate changes in performance and potential since the previous assessment showing whether the ratings have improved, remained the same, or deteriorated. When a group of employees work together on similar work, some form of performance ranking should be used wherever possible for comparison with a similar ranking of salaries.

Job opportunities

The possibility of avenues of broadening or promotion for staff with potential is vital. Succession planning is usually organized to cover long-term replacements for most of the senior posts in a large company, but lower down the tree such a plan is generally less clearly formulated and co-ordinated. Promotion and movement in the middle and lower levels of an organization tend to be restricted to the immediate area, or location or function, so that individual managers and their personnel managers need to be aware of these shorter-term and local prospects.

These promotion prospect factors should be taken fully into account at each salary review. Succession planning charts and all other available information should be checked to establish planned career moves at all levels. If possible, promotions should always be planned well in advance to enable the employee's salary to be moved towards the appropriate level and avoid the necessity for excessive salary adjustments to rectify a low-payment situation.

Comparable staff

Individual salaries should rarely be looked at in isolation. Salaries and appraisals of other staff in a section, department or division carrying out comparable work (or work at an equivalent level), should be studied when planning salary adjustments. This is to ensure steady movement towards correct salary relationships. It is unlikely that perfection will ever be attained, partly because individual views colour the picture, but primarily because the ideal itself is constantly developing and thus changing the proper salary relationship between any two men in a grade. Where one is a young, good performer of high potential but limited experience, and the other is an older, experienced man of average performance their salary relationship may lead to many arguments until the younger man is promoted clear of the other. Perhaps the factors influencing the setting of salaries for these two individuals are so complex that any attempt at establishing, as a bench-mark, any 'proper relationship' between them is doomed from the start. Efforts should be concentrated on the respective salary positions of less contrasting cases—a comparison of salaries paid to young economics graduates in widely differing jobs might present less difficulty.

Salary budget

In organizations where salary adjustments are planned within a budget, and this surely covers most organizations of all sizes, the budget will set an overall limit and decide the probable pattern of individual increases which may be given at the particular review. This subject is covered in greater detail later in this chapter under the heading 'Salary Reviews'.

Salary policies and procedures

Finally, all salary adjustments must be planned within the guiding framework of the individual organization's Salary

Administration Policy. Clearly this basic policy, which will establish classification procedure and merit or incremental salary scales, also establishes the fundamental framework within which one must administer salaries. This should normally include a pattern of rules regarding the size and permitted frequency of salary adjustments, and an indication of the intended rigidity of their operation, all of which must be taken into account in salary planning.

We believe that the most important single factor in salary administration policy is flexibility of approach. Certainly procedures and restrictions are required to control this major administrative function, but these should cover only ninety-nine cases out of a hundred. The hundredth case concerns the odd man out, where any rigid application of rules would kill the effectiveness of the whole system. What value has a 'perfect' system which lacks the facility of being logically adaptable to sympathetic consideration when required by individual circumstances?

But here we must add a reservation, a gentle note of warning on flexibility outside formal policy, for the administrator who is too flexible, by his own choice or under pressure, will surely kill the whole value of his plan by gradually conceding points where these are unnecessary—by applying special circumstances in all cases until normal standards suffer severe inflation. (Here is a snake of enormous proportions in the snakes-and-ladders game, leading straight back to Chapter 1 of our book!)

Use of scattergraphs for salary planning

Of all the visual aids that Salary Administrators can use, the most valuable for salary planning is the scattergraph (Fig. 12.4).

On this graph it is possible to portray most of the factors discussed above in simple pictorial form in a way that permits the whole 'story' for a group of staff to be seen at one inspection. All the essential criteria for salary planning, for any number of individual salaries, become clear. Basically, the scattergraph consists of a chart with a salary scale on the vertical axis and an age or time scale on the horizontal axis. Each employee's present age and salary position is first of all plotted on the graph. Subsequently, a diversity of refinements can be added to show off those points of particular interest or significance in the current study.

As examples of refinements, the *vector* (amount and timing) of his last salary adjustment can be drawn; the salary plots of

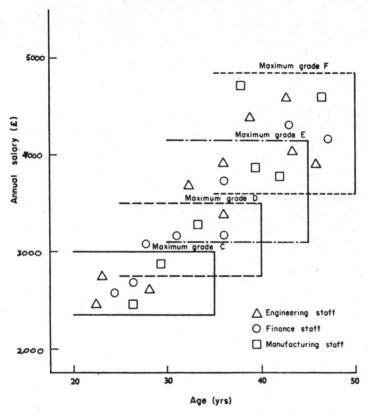

Figure 12.4 Scattergraph of salaries for various types of staff

staff in different *salary grades* can be identified by the use of various colours with the salary ranges indicated in the same colours; and *functions* or *departments* such as finance, engineering or manufacturing can be denoted by differently shaped symbols. Some of these refinements are illustrated in Fig. 12.4.

I

Where scattergraphs are used for salary reviews spread throughout the year, where it is essential to plot exact age to the nearest month rather than year, special graph paper graduated in twelfths for months on the horizontal scale, and tenths on the vertical scale, for money, should be used.

As a practical exercise in the use of these graphs we will carry out a hypothetical review of the salaries of three Development Engineers as represented by the career plots *A, B* and *C* in Fig. 12.5.

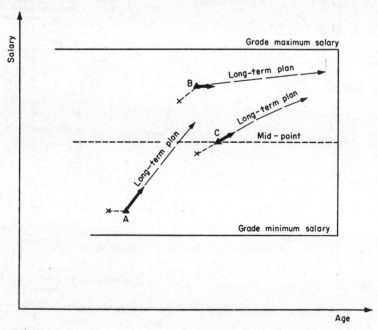

Figure 12.5   Salary scattergraph covering three Development Engineers, showing short-term and long-term plans

Let us assume that the facts of each case are as follows:

Engineer A is near the minimum of the salary range for his job. He has a performance rating of 'outstanding' and high potential rating. In fact, he is ready for immediate promotion and there will be a post one grade higher available for him in about one year. As can be seen by the dotted line behind his salary plot he did not receive a salary adjustment at the last review, but received a promotional adjustment of 9 per cent approximately fourteen months ago.

Clearly *A* is low paid in relation to *B* and *C* and his past salary treatment has probably not adequately reflected his rapid previous progress. He should be moved towards the minimum of the salary range of his next position in anticipation of this further promotion. This means that his salary vector should be steepened by an above-average adjustment as shown by the arrowed line leading from the salary plot. This treatment also starts to correct the relationship between his salary, and those of the other two Engineers.

Engineer B is very high in the salary range. His performance rating is 'below average' and he has no potential for further promotion. His present grade level will be his terminal one and his retirement salary should thus be somewhere between the mid-point and the maximum of the salary range, and not necessarily the range maximum unless his level of performance improves.

The dotted line leading to his present salary plot appears to indicate that his recent salary treatment has been too fast in relation to his current appraisal ratings and he should obviously be slowed down, perhaps to routine merit increases at twenty-four- of thirty-six-monthly intervals.

It is usually worth investigating a case of this sort to ascertain whether a change of supervisor has resulted in an unjustifiably hard appraisal, or whether previous appraisals have given a totally erroneous impression. Staff appraisal systems are not yet so perfect that a substantial change of appraisal level, if this occurs, should be automatically accepted.

It would seem appropriate to give no salary increase to *B* as indicated by the arrowed line leading from his salary plot. Moreover he should be properly counselled and encouraged to improve his performance. Where appropriate, constructive advice should be given to help him correct any shortcomings.

Engineer C is near the mid-point of the range. He is rated as an average performer with some potential for promotion to a more responsible position at some time in the future. He received an average merit increase at the last review.

A further average increase would seem appropriate for Engineer *C* in the light of the appraisal ratings. He is suitable for promotion later on and a modest increase will only take his salary just past mid-point. However, he may have to slow down within a further year or two, by stretching his adjustments from twenty-four to thirty-six monthly periods, if no promotional opportunity occurs for him.

It will be understood that the above explanation is an over-simplification of a fairly involved and lengthy process, particularly where staff are involved, but it shows the 'opposite side of the coin' from the 'pound all round' type of salary planning which seems all too common in some United Kingdom organizations. It is only fair to add at this point that while salary planning plays a vital part in the salary administration of senior or career staff, lower-level staff with more limited career potential and prospects do not justify the same detailed attention. Naturally, these staff will also progress through the salary range by means of a series of merit increases. However, tradition and modern pressures adapt the 'merit' concept to take greater account of such factors as service, justified as 'increasing experience' and therefore value as merit. The result is a wide spread of salaries within the salary range with an average level round the competitive mid-point, which is perfectly acceptable. A scattergraph may add to the clarity of the picture and may reveal faults in the form of a biased distribution of actual salary plots.

Graduate guide lines

While on the subject of visual aids for salary planning it seems appropriate to cover the use of salary guide lines for the planning of salaries for young, high-potential staff such as technical graduates, also mentioned briefly earlier in this chapter.

This technique consists of reviewing the salaries of this category of staff covered against a national or industry-wide salary distribution of comparably qualified staff.

As a basis for this type of review, it is necessary to obtain,

Company: ....

Salaries effective at:................................

Salary, £	Year of birth												
	1954	53	52	51	50	49	48	47	46	45	44	43	42
1200 – 1249													
1250 – 1299													
1300 – 1349													
1350 – 1399													
1400 – 1449													
1450 – 1499													
1500 – 1549													
1550 – 1599													
1600 – 1649													
1650 – 1699													
1700 – 1749													
1750 – 1799													
1800 – 1849													
1850 – 1899													
1900 – 1949													
1950 – 1999													
2000 – 2049													
2050 – 2099													
2100 – 2149													
2150 – 2199													
2200 – 2299													
2300 – 2399													
2400 – 2499													
2500 – 2599													
2600 – 2699													
2700 – 2799													
2800 – 2899													
2900 – 2999													
3000 – 3099													
3100 – 3199													
3200 +													

Figure 12.6 Technical graduate salaries survey sheet

by salary survey, a substantial volume of information to build up the distribution pattern. This is achieved by obtaining the ages and salaries of a large number of technical graduates, or other required group of staff, from co-operating companies on sheets similar to Fig. 12.6, then merging the information provided by all participants, and plotting percentile distribution lines (such as the 10th, 50th and 90th percentiles) on a graph similar to Fig. 12.7. The procedure is as follows.

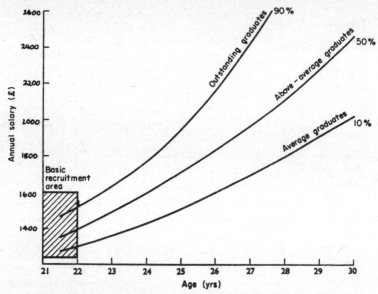

Note: The word 'average' implies acceptable quality only, in line with current usage

Figure 12.7   Graph of technical graduate salary percentiles

The percentile plot-points at each age group are arrived at by setting down all the salary plots in descending order, and then making use of the following simple formula :

$$P(N + 1)/100 = X$$

where

P is the percentile selected (say the 10th, 50th or 90th),
N is the number of salaries available at the age, and

X is the number of the salary on the list.

For example, if there were nine salaries at one age and we wished to find the 50th percentile the formula would be as follows :

$$50(9 + 1)/100 = 5$$

i.e. the fifth salary in the list is the 50th percentile plot point.

If there were eight salaries the calculation would be :

$$50(8 \times 1)/100 = 4.5$$

i.e. the 50th percentile would be mid-way between the fourth and fifth salaries. If these salaries were £1400 and £1500, the exact percentile plot-point is obtained by deducting the fourth salary from the fifth, multiplying the difference by the figure *after* the decimal point (0.5 in this case), and adding the answer to the fourth salary, as follows :

$$£1500 - £1400 = £100 \times 0.5 = £50$$

$$£1400 + £50 \quad = £1450 = \text{50th percentile}$$

The resultant percentile points at different ages can be joined up. These lines can subsequently be smoothed out statistically by using the least-squares formula to give clear-cut guide lines which are easy to explain and understand. This formula is best obtained from a textbook on basic statistics.

The resultant percentile lines, which reflect the competitive picture for the category under study at each age level, should be used as an audit tool; for example, to ensure that the organization is achieving realistic salary objectives for a valuable group of young technical graduates during their early career years.

The salaries of these young graduates, when plotted on this graph, should form a scatter right across the percentile lines. In subsequent administration of their salaries, the lines should never in any sense be used as tramlines along which salaries should rigidly be progressed, but should be used as a continuing audit to ensure that a competitive situation is maintained.

The position of any young graduate's salary in relation to the guide lines will mainly be dictated by his potential, with performance as a secondary factor. Thus, the salaries of very-high-potential graduates should be distributed across the upper part of the scattergraph. For example, those considered the best 10 per cent in the company should normally fall above the 90th percentile line. The majority of salaries will scatter around the median or 50th percentile, and only the salaries of poorer employees of very limited potential should fall around and below the 10th percentile. This last category contains the people who gradually drift out of the graduate stream into low-level routine posts, and a variety of individuals who maintain their levels but stick there for the greater part of their careers, lacking either ability, initiative, or perhaps opportunity, to achieve promotion.

By the time that graduates have reached their middle to late twenties their careers should have 'firmed up', and when they are established in a more permanent post, it will be possible to assign them to posts with definite job grades. From this point you make use of the appropriate salary ranges for progressing their salaries. Use of guide lines for graduate staff during their early formative years should ensure that their salaries have been fanned out from the close limits of recruiting rates towards more appropriate levels by the time their middle career possibilities have become apparent.

As a word of warning, if the salaries of high-potential staff of this type are not progressed at a rate faster than is possible with the routine merit increases appropriate for other staff at the same level, they will tend to move in search of high salaries, that is, to a company where salary administration thinking is more enlightened. The slope of the guide lines indicates the rate or normal salary increases appropriate for low-, medium- and high-calibre graduates, and these rates will be seen to range from approximately 3 up to 12 per cent of basic salary, apart from any inflationary uplift (see again Fig. 12.6).

Maturity curves

We have suggested above, that middle career patterns have become apparent by the time individuals reach their late twenties. This rather arbitrary statement is based on the statistical fact that average career salary paths do follow patterns, and there is a distinctly better-than-average chance that the individual who achieves a salary of £*X* in a post in grade '*M*' by age 28, will achieve a salary of £*Y* in grade '*P*' by age 40. But no irrevocable forecast on individual salary progress should ever be made on the basis of these 'average' lines, pending the development and proving of reliable methods of assessing the validity of such forecasts.

Maturity curves or salary-growth curves are a comparatively recent salary administration development for salary planning and audit purposes. There are wide variations in the forms which these curves take but basically they all stem from the same data, the salary distribution at various age levels. They are used mainly for planning the salaries of professional staff such as Engineers, Chemists, and Physicists, as some organizations consider that ordinary grades and salary ranges will not provide satisfactory salary progressions for these people.

In the simplest, basic form only the median salary curve is plotted. A salary survey is set up with a number of other organizations either locally or nationally and salary data obtained at each age level to be surveyed, and when all the information has been received median salaries are plotted against each age level on a graph.

This median salary curve, although limited in value, has a number of uses, the main one being the comparison between the surveying company's curve and the local or national picture. It may even be desirable to compare the position with one or more other industries. From the relationship between the curves it is possible to identify dangerous areas of low pay and to rectify salaries in such areas to match competitive levels.

A less general use is to plot the current salaries of comparable staff on the graph, mainly to see how they relate to the competitive median salary curve. Ideally, the salaries should form a scatter all round the line, but this rarely happens in practice. Furthermore, the salaries of the best people should all plot above the curve, the average performers close to the curve, and the less able employees well below the curve.

More often than not there is far less logic in the actual plot of salaries, and action should be taken to readjust individuals' pay to reflect their true worth. Some form of employee appraisal or ranking technique will be essential to indicate the relative values of employees when determining the appropriate relations between salary levels and position against the median curve.

A more sophisticated approach to the use of salary growth curves is to plot the 90th and 10th percentiles in addition to the median, or 50th percentile. If the use of percentile distribution curves is not considered appropriate, a more simple adaptation is to plot the medians of the top or highest 10 per cent of salaries as well as the lowest for each age block or level. The resultant lines can either be left in their original irregular shape or smoothed by use of the method of least-squares, according to taste. A loose interpretation of these three salary guide lines might be to use the highest curve for planning Senior Engineers' or Technologists' salaries, the middle line for Engineers and the lowest for Assistant Engineers.

Some organizations using this approach do not impose any salary maxima for any of these groups of staff, regardless of their current jobs or future prospects. They claim that this approach tends to retain valuable career staff in the organization, and also that this salary treatment maintains interest and incentive. The opponents of this concept consider that it is possible to grade such jobs and to employ the appropriate competitive salary ranges. They point out that there are economic salary limits for every job and that to have unlimited maxima may be unnecessarily expensive.

Salary growth curves also give an indication of the expected differential between salaries at each age level and thus help to determine the approximate rate of salary increase which should be paid at periodic, say annual, intervals. These growth curves indicate possible percentage increases on an annual basis for different levels of Engineers and are typical of the guide lines used by a number of organizations for planning the salaries of professional groups of staff.

The main danger associated with the use of these curves is to use them too rigidly, like tramlines, so that all employees' salaries move along them together regardless of individual performance or potential. This type of salary administration would create nearly as many salaries inequities as the old-fashioned haphazard approach!

Probably the safest and most effective use of salary growth

curves is as an audit tool to ensure that the overall salary picture is competitive with comparable organizations. If in achieving this a more careful look is taken periodically at the salaries of all staff a useful objective will have been achieved.

Another type of growth curve can be plotted by graphing actual annual salary increases for select groups of staff over a number of years. It is interesting initially to plot the total annual increases which would include elements of merit, increases in cost-of-living, promotions as well as other general wage and salary movements, and then to extract from these data all elements other than merit increases to obtain the often elusive factor of salary growth rate.

Such a study may lead people responsible for salary administration to think carefully about the relative worth of their organization's merit plan, and also to consider the effect of extraneous factors on salaries and salary scales.

All too often salary growth is utterly haphazard, and this usually results in ultimate deterioration in pay relationships and increasing inequities. In any organization, however small, it is possible for someone to study and evaluate the overall, as well as individual, salary positions using the simple techniques we have described, and to formulate a meaningful salary plan which will achieve the equitable and controlled growth of salaries across the whole organization.

Salary guide curves

Certain organizations, particularly in the USA, have developed complete salary planning systems based on a series of exponential curves. These are used as grading structures, taking the place of formal salary ranges and merit progression. Employees are appraised, with varying degrees of sophistication, for performance and promotability and moved from one curve to another according to their yearly rated value (see Fig. 12.8).

Theoretically, evaluation considers the long-term growth potential of an individual and pays him for this rather than for his current value, so that he can be employed on varying types of work with greater mobility and opportunity for development than is provided by the 'normal' structure.

It is essential that the curves used should be relevant currently to typical salary patterns of comparable people. As these patterns are constantly developing and vary also between different groups, producing and maintaining acceptable guide curves is not easy. Inevitably, some adjustment becomes necessary in order to fit in individual market values, but this is just one disadvantage.

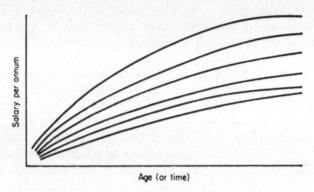

Figure 12.8   Salary guide curves

A more fundamental disadvantage is the way in which individual careers develop at varying pace—often by a series of steps as energy, drive and success fluctuate, and real values vary. To continue to progress an individual's salary on vague assumptions of long-term potential is unrealistic. How often are we accurate about development and training for more than one career step ahead?

Another real disadvantage of such a system is that long service or older employees of limited value can carry excessive 'weighting' for long service and be at the same salary level as younger high flyers, a concept much admired in Japan but not really appropriate for advanced thinking companies who are trying to retain thrusting young professional staff and managers.

Another synthetic salary progression technique (particularly for young career staff) is to plot salary progression curves calculated for a specific category of staff from a combination of cost of living, merit and market value data (see Fig. 12.9).

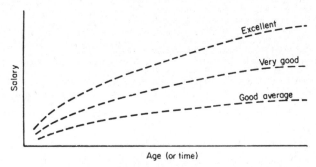

Figure 12.9 Growth-of-income guidelines for specific staff category

These guides are based on the premise that merit should not be less than, say, 5 per cent of salary each year for an acceptable performer (the alternative for less than acceptable performance being nil). However, the average salary increase for good performers is around 7 to 10 per cent, with outstanding people getting up to 15 per cent. Such increases are modified according to the employee's position in the salary range if this exists, or may be subject to an economic limit. That is, if he was already in the top quartile of his salary bracket and an outstanding performer, the appropriate 'automatic' increase would be reduced to, say, 5 or 7 per cent with nil for merely 'acceptable' performance.

A further alternative, developed by numbers of American companies for the bulk processing of lower level salaries, is to tabulate percentage sizes of increment on the basis indicated. The size of increment becomes dependent on the two factors of performance and place in the salary range. This seems logical enough and certainly reduces the administrative burden. It may even be computerized! But the real evaluation of the pace of the employee's development and changing value cannot be covered by so coarse a mechanism.

This approach is altogether too rigid and unsophisticated—sound salary planning requires a great deal more thought and consideration of many factors.

Salary reviews

Annual salary reviews

The majority of large organizations in the United Kingdom carry out a review of all staff salaries once a year, usually culminating immediately before the Christmas holidays when the lucky recipients of salary increases are notified of their good fortune and the remainder spend a miserable Christmas wondering whether they were overlooked or will get their reward after the holiday. The major drawback to this traditional ritual is the inevitable consequences of a blend of Christmas spirit and compassion on the part of managers which comes into direct conflict with some form of salary budget and with salary planning. Often the result is that small routine increases are doled out indiscriminately to as many people as is humanly possible, good and bad performers being treated alike, so that as few staff as possible are disappointed. As we have pointed out elsewhere in the book, this system provides little incentive to work harder or to do a better or more responsible job than the other fellows—everybody gets the same anyway, so why try for more?

Clearly, it is advisable, if not essential, to carry out a co-ordinated review of the salaries of large groups of staff at a set time in the year. Tradition plays a strong part in this decision for many organizations and it may be that staff like the Christmas timing. In these circumstances, the Salary Administrator has a responsibility to his organization and to the staff to reduce the emotional aspects of the review to an absolute minimum. After all, the salary paid to an individual should be associated more with his value to the company throughout the year than to the feelings of *bonhomie* preceding a holiday. However, we do not propose a total exclusion of Christmas as a review time. We merely suggest that the timing need not coincide with Christmas; that the salaries of career, or monthly, staff are reviewed at one period, and those of other staff, mainly weekly (unionized) at another.

Carrying the suggestion one stage further for career staff, to get away from the Christmas box, 'one-gets—all-get' spirit, why not review these staff, say, during March, April, and May, working from appraisals and other review data, and forecast a next salary increase, or nil as may be appropriate, for each member of the staff to be effective at any time during the following year, or at some future specified time? The 'year' for this purpose would be a review year, perhaps from the beginning of July to the end of June next year.

To help select an appropriate time in the year for an adjustment, such meaningful anniversaries to the employee as the date he joined the company, or the date of his last promotion could be considered, but the concept of twelve months as a standard interval between salary adjustments can go. Any interval, such as 9, 12, 15, 18 months, can be used and maximum flexibility of timing attained.

The advantages of this type of flexible timing review are as follows.

1 As people receive increases throughout the year they are less aware of the awards being made to their associates and therefore are less concerned. There is less comparison of increases.

2 There is none of the triumph or shame or jealousy normally witnessed at Christmas-time indicating the lucky and unlucky staff.

3 As the atmosphere of emotional drama associated with Christmas is removed by year-round increases, salary planning is conducted on a sane and more logical basis.

4 The feeling that everybody must get a Christmas box is removed and the available salary budget can be allocated where it belongs, to the good performers and high-potential staff.

5 The timing of individual increases can be adjusted to provide maximum incentive power, associated with individual achievement. Reviews should not be allowed to become too flexible so that certain groups may be overlooked. Staff should always be covered by co-ordinated reviews of significant groups or all at the same time, after which the salary adjustments can all take place at the same date or can be spread out if desired.

The co-ordinated review for weekly staff, or possibly staff who received general awards, could be carried out preferably by October or some other time to fit in with company programmes generally.

Amounts of salary adjustments for non-career staff will tend to be more routine in amount, augmenting the periodic general awards, and the number of increases in any review should be proportionately fewer than for career staff.

Staff on incremental salary scales

As is the case stated elsewhere in this book, the position in respect of staff on incremental scales is quite different. For these staff there is very little discretionary element in their salary adjustments and the timing is established on an anniversary basis. Under the, virtually, 'all-get' principle, there is little to be gained from a co-ordinated review of individual salaries.

Footnote

The special circumstance of a partial or complete National wage freeze is ignored in this chapter. To the extent that normal salary planning can continue, it should do so. On conclusion of a period of freeze, it will be necessary to move steadily back to the matching of salary progress with developing career.

This does not apply to the Civil Service and Local Government, where the award of annual increments continues through periods of National wage freeze.

Chapter 13

Salary Policies and Procedures

There are three main parts of this chapter; the first covers the various operational procedures in use in salary administration, the second is on salary administration statistics, and the third discusses the process of policy development and communication.

Operational procedures

A Salary Administrator's responsibilities do not end with the creation of a job classification, salary structures and a policy. Operational procedures are required to weld the plan together and, of course, active operational support from all participating individuals is essential.

If line managers and local personnel managers are left with only the basic elements of salary administration, they will create their own local systems and procedures, such as fragmentary, sub-grade structures and complex arrangements for allocating salary adjustments, and chaos will result. The basic structures must be tied together with effective operating procedures which will provide a standard pattern, company-wide, as well as fast and smooth-flowing paper-work.

Many of the operational procedures relevant to the individual elements of salary administration have been covered separately in the appropriate chapters. These individual processes culminate in the co-ordinated salary review, the principles of which were covered in the previous chapter. However, the actual review procedure and the associated control and audit of year-

	Name	Initials	Age	Service	Job title	Job grade	Last salary increase			Salary range		Present salary	Recommendation		
							Date	Amount	Reason	Min.	Max.		Amount	New salary	Bonus
1															
2															
3															
4															
5															
6															
7															
8															
9															
10															
11															
Totals															

Figure 13.1 Salary review sheet

wide salary adjustments, deserve separate coverage as distinct and major elements in the salary administration process.

The annual salary review

The following pages set out a basic routine procedure which is used with variations by many British companies in their annual salary reviews, and which can be taken as a practical operating pattern. For the purposes of this example we have used an imaginary setting of a large organization undertaking a co-ordinated review of all staff salaries at Christmas. The time-span of the operation would be similar at any other time of the year, for example, even if it was effective in July. In smaller organizations, the procedure would take a shorter period of time so that the programme should be readjusted to suit individual conditions.

In September, salary review sheets (see Fig. 13.1) are prepared covering all staff. Usually, four copies are printed; two for the head of the organizational unit concerned, one for personnel department, and a file copy for the payroll section preparing the sheets.

As can be seen from the example, salary review sheets should incorporate essential data on which a review of each salary can be based. Job title and grade are basic essentials; salary ranges may either be included or covered on a separate document; recent salary changes as well as current salary and bonus data are essential; age and service occasionally have relevance; performance and potential ratings are necessary and can be coded or attached on separate documents. On the other hand, time-keeping and similar matters which should be more a matter of immediate supervisory control or discipline have no place on a review sheet and should be excluded.

The two sets of review sheets are sent out to the organization heads together with sets of special instructions for the administration of the review. These will vary from year to year as circumstances change, and much thought should go into a clear explanation of intention and operation. The form of analysis and statistics required are also subject to evolutionary development from year to year. Figure 13.2 shows a typical salary review data sheet.

The salaries of all staff are reviewed by the various super-

DEPARTMENT..................

(All figures in £'s a year)

Job grade	Mid-point of salary range	Part I: PRESENT SALARY POSITION			Part II: SALARY RECOMMENDATIONS				
		No. of staff	Total salaries (£'s a year)	Average salary (£'s a year)	No. of salary increases	Total cost of increases	Total salaries after review (£'s a year)	New average salary (£'s a year)	New average salary as percentage of mid-point (£'s a year)
(1)	(2)	(3)	(4)	(5)	(6)	(7)	(8)	(9)	(10)
Totals:									

Bonus:

Number of recommendations..................   Total cost of bonus recommendations..................

Figure 13.2 Salary review statistics sheet

visory and managerial levels as described in Chapter 12, 'Salary Planning', and the initial salary and bonus recommendations are recorded in pencil on the review sheets.

Totals are then calculated for each department to check whether they are within their agreed budget; scattergraphs are plotted to see the effects of the changes, and grade average salaries calculated to review the new balance of salary levels created. When any necessary adjustments have been made **the**

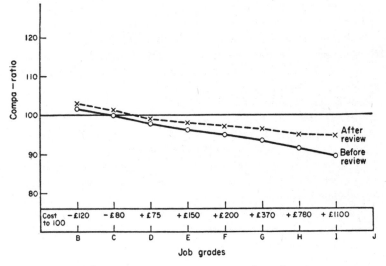

Figure 13.3 Compa-ratio chart

recommendations are inked or typed in and the sheets signed as approved by the manager, in line with the responsibilities and authority which have been delegated to him.

One of the two sets of sheets is then sent to the salary administration or other department responsible for auditing the recommendations, to ensure that they conform to the company's policies, and for obtaining the final approvals of top management to the recommendations. During this phase, individual exceptions to company policy or to budget limits are checked and referred to the appropriate executive.

One of the visual aids recommended for reference to top management is the compa-ratio chart shown in Fig. 13.3. This illustrates the salary position prior to and after a salary review, and spotlights high and low payment areas. Additionally, in the form we have designed, it acts as a cost control and budget forecast document by giving details of salary adjustment costs.

If the salary objectives for the whole company and for the individual organizations in the company have been achieved, the recommendations will be authorized and confirmed by sending a photostat copy of the authorized sheets back to each manager before the effective date.

A typical programme for organizing the annual salary review 'announcements' is as follows :

All staff receiving a salary adjustment or bonus are seen by their supervisor or line manager, not only to be told of the award, but also for a discussion covering their performance and possibly associated matters.

Some companies insist on *all* staff being interviewed at least annually for a discussion of appraisal and salary, preferably on separate occasions, whether or not they receive an increase. This seems extremely sound to us. If the employee is a poor performer, his salary treatment is affected by this and he should be told of the position and counselled to assist him to eliminate or improve faults where possible. Also, if the employee is a good performer, but is already on a salary high in the salary range so that his salary progress needs to be slowed down, an explanation to this effect should be given and future opportunities discussed where these exist.

The need for detailed appraisal and salary discussions for non-career staff may be considerably less than is the case with more senior people, but it still exists. These employees should always have the opportunity to discuss their salary position and performance if they wish.

The flexible salary review

A 'Flexible' Salary Review is one which is carried on throughout the year instead of at one point in the year.

We have explained the advantages of this type of review, particularly for career staff, in removing the study of their salaries from the emotion and sentiment of Christmas and in adding flexibility of timing to flexibility of increment.

Sheet no.	Name	Age	Sex	Job title	Job grade	Last increase			Recommendation												Reason
						Amount	Reason	Date	J	A	S	O	N	D	J	F	M	A	M	J		Reason
1																						
2																						
3																						
4																						
5																						
6																						
7																						
8																						
9																						
10																						
Totals:																						

Figure 13.4 Flexible salary review sheets

Basically the method of operating this type of review is as follows. In March, the co-ordinated review and forecast is begun. Salary review sheets, see Fig. 13.4, are prepared for all staff covered in the flexible review. Sets of sheets are issued to line managers, together with any review instructions covering budgets and company or department salary objectives.

Using the review sheets, scattergraphs and employee appraisals, managers carry out a co-ordinated review of all staff during which they forecast appropriate salary increases for those staff who are to receive adjustments between the coming 1 July and the following 30 June, and may also indicate approximate timing for a next adjustment for other staff. These increases can be forecast for any month during the fiscal period. While such anniversaries as date of joining the company or date of last promotion are borne in mind, there is no obligation to follow twelve-monthly cycles. Nine-monthly increments for young, high-potential staff, and eighteen- or even thirty-six-month cycles for staff progressing less rapidly, are totally acceptable on the basis of individual requirements.

For flexible reviews it should be remembered that salary adjustments are planned for the most appropriate time, i.e. for when they will do most good, or to fit in with current circumstances of each organization. They can be given at any incremental interval and need not be given necessarily each review period.

The forecast increases are recorded in the review sheets against the appropriate month during the fiscal period, and the total cost of the adjustments is calculated to ensure that they are within budget. The review sheets are then sent to the Salary Administrator for audit and advice before being approved by the Chief Executive.

When the forecast adjustments have received overall agreement, the second phase begins immediately. The first batch of increases, which will be effective from 1 July, are referred to the line managers in June for reappraisal and confirmation. This is carried out by using the monthly reappraisal sheet, Fig. 13.5. If they have any amendments these are made and the sheet is then sent for final approval and payment.

Each month the reappraisal sheets covering adjustments to be

(I plus 3 copies required)

Location: ....   Division: ....   Effective date..............

Department: ....

Employees affected:

Name	Sex	Job title	Grade	Present salary (£'s a year)	Proposed increase			Proposed salary (£'s a year)
					Date	Type of change	Amount	

1. Reappraisal by: 2. Personnel Manager: 3. Approved by: 4. Final Review by:

Remarks and explanations:

Figure 13.5 Flexible review – monthly reappraisal sheet

effective on the first of the following month are sent out to line managers and recommended changes are recorded.

It is almost essential to use punched card equipment to support this type of review as speed and accuracy of paper-work are essential to its effectiveness. If a company is fairly small, this type of review might be handled without such equipment, but otherwise it would be difficult, if not impossible. The use of punched card equipment is discussed more fully later in this chapter.

Salary budgets

In most companies using modern management techniques, there will be as part of an overall company salary plan a predetermined annual salary budget. This is usually planned with the Salary Administrator on a three- to five-year forecast basis and reviewed annually.

In highly complex organizations each department or division has to decide what they need to afford in the way of salary increases, working from data shown on compa-ratio charts (see Fig. 13.3), information relating to cost-of-living, and general increases and national awards or similar union-negotiated increases, and general salary movement amongst competitive companies. More usually, these factors are computed centrally to reduce the work of busy line managers.

In an economic climate of good profits and full order-books the salary budget often tends to be generous, with or without cause, but when money is tight the salary budget is pruned to the minimum. Although these policies are understandable they may well be very wrong. Low pay conditions in a company may have helped to worsen already poor morale and produce or aggravate lack of desire to make a profit. Judicious increases to the better performers can do much to boost morale and recreate interest and incentive in a tough business situation. Conversely, over-generous treatment during periods of prosperity can lead to a gradual deterioration in profits due to high wage and salary bills.

Salary payroll forecasting

If any attempt is to be made to make short- or long-term company business plans, particularly with profit planning in mind, or even, at a much simpler level, if Personnel Department or the Finance people want to budget for payroll costs and to control them; then the following factors must be taken into consideration :

1 *Numbers of people* employed have the greatest influence. If we allow numbers to rise without any proper control our salary costs may rocket. Hence the need for scientific manpower planning linked with work measurement techniques.

2 *Mix of categories* employed may change within a stated number of people. If we substitute more expensive types of staff for those previously employed, our cost per employee will rise.

3 *Attrition* has the effect of reducing average salary levels where there is personnel movement within a staff category and less experienced replacements are hired on lower salaries.

4 *Inflationary* movement of salaries will change our standards of assessment. However, usually salary ranges are moved to reflect the higher market rates for personnel brought about by increases in cost of living.

5 *Overtime payments* can make a significant addition to payroll costs and need to be properly controlled, where possible by prior request for overtime to be worked and analyses by Management and Personnel Department of reasons.

What information do we need in order to establish reasonable control and a basis of forecasting? The primary need is for a simple analysis of our existing staffing and future requirements, with an assessment of the changes which will take place. Each department should be helped to prepare a schedule showing the forward staff budget, by types of employees, and with their forecast salaries totalled month-by-month. Adjustments should be made for the year's attrition forecast, merit increases, awards and planned starters and leavers, and also for expected inflation. This salary summary will form part of each department's budget for the fiscal year.

A small company may be able to forecast with reasonable accuracy the probability of each individual staying in the unit, the post he will fill and the salary necessary to hold him. Similar assessments covering new personnel will enable quite precise total forecasts to be made. Basically, the factors used in such a study are exactly comparable with those outlined above, but the calculations are made individually on the smaller numbers of personnel involved.

As we have already said, the central point in salary control is variation of average salary figures from the mid-point or other control point within a salary range for each category of employee (compa-ratio). Statistical analysis of this movement is the basis for large company salary bill forecasting.

An important factor in considering mid-point control ratios for salary planning is the overall state of each operating organization or budget centre. One division of the company may be on a high average salary generally, although their profitability and output are low. It has to be decided whether their annual increases should be throttled back, and what effect this will have on morale and possible losses of employees. It is even possible that this may be a desired state, e.g. that the division is overpaid, overstaffed and not working very hard.

Another division may have a low average salary, compared with the company average, and this might be due to their having a very young but high-powered staff team. In this case, it may be necessary to inject far more than the average salary increase to boost morale and to retain the team with, as usual, more being given to the better performers and high fliers.

So each division must review *all* its staffing criteria when recommending the amount of salary roll increase at review time and during the budget year. One of the most dangerous people in a company can be the division manager who openly boasts how tight he is with his pay rises. It could be found that he has the highest turnover of employees in the company after analysis by Personnel, and the cost of replacing his staff far outweighs his so-called savings.

Attrition

A key figure in any analysis and forecast of salary roll movement is 'attrition'. Attrition is the process of gradual erosion of payroll; the gradual reduction of average salary levels for each type of work. This results from a number of factors best explained by a series of brief cases :

1 Where a senior man retires, on a salary high in the salary range, he may be replaced by someone whose salary is much lower in the salary range. The effect of this is reduction in the average salary for the staff in that grade. (See Fig. 13.6a.)

2 Several new jobs may be created which are filled by people on salaries which are low in the salary range for the appropriate grade. This will tend to reduce the average salary for the grade. (See Fig. 13.6b.)

3 Jobs may be reclassified following gradual change in duties to either lower, or higher grades, which again affect the average salary positions in those grades concerned. (See Fig. 13.6c.)

4 When an employee is promoted from, say, just above mid-point of one grade to just below mid-point of the next grade, this action is likely to reduce the average level in both the grades.

These various factors have the cumulative effect of reducing

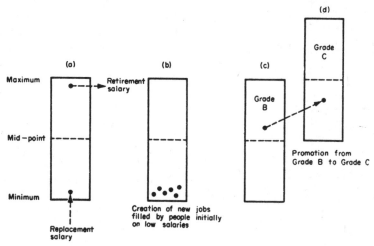

Figure 13.6 Block diagram showing examples of average salary attrition

the average salary level for each category of work over a period of time so that part of the salary adjustments given during any period is to offset attrition and hold the company's salary levels steady at a particular point, or standard.

For example, we may employ six design engineers, and expect to employ seven in a year's time. The six may cost us an average of £2400 each after the present salary review, a total of £14,400. As we should have the seventh man from the middle of the year, we can add on half of £2400 to make £16,800. Very simple, and possibly quite adequate.

However, we expect to lose two engineers and to promote two others during the year, and will be replacing them—and obtaining the additional man—from the junior engineer category at an average of £1800 a year. The average of the seven by the end of the year will be about £2000 and the total bill for the year will be about £14,400.

What has happened is attrition: the phenomenon of falling average salary which exists for *every* staff group where any movement takes place, which offsets the injection of money for merit increases.

In its simplest form, attrition can be examined by watching the movement in average company-wide salary. This overall figure is most meaningful in a fairly static situation, i.e. where the company is neither expanding nor contracting and has a fairly low turnover rate.

For straightforward costing purposes, attrition is most clearly seen by a regular calculation on the total salary roll. In most organizations it will be seen only at major salary reviews that the total salaries for all employees is lower than the sum of mid-point salaries, i.e. the product of multiplying the number of employees in every grade by the grade mid-point.

Over a year this differential widens until salaries are increased to reinstate the previous level of average salaries. As trend lines are worked out over a period of time, it is possible to forecast approximately the amount of money which should be fed into the payroll in the form of salary increases in order to hold average salary levels at a static level across the company.

Normally, attrition should be measured for specific categories of staff, e.g. engineers in grade 'x'. Where differentials between intake and output are substantial, or where a large proportion of the category move during a year, attrition may amount to figures as high as 5 per cent. In other words, the average salary for the group decreases by 5 per cent; the average level of knowledge and experience is lowered and salary levels are lower proportionately.

Within a category, whether the employee situation is static or turbulent is relatively unimportant, in that attrition arises from change and is a measure of that change; for example, in a company where there is a substantial amount of promotion.

Where a group of low calibre employees are gradually replaced by higher standard personnel, the incoming group is more highly paid and attrition for the overall category may be offset, i.e. the average salary may rise considerably.

In considering the implications of attrition, one needs to look at the *target* average salary figures for personnel in each category, allowing some weighting for the newness or experience contained within each group. For example, within a rapidly changing team where none of the staff in a particular category has been longer than two years in his job, one would expect the average salary to be well short of the mid-point of a range. By contrast, average salaries in a long-established and fairly static department tend to be justifiably above grade mid-points.

This movement in average salaries should be presented grade-by-grade, for the whole company or for each division. This provides the most important basic salary administration statistic, the compa-ratio, which is discussed above.

Salary bill forecasting poses two questions: 'What is the actual average salary position?' and 'What should it be at any particular point in time?'

In this forecasting activity, attrition gives a measure of how the position has changed. In looking at attrition historically, one can build up an understanding of the events which explain the change. If one is looking forward, the attrition forecast must be based on the expected rate of personnel change, linked to knowledge of existing salary distribution.

In a static situation, the attrition rate is likely to be of the order of 1 per cent, or even less, while in a turbulent situation it may be around 5 per cent, possibly even higher. It is important to recognize that in the static situation, average salaries are likely to be around mid-point, or perhaps even higher, while in the turbulent situation the average may be as much as 10 per cent below mid-point, being pushed back to a low of 15 per cent by attrition, further helped by inflation.

Attrition indicates the amount by which average salaries for specific groups of staff have been pushed back, so that it indicates the amount required to restore a previous average salary position.

All these, and many more factors, such as Government action, economic crises and manpower problems, must be considered when budgeting and salary planning. It is like all business planning, a combination of Statistical and Personnel Analysis plus experience in this rather difficult field.

Inflation

In forecasting future salary bills, an assessment of the rate of inflation is necessary. In an early edition of this book, we spoke of 4 per cent as a useful general guide, but experience in the early seventies has raised our sights to totally different levels. In spite of all the problems of assessing how the rate of inflation is going to evolve, a forecast is necessary year by year for salary budgeting.

Of course, market value movement varies enormously between different types of jobs and it is possible to make allowance for this in departmental budgets if enough knowledge and information about the market are available.

Attrition is quite separate from inflation (although sometimes confused with it). It is a measure of the extent to which average salary per grade in a company has reduced during the year, due to changes in personnel, and therefore a measure of how much salaries would need to be increased in order to maintain the average salary at the level following the previous review. Normally, staff leave the upper part of a salary range for promotion and retirement, and their replacements come into the lower part of the range, thus gradually reducing the average of salaries currently paid.

Control and audit of year-wide salary adjustments

It is a practice in the majority of companies to operate some form of control and audit of salary adjustments, both for the

Copy: **To:**
1. Salary Administration Dept.
2. Treasurer/Payroll
3. Location Personnel Dept.
4. Dept. originating form

CHANGE IN STATUS OR SALARY

Surname	Initials	Type of change				Salary change	Date form prepared:
						Yes/No	

Sex	Age		Service		Basic hours worked	Monthly/Weekly staff	Regular day work	Part time	Shift allowance	
M.	Y	M	Y	M			Shift:		Present	Recommended
F.										

Present job classification	Grade	Job number	Department

Proposed job classification	Grade	Job number	Department

Previous salary adjustment	Salary from	Salary to	Effective date	Type of salary change	Present salary	Recommended salary	Effective date
Type:							

Supervisor	Function head or Group/Division/Department Manager

Location Personnel Manager	Salary Administration Dept.

Remarks and explanations

Figure 13.7 Salary change form

purpose of budgetary control as well as to ensure that adjustments are within company policy and are changing individual salaries where there is most need.

As we have shown in the chapter on salary planning and in the first sections of this chapter on annual salary reviews, there are numerous methods of controlling and auditing increases during co-ordinated reviews of all salaries—organizational budgets, statistical summaries, compa-ratios, and other analyses all serve to this end.

However, salary adjustments which are processed separately throughout the year are far more difficult to control unless there are clearly defined policies and procedures governing their award, either on a local control basis for each single operating unit, or alternatively on a much wider scale, from an overall company view through a central authority. Apart from ensuring that year-wide salary adjustments covering promotion, in-grade promotions and low payment are normally within policy limits, what else should be considered and how can the controls and audits be administered?

There are various ways of setting up a system, but basically, in every case, the proposed salary adjustment should be recorded on some kind of salary change form or salary adjustment form (see Fig. 13.7) which will give the full facts of the recommendation as well as relevant current and previous personal and salary information.

This form, with an appropriate number of copies, is originated by the employee's supervisor or manager well in advance of the proposed effective date of the salary recommendation. It is routed only through essential people in the chain of command to the manager delegated to authorize the adjustment. There is sometimes a tendency for large numbers of people to sign or initial these forms for 'status' reasons; this is unnecessary and should be resisted, if necessary by taking positive action to trim down the number of 'approvals'.

The Local Personnel Officer or Manager should automatically be included among the signatories as it is part of his function to carry out the local control and audit operation on behalf of management. In companies where there is a central salary administration organization, this unit will carry out the final review of adjustments for 'career staff' and possibly all staff, except in simple routine cases such as automatic increases for junior staff.

This review by a central adviser can take the form of a post audit, after the increase has been made effective, but it should always be made. The advantage of the post audit approach is that it speeds up the processing of salary adjustments by cutting out a signatory and also removes much semi-routine paper handling and checking from Salary Administrators, leaving them more time to carry out their main function of policy-making and advising.

Once the salary change form has been fully authorized and cleared for action the various copies are routed to the managers concerned. The originating supervisor will need a confirmatory copy, as will the local Accountant for payment and the local Personnel Manager for recording the salary change in the employee's records. In the central personnel organization of a large company, the salary administration copy should be routed to central personnel records for processing, including the punching of a new card where electronic data-processing equipment is in use.

These year-wide salary increases should be analysed periodically to see how much money has been spent, where it has been spent, and for what reasons. The form in Fig. 13.8 shows the way in which these data can most effectively be produced for use by salary administration and top management.

As we have stressed, it is part of the salary administration function to see that the money employed for salary increases is being used effectively, that it is going to the right people in the company and is not being shared around in the form of miserable hand-outs for everyone like some 'Christmas Slate Club'. All too often the old-fashioned, more limited type of manager still retains a pathetic belief that he can purchase the love of all the employees who work for him by giving each of them 'a little something all at the same time'. Such a man is immediately in trouble if he ever directs the work of high-calibre staff, as they will not be interested in this kind of salary treatment.

The main statistics, which will generally be required either half yearly or yearly, will include the number of increases and total money spent for each organization in the company. These figures can be further broken down into types of increase, such

SALARY INCREASES STATISTICS FOR ....

Reason for increase	No. of increases effective												Cost of increases											
	Jan.	Feb.	Mar.	Apr.	May	June	July	Aug.	Sept.	Oct.	Nov.	Dec.	Jan.	Feb.	Mar.	Apr.	May	June	July	Aug.	Sept.	Oct.	Nov.	Dec.
INDIVIDUAL MONTHS																								
1. Promotion																								
2. In-grade																								
⋮																								
9. Merit																								
Total:																								
CUMULATIVE																								
1. Promotion																								
2. In-grade																								
⋮																								
9 Merit																								
Total:																								

Figure 13.8 Year-wide salary statistics sheet

as promotion, rate-for-age and underpayment, at least for central information if not for the line organizations. These statistics should be sufficiently comprehensive to enable the Salary Administration Adviser to comment on what is happening within the organization and to advise, and take action, if money for salary increases is being badly spent by any department.

Compa-ratio graphs are probably the most meaningful way of seeing if the money is broadly going where it is most needed and that salary objectives are generally being achieved.

Delegation of authority

Whether official or tacitly agreed, there is usually a clear-cut understanding in most companies of who is empowered to authorize various things, such as purchases, tenders and, of course, salary adjustments for his staff. Usually the manager who is delegated to authorize pay increases is responsible for the overall budget of an organization, so that he has a knowledge of what money is being spent and where it is going.

However, to lighten the inexorable burden of paper-work landing on a top manager's desk it is not unusual for him to delegate certain responsibilities to his senior executives. Considering the salary administration field only, let us see how this delegation might work in practice.

Where sound job classification and salary structure exist a top-line manager may decide that he does not want to have to authorize routine salary increases for junior staff under age 21, or for clerical staff in certain lower grades. He would, however, need to know the number and cost of such increases periodically and their effect on his budgets.

It is rare for the authorization of job grade and classification changes to be delegated to anyone other than the top manager, as these are fundamental changes in job values which can prove costly if they affect many employees. Moreover, changes in job classifications have a way of chain-reacting not only on other allied jobs in the local organization but also throughout the whole company.

Delegation of authority is often published officially in the form of a series of schedules covering different subjects, such as purchases, expenses, staff salary increases, etc. (see Fig. 13.9).

A manager may delegate responsibility for authorizing adjustments for the more junior levels of monthly staff, but he should always retain authority, and a keen interest, regarding all adjustments for his senior people. This could be all his career staff, or could cover the people reporting directly to him and their immediate subordinates only.

	Rate for age increases for junior staff	Weekly staff increases	Monthly staff increases	Senior staff increases
Originated by:	Immediate Supervisor	Immediate Supervisor	Line Manager	Line Manager
Checked by:	Personnel Manager	Personnel Manager	Personnel Manager	Personnel Manager or Director
Authorized by:	Line Manager	Line Manager	Top Line Manager	Chief Executive (M.D.)
Audited by:	SALARY ADMINISTRATION			

Figure 13.9 Salary administration authorities

It is always wise to have some form of audit check, as for any other function where company money is being spent, to ensure that all salary increases are normally within official company policy and that any exceptions are satisfactorily explained and thoroughly documented.

The external Auditors will usually want to check that all the correct signatures are recorded on the accounts copy of salary adjustment forms, so it is essential to obtain these at the time of the salary action.

Naturally, salary administration and line personnel staff have a responsibility to check and advise on all salary adjustments, and many totally unjustified recommendations are indeed dealt with by these staffs in the course of processing increases through the delegated chain of command.

Salary administration statistics

Compa-ratio

The compa-ratio is the ratio between the average salary for a particular grade and the mid-point of the salary range for that grade, calculated as follows :

$$\frac{\text{Average of all salaries in the grade}}{\text{Mid-point of the salary range}} \times 100 = \text{compa-ratio}$$

The compa-ratio has significance only where merit salary ranges are in use and where the mid-point of the range is given the significance of being a target average salary, i.e. a good competitive level which need not, on average, be exceeded. Where the compa-ratio is precisely 100, the average salary is obviously identical with the mid-point of the salary range, which is probably the target in the salary administration programme.

In a salary range in which the maximum salary is 50 per cent higher than the minimum, a compa-ratio of 80 will show that the average salary is identical with the minimum, and a compa-ratio of 120 will indicate an average salary in line with the maximum. However, in most situations the compa-ratio is unlikely to move much outside the limits of 95 to 105.

The compa-ratio has a wide use in determining, within a structure, where money available for additional salary increases should be spent. Where the compa-ratio has reached the 100 mark, it is likely that salary levels are generally acceptable to most staff and the need for widespread salary increases is limited.

When the compa-ratio rises above the 100 mark, this may indicate that average salary levels are riding too high, or alternatively, may result in an organization which is fairly static so that the people concerned are established, experienced staff whom one would expect to have salaries generally in the upper part of the salary bracket.

Where the compa-ratio is below the 100 mark, and particularly where it is substantially below, some degree of underpayment may be indicated in relation to competitive rates and the need for a greater proportion of salary adjustments is indicated. However, in a newly formed department where most staff are young and relatively inexperienced, a low compa-ratio may be clearly justified for a certain period of time.

The preceding paragraphs give emphasis to the use of compa-ratios in organizations using merit salary ranges, where mid-point control of salary levels is relevant. However, compa-ratio calculations may have some application in use with other types of salary structure. For example, grade average salaries in different departments may give useful general information on departmental structure where incremental scales are in use.

Use of computers

Any organization with a staff strength approaching 1000, and certainly those with larger numbers of staff, can justify at least the partial use of punched card machinery for personnel statistics and salary administration purposes.

The primary use of this equipment will, of course, be for the production of statistical analyses which will aid the day-to-day control of salary administration; analyses which are equally relevant in the smaller companies, but which do not need such sophisticated machinery to produce them.

The type of information produced can vary substantially and we describe below some of the most usual pieces of information which can be extracted by using electronic equipment.

Salary surveys   These surveys can be carried out in order to contribute to a study being made by some other organization, or for purely internal purposes to find out more about the existing salary position within the company. One might, for example, want to know within the company the actual salary structure applying to Typists or Development Engineers, which may be substantially different from that indicated when looking at the appropriate grade salary range. When a study of this sort is done, it is possible to list a complete category, showing job grade and salary, and perhaps age, some indication of level of performance, and any other information recorded. Where a machine run is used the median salary and possibly percentiles might also be calculated. At the same time all this information might then be used as a basis for preparing a scattergraph (see Chapter 12) which will show clearly, in pictorial form, the actual salary structure for the group of people under study.

Where an external study is concerned, most punched card equipment would enable statistical information requested to be produced easily.

Of course, there are other internal studies which one would wish to make apart from those covering specific jobs. One may want to calculate the total salary cost of various company functions or the average cost of various types of activities, any of which can be done speedily from these basic records, rather than through the company's normal cost accounting system.

Salary controls Statistics for salary control purposes lead directly on from the survey analyses discussed above. Within a company with an established salary structure one would expect regular analyses of average salary and salary distribution within each grade and within each sub-organization (division, department, etc.). Always provided that the breakdown was not in the components containing such small numbers of staff that the resultant statistics were not significant.

Movements in grade average salaries within organizational units are of particular value, but need careful study as a large number of factors influence movement in these levels.

Salary reviews Punched card equipment clearly provides an ideal means of producing, quickly and easily, the salary review sheets. Examples 13.1 and 13.2 showed typical salary review sheets used by major companies which might be produced from this equipment.

As the salary review sheets are run off, the tabulator or printer can be set to summarize the salary information shown on each sheet, and probably also make further simple analyses for straightforward salary review costing.

Policy development and communication

Responsibility for salary administration policy

Each organization has its own procedures for the allocation of company responsibilities to managers. Among these responsibilities will be those for all personnel management policies and for personnel operations, which includes responsibility for salary administration policies and operation.

A large organization, with a Personnel Director or Group Personnel Manager, may carry an establishment for a Salary Administration Adviser, or Manager, who is responsible for policy and for ensuring that this policy is fully understood and correctly operated. In smaller organizations the salary administration function may be one of the functions of a Personnel Manager, whose staff is too small to include specialists. Exceptionally, the function may be incorporated with accounting or secretarial duties, but this set-up is outmoded.

However, no matter who has the basic responsibility for salary administration policy in an organization, certain aspects of policy should always be determined by consultation with other company officials. For example, the Chief Executive and Finance Director in particular should participate in any decision on the overall level of a company's salary structure.

Who should participate, then, and on what aspects of policy making? In broad terms, the main breakdown is as follows. The Executive Board together with the Salary Administration Adviser determine the basic aims of salary plan. This would include decisions on the overall levels of salary and bonus; the type of emphasis to be given to salary adjustments for various reasons, particularly to degree of salary variations to be associated with performance variation, the frequency and form of salary reviews; the type and method of job analysis and evaluation, and other factors of a fundamental nature. They should always be consulted, usually by way of a written case and recommendation initially, whenever any significant change of the classification or salary structure appears appropriate.

The Personnel Director or his equivalent will be consulted on all significant policy changes of a less general nature, again usually by having a properly prepared and supported recommendation put to him.

It is reasonable, also, to keep him informed of those special cases outside policy which are processed from time to time; cases which exceptionally may be brought to the attention of the Chief Executive as well when very senior staff or important principles are involved.

Adjustments affecting individual senior staff throughout the company should generally be advised to the appropriate Functional Director to enable him to keep an eye on the overall personnel picture within his field for career planning purposes.

Apart from the participation of the Executive Board and its members on salary administration, operational line management also has an important role to play. Any significant policy development inevitably affects the line manager, and failure to let him have a say in its development, or at least to comment on the proposals and what they may mean to his organization, hardly encourages him to support the new policy subsequently. Nor will he feel confident of a method of policy determination in which he cannot participate.

Normally, company policy-making procedures require the co-operation and participation of all major interested parties, at least in the final stages. However, where this approach is not formally required we have found that line support is very greatly improved where deliberate efforts are made by Salary Administrators to consult with, and take note of, sound comment from line managers.

Similarly, in a large company with a number of Personnel Managers, the Salary Administration Adviser will be unwise to ignore the opportunity to consult his line colleagues both on present as well as proposed policy.

Today, very many companies involve representatives of members of their staff who belong to trade unions. In these situations, the staff members' viewpoints on facets of salary policy are heeded, and contribute to the end result. It is relevant that managements should be influenced by the people on whom they are spending a considerable proportion of their company's total expenditure, to ensure that it is spent as well as possible.

Policy communication

As policy is established, whether on salary administration or on any other important facet of business operation, it is essential that executives who will have responsibility for any part of the subsequent operation on the organization should be fully informed of their roles. Communication of policy information will be either in written or oral form each of which has its own particular applications.

Written communication

Basic statements of policy and procedure are essentially in written form, available for reference at any time

Policy statements are usually fairly brief documents; straightforward precise statements of the basic policy plus primary interpretation of important points and essential supplementary detail. Modern practice shies far away from old-fashioned quasilegal jargon, in favour of maximum simplicity without loss of meaning.

Operating notes provide the 'padding', that is the operational detail required by staff concerned with the day-to-day routine operation of a policy.

Operating notes must cover all possible queries, interpretation and other queries likely to be raised, so that the policy can operate smoothly without constant reference to policy makers for decisions on intention as 'special cases' arise. If the policy and procedure development team do their work properly, all potential events and combinations will have been catered for in the procedure guide.

In spite of the detail required in a guide, the same application of simple basic English should always be made. Only queries come from the use of 'legal' language by non-legal people.

Manuals are often prepared to cover particular areas of policy, consolidating all the more important detail in easy reference form for busy supervisors and managers who have a regular interest in the subject. Salary administration policy lends itself particularly well to manual presentation.

Distribution of policy statements is likely to be restricted to senior executives; operating notes will be distributed to staff concerned with detailed operation; the manual of salary administration can be handed out to all those middle managers with a responsibility for administering the salaries of their staff, but who may not have time to absorb the detailed procedures. The manual provides the reference book which should answer most of the questions they are likely to ask.

Once again, a simple, easy style of writing should be adopted for this manual to avoid any difficulty which might result in a barrier or objection to interpretation.

Oral communication

Supplementing the basic written statements must come the face-to-face sessions with supervisors and managers to clarify all aspects of the subject. All the misconceptions and wrong interpretations come out of their dark holes into open discussion of philosophy and intention, plan and operation.

What form should this take, in particular for salary administration? Salary Administrators should be approachable. They must be available and willing to help to clarify all doubtful interpretations, no matter how petty these may sometimes be! They must get out of their offices and meet the people who operate their policies; to gain the confidence of these people and sort out the doubts and reservations, if necessary by evolving new policy.

Line managers and supervisors, in particular, should always have the opportunity to raise their doubts openly and have the fundamental right to have their questions answered satisfactorily. These open sessions have a strong training flavour, as the questions, in a relaxed atmosphere, provide leads for short lectures on aspects of policy and discussion-group approach to operational difficulties. Indeed, informal communication and training of managers and supervisors are an essential part of effective salary administration.

Chapter 14

Bonus Plans (and Premium Payments)

'Our bonus plan is designed to motivate our executives to achieve their stated objectives—and more. We believe that our managers strive harder, attracted by the prospect of a 20 per cent potential increase in their total earnings.' Comment by the managing director of a substantial organization, and typical of attitudes to executives' bonus plans.

Our attitudes to bonus payments are varied, but important. In general, attitudes of bonus recipients are not favourable, in spite of the widespread use of the bonus concept in many organizations.

Bonus is looked on by some people as a 'withholding of income'. If it is part of the remuneration for successful performance of a job, why, they ask, should it not be paid like salary? After all, if the individual fails in his job, loss of bonus which is not significant when compared with loss of employment.

Faced with the choice of variable bonus or fixed salary, the majority of staff at all levels appear to favour the known fixed figure on which they may budget and plan. It is the entrepreneurial type, such as the salesman, who wants his income linked more directly with results, and who is motivated to increase his work pace by this direct incentive.

The professional manager does not wish to be 'paid by results'. He recognizes that he *is rarely in total control of a situation* in that the factors which influence his results are partially external. Also, *his effort will be at maximum anyway, regardless of any 'bribes' offered to achieve more.* He cannot be bribed for he is already at full stretch, but if the bribe is big enough, he may be tempted to make some adjustments in a favourable short-term direction !

Purpose of bonus

Virtually every bonus is a supplementary rather than a primary payment. It is an addition to the primary payment, which is salary.

The manager is paid a salary for the effective performance of his job. In simple terms, if he fails at his job, he is fired. If he merely 'gets by', his salary progress is restricted. If he achieves more than the basic job stipulates, his salary and career are advanced.

This concept of good salary for good performance and firing for failure is really only acceptable when the level of salary encourages the manager to act and accept risks in his determination to perform to high standards. An 'ordinary' level of salary encourages only 'ordinary', riskless performance, but is accepted as normal by many UK companies. Perhaps they are making assumptions which are incomplete; that as a manager is likely to be motivated to achieve results for reasons of job satisfaction rather than purely remuneration, and as one of the strongest motivational factors is opportunity to advance one's career, where does bonus come in ?

In theory, most bonus schemes are created and justified on the basis of their value to motivate, to provide extra incentive, or to develop the 'owner's eye'. Perhaps, for the entrepreneurial type who seeks reward directly related to effort, bonus may provide some part of these things, but what of the professional manager, employed and not owning ?

In an era of bigger and bigger industrial units with progressively reducing opportunity for direct ownership or significant share of equity, the successful manager's ability to share directly in the profitable results of his personal efforts are disappearing.

The bonus plan linked to profits overcomes this to a slight extent. A proportion of the achieved profit is paid directly to the achievers. It seems right and proper. If there had been no profit, then there would be no bonus. Again, this appears to be 'fair'.

I suggest that this wish to be 'fair' is at the root of a large proportion of UK bonus schemes, however much the motives are concealed behind pompous and grandiose expressions.

I suggest that an executive bonus scheme should provide the opportunity for a key man to acquire sufficient capital reserve to give him some independence and security, so that in carrying out his job, he is fully encouraged to exercise his judgment and take the business risks necessary for fast, profitable (but controlled) company growth. Success will be well rewarded. If his judgment proves sufficiently wrong to justify his removal from office, his earlier rewards cushion any hardship.

Incentives and targets

Direct incentive payments must be linked to targets, so that achievement leads to reward and shortfall to penalty. If targets are not set, or are set without adequate precision, the executive cannot assess what he has to do to obtain his bonus and the incentive value is largely lost.

One can draw a useful parallel with salesmen on commission. Where the commission scheme is simple, and the salesman can calculate his earnings immediately he makes a sale, the incentive is at its highest. Where the plan is more complex and commission is built up on a number of factors such as 'maintaining good customer relations', the impact on earnings is less immediate. The salesman may have to wait for a monthly statement, which arrives several weeks later, to find out what he has earned. In such cases, high basic salary and good supervision would often produce better performance!

So with the executive in a bonus plan. If the scheme is designed to enable him to assess the effect of his activities on his bonus, then there may be incentive. In most other situations, the professional manager's need for job satisfaction and personal credit will keep him at full stretch, and bonus has a negligible impact.

On the incentive aspect, there may be incentive where targets are clearly defined and achievable by the manager concerned, but most situations involve some degree of team effort which bonus schemes should recognize. Even so, factors outside the control of the group concerned are invariably present and can more than offsets the efforts of the team. Revision of targets only partially offsets the frustration and, as targets can be revised upwards as well as down, a further element of frustration is added.

Some effects of bonus plans

Bonus amounts Bonus payments may be so insignificant that they are ignored by the employees they cover. Where the benefits are sparse and automatic, and looked on as extra salary, such schemes are better dead.

Effect on staff mobility If the amounts are large, the side effects of retaining staff who should 'move on' in their own as well as the company's interest, or the 'cycling' of terminations to the months immediately after bonus is paid, can be infuriating. Staff 'locked in' by 'deferred payment' bonus schemes get frustrated and may become a positive nuisance.

Impact on decision-taking In my experience there is real pressure on a manager within a bonus scheme to make short-term decisions to increase immediate profitability at the expense of the long-term good of the organization.

> 'Profits could be higher if we cut our R&D budget, trim down on training, and avoid spending £30,000 consultancy fees to get our stock control right. And, the benefits from all that will be taken into account in setting tougher targets next year. If our profit this year is high enough, and the plans for next year look good, I may get promotion before trouble breaks!'

The 'owner's eye' theory that participation in profits or a stockholding encourages managers to think of the business as partly their own is not accepted within the UK as part of the normal pattern. Tax difficulties of building a stockholding may explain this view. The individual's chance of accumulating a stake significant to him in terms of after-tax income is slight.

Control over targets The factors on which bonus may be based may not be under the full control of the individual whose bonus will be affected. For example, in a highly competitive market, action by other competing companies cannot be foreseen. If unforeseeable activity cuts back profits, is it wholly logical to cut the bonus of a production manager who met every target set for him?

A personal view

Recently, I had cause to set out my attitudes to incentive payments in a brief memorandum:

> Remuneration is not the most important motivational force—job satisfaction, personal credit and career growth are at least as important.

> 'Incentives' can involve some form of supplementary payment which is made for specific achievement. However, sound basic remuneration backed with good management do not need added 'incentives' to produce effective operation.

> Where 'additional financial incentives' are to be used, they must be linked as clearly and precisely as possible to the achievement of targets. This is normally possible on the shop floor or for salesmen, but is ruled out by the complexity of most management activities.

> The 'professional' manager, motivated by the non-financial factors will be working at full stretch and may even react badly to 'bribes' offered to improve performance. The entrepreneur thinks differently.

> *The major factor in 'bonus' schemes for senior executives in UK is the opportunity they may provide to assist personal saving or capital accumulation, rarely possible out of normal income in view of taxation.*

'Incentive' bonus schemes for professional employed managers are largely worthless—at least in the present UK economic situation and personal taxation policies. Most managers now know their value. It annoys many of them to have part of their value paid uncertainly in deferred form. It annoys them as much to be bribed over their value for 'extra effort', which they give anyway for non-financial reasons.

Lastly, I am concerned at the pressure on managers to take short-term decisions. Management mobility is increasing and the philosophy of a minority may be to remove themselves after short spells of high profit and bonus, leaving others to clear up the mess resulting from a lack of longer-term activity.

There is considerable value nationally to be gained by encouraging long-term savings/investment schemes. But I should feel uneasy about a scheme which excessively reduced an individual's freedom to move.

Profit-sharing

The straightforward profit-sharing scheme has no incentive value or intent. Often valued at less than 10 per cent of salary, and varying by minute amounts from year to year, it aims to treat employees in a similar way to shareholders and to allow them a small share of the profits.

Many of these schemes are based on formulae which produce a total amount of money, a percentage of profit in most cases. for proportionate distribution to eligible staff. In a few cases, some merit element may be involved. Invariably ill-defined, this merit element allows managers to vary the amounts awarded to their staff, and perhaps increase bonus for such criteria as long hours or special effort.

From this simple beginning we add complexity as we begin to build in provisions for 'incentives'. Firstly, the amounts of money involved become larger as incentive will not exist at all unless the potential variation in bonus is significant. Secondly, variable payments involve defining the factors which are to affect variance. There is no incentive in schemes where the employee does not know the basis of his possible award, as he does not know how he may influence the desired result.

Sharing the group bonus pool

The type of formula used to calculate a bonus pool may be more complex. For example, it may take a percentage of profits, but deduct from this a figure related to capital employed, so that the pool is increased if the return on capital is increased, and vice versa.

A 'management' bonus scheme which opens participation in the bonus pool to a large number of people immediately reduces its effectiveness. For one thing, it reduces the amount of money available per head, and thereby the attractiveness of the amounts involved, and reduces any incentive potential it might have had.

Many schemes which have allowed lists of eligible staff to grow annually have reached stages where they have found it essential to cut back numbers in order to make sense of the scheme. As this can involve 'buying-out' by consolidating previous bonus levels into salary, it is to be avoided where possible.

Who should participate? Those individuals in a position to make significant decisions—decisions likely to have impact on profit—or whose advice from a staff role may have comparable impact. In a moderate sized company, or division of a large organization, this might restrict eligibility to the chief executive and the heads of each major function—say half a dozen people, probably earning salaries in excess of £6000 a year. Variations in the size of pool from year to year will now be appreciable to those involved.

Distribution of the total within a small group should probably be on a percentage of salary basis, with a '× 2' factor applied to the chief executive. Calculation of the 'norm' percentage is easily calculated from the ratio between the total bonus pool and the total salaries of eligible staff, counting the chief executive's salary twice (to cover the × 2 gearing).

This procedure leads to standard bonus figures for all eligible staff. However, some executives will be considered more effective than others, or to have made special contributions during the period. From the starting-point of standard figures, adjustments up and down may be made to produce final awards. There is unlikely to be very much science in this last stage, but it seems to be fairly popular as management exercise their rights to take decisions over what is imposed by computer! And it should produce an acceptable result.

How big ought variations to be? Some theorists incline to the view that a bonus should be 20 per cent of salary or nothing. Faced with a decision on this borderline, most managers compromise. While I believe that bonus of less than 10 per cent has no incentive value, partly because variations would be marginal, variation steps of 5 per cent of salary are quite significant.

The ability to reward key people with substantial bonus at the expense of the ordinary contributors, had the management guts to do this and justify their actions, can make a big difference to a scheme. Where the average award is 20 per cent but individual bonuses are spread over a range of from 10 per cent up to 40 per cent, the man with the largest bite off the carrot really knows he is successful and is directly aware of his Board's appreciation.

In the larger organizations, competitive spirit between units may be generated by linking bonus pool contributions to divisional results, or to whatever profit centres exist.

In these circumstances, it is not appropriate to link the pools directly to profitability or return on investment, as these figures vary outside the control of management. It may be possible to relate targets to standards of return which are relevant for the industries covered, but more usual, it is appropriate to link targets to assessments of what is achievable, so that all units start equal. To equate the division in a very tough market with low profit opportunity, with another in a high profit near monopoly situation, by this means is fairer to all concerned and will be appreciated at least by managers in the tougher situations.

The need for realistic assessments of what is achievable is obvious. The difficulty of making sufficiently precise assessment is the major stumbling block for schemes of this type. An organization without an established pattern of forward business planning stands virtually no chance of producing adequate bonus criteria, while experienced companies need no additional comment from me. (Few would deny the value of planning but recognize its value in their awareness of the future rather than the precision of its figures.)

'Reasonable bonus'

The potential size of a bonus must be significant if the scheme is to have any real incentive value. Figures of less than 10 per cent are 'interesting' but not 'exciting', while the prospect of raising incomes by 20 to 30 per cent may reasonably be called exciting'.

Provided the bonus is genuinely achievable against balanced and logical objectives, an exciting size bonus will certainly provide some incentive for a year or two. Even so, there are managers who object positively to this carrot-and-stick approach and the implication that they would not otherwise strive so effectively!

Where management bonus figures ride up to and over the level of salary, I suggest that the pressures are unreasonable and the justification for such a scheme is very difficult to provide.

Capital accumulation

Crawford Greenwalt's view was that while only one executive could have overall financial control (in that this involved owning at least 51 per cent of a company's stock), it was possible to give thousands of executives the 'owner's eye'. He asked the question 'How much stock did a man have to own in order to acquire the owner's eye?', and suggested that income from this stock needed to be significant in relation to expected pension—perhaps at least half as much as pension.

(The 'owner's eye' is achieved when the executive begins to feel that it is his own money which he is spending rather than an impersonal 'the company's money'. He begins to look more carefully at expenditure, and to encourage investment, which should improve the company's profitable growth. Success means that the value of his stock will grow.)

In developing any form of share ownership or *stock option plan*, one has in mind that the business owner has a tax avantage over employed managers in cumulating capital, in that the rate of long-term Capital Gains Tax is 30 per cent of 'earnings', while on normal earned income tax rises to the region of 90 per cent.

In the UK tax situation, few employed managers are able to accumulate personal capital on the American pattern. The most valuable aspect of any bonus scheme from their viewpoint would be to provide this opportunity, yet taxation cuts viciously into the top slice of income.

A recent survey showed that something like 80 per cent of salaried and professional directors would like to see tax-free bonus payments for themselves and similar people. A minimum of one third, and generally well over 50 per cent of any bonus payments made to executives would be absorbed by taxation, yet companies depend upon their top management taking the initiative on profit-increasing activities. Survey participants agreed that the possibility of higher net remuneration would make it possible to get a higher standard of efficiency : 'Management discipline requires large incentives associated with large penalties, and it is not possible to impose large penalties in the shape of the only ultimate penalty which a company has—dismissal for failure—if it was not possible to offer correspondingly large benefits for success.'

Stock option plans

Accumulating capital need not involve the payment of cash sums, but can be achieved by acquisition of assets with high capital appreciation potential. If this is made possible by some stock distribution plan, the employed manager would share the owner-manager capital appreciation advantage with its lower rate of tax.

Normal stock option plans attract a tax charge at the time an option is taken up, based on the difference between the market value of the shares at that time and the lower special purchase price. Where the purchase price and share value equate, there is no immediate advantage, nor tax liability. But there is a requirement to produce the capital sum to purchase the shares.

Few employed managers have significant capital for investment in this way, and the purpose of normal stock option is defeated as it becomes necessary for the recipient to sell most of the shares to cover tax and capital payments on those retained.

Dr George Copeman, with the Wider Share Ownership Council, has investigated the possibilities of a scheme within existing tax legislation which would enable a man to accumulate a significant stake in the company which employs him. The main characteristics of the scheme developed by Dr Copeman are :

1   That shares should have minimum rights and value at the time of issue (and therefore minimum cost and tax commitment).

2   That they should acquire rights and value as pre-set profit and growth targets are achieved.

3   That they should normally acquire rating and value as full ordinary shares at the end of a ten-year period.

In the UK tax situation, this approach appears to attract minimum tax commitment on issue, in that the shares would be sold to executives at a low figure in line with their low initial value. Over the years, their value would increase but would attract no further tax until the time of sale when long-term Capital Gains Tax (at present 30 per cent) would be payable.

This concept appears to be very sound. To the executive, the day-to-day incentive is slight as it is likely to be in most executive bonus schemes, but the accumulating rights over a period of years will add up to a very attractive package—and ultimately to a substantial capital investment.

The concept behind share schemes is to allow highly taxed executives to accumulate capital, and in so doing to provide an incentive for them to remain with their companies and to increase profitability.

Until 1966 Share Option Schemes were increasing in popularity as they gave senior executives the chance to make considerable capital gains without tax liability. Basically these schemes offered senior employees the option to purchase shares at some time in the future, but at a price agreed on the day the option was offered. If the share price had not increased sufficiently by the day of exercising the option it was not taken up.

The 1966 Finance Act ended Share Option Schemes almost entirely as it decreed that gains from options would be taxed as income at the time the option was exercised.

Share Incentive Schemes were not affected by the Act as the shares in the schemes were purchased by the participants immediately they entered their Scheme, either for the full price, or for a price reduced by up to 20 per cent due to restrictions on dividends or voting rights. Interestingly, in many cases of Fully Paid Schemes where the executive is required to find all the money for the shares immediately, he can be allowed to borrow the cash from his company at low or nil interest. In some schemes profit targets are set for the company which must be achieved before participants may sell their shares.

The 1972 Finance Act considerably changes the law affecting

the taxation of Share Schemes, removing the oppressive provisions introduced in 1966 and allowing for the approval of satisfactory option and incentive schemes by the Inland Revenue.

The rules for approval of share option schemes and incentive schemes are alike and are as follows :

1   The nominal value of shares allocated under the scheme must not exceed 10 per cent of the nominal ordinary issued share capital, providing the capital is less than £1 million. Otherwise the nominal value of shares allocated must not exceed 5 per cent of the nominal ordinary issued share capital, or £200,000 if more.

2   The shares must be in the company employing the participants, or in a company controlling that company. There are special rules for consortia. Unless the shares are quoted, they must be in a company which is not controlled by another company.

3   The value of shares available to any executive may not exceed four times his salary.

4   Incentive shares and options are not transferable.

5   Only a director or employee who is basically fully employed on the company's operations may participate in a share scheme.

6   The scheme must not last for more than 10 years.

7   No option may be exercised more than seven years after it has been given. Also seven years is the limit for restrictions on incentive shares.

8   The price paid for shares must not be manifestly less than the market price when the option was conferred, or in the case of incentive schemes, the shares acquired.

9   Shares must be retained for at least three years.

10   Shares under an option scheme may not have any special restrictions.

11   The scheme must be approved by the shareholders.

12   The scheme must be approved by the Inland Revenue.

Other types of bonus

Merit bonus

The most important single reason for awarding a bonus is to use it as a means of rewarding the employee for some special act of service to the company, or for an *outstanding* contribution over a certain period of time. Such a contribution could take the form of an exceptional job on a special assignment outside an individual's normal range of work or, alternatively, could result from special effort or circumstance directly related to an employee's job, but beyond the normal call of duty.

At executive levels the award of merit bonus is more general and is often an integral part of normal remuneration. For senior executives, however, the interpretation of the word 'merit' is rather different and this 'integral' part of remuneration is subject to substantial fluctuation depending on the individual's contribution to the organization's profitability over a particular period.

The size of a merit bonus may vary very substantially, but such awards are rarely small; 5 per cent of basic salary probably constitutes the minimum bonus payable under this heading, while from 10 to 12 per cent of salary is a normal level for middle or senior staff. As we stated above, the picture becomes quite different at executive levels and here the amounts may be very substantial. While 20 per cent of salary provides a 'norm', 50 per cent of basic salary would not be exceptional for an executive in charge of a highly profitable small company, or profit centre within a larger organization, and figures up to and exceeding 100 per cent of basic salary are not all that infrequent.

The value of bonus awards of between 5 and 15 per cent of basic salary is significant for people at levels where the 'tax bite' is not normally too savage. However, at the very senior executive levels the 'tax bite' into an apparently substantial payment is so great that very large amounts are necessary in order to give the individual any appreciable amount of real benefit, which is the purpose of the bonus award, rather than a feeling of disappointment and doubt about the value of his extra effort.

'Continued good service' bonus

A number of companies adopt, as part of their salary plan, the policy of giving a bonus for continued good service. Such bonus payments are primarily awarded to staff who are on the maximum salary for their grade, as an incentive to keep up a reasonably high level of performance which will not be rewarded by further salary increments. Where the incentive of further promotion prospects either does not exist or is not appropriate, this form of bonus provides an alternative incentive.

These awards are normally granted at intervals of from two to five years; the average period is probably three years and the size of bonus is normally about the size of the last few salary increments given to the individual concerned.

This form of bonus appears to have a real incentive value for certain people with no further career potential or prospects, but who are clearly better than average performers in their current job.

Traditional bonus

Salary surveys indicate that a surprising number of organizations with remuneration policies which are old-fashioned tend to make very wide use of the small bonus award, associated apparently with continued *service*, not continued *good* service, and apparently given in the spirit of a traditional 'Yuletide' gift. Bonuses of 1 per cent or less for quite senior people appear normal where these policies exist and individual payments may tend to spread to most members of the staff, particularly in years when the annual salary 'Christmas Box' review is even more restricted than usual.

Traditional bonus is generally associated with a paternalistic attitude to (usually low calibre) staff, perhaps as a token of appreciation to them for putting up with low salaries. There appears to be no real value whatsoever in granting bonuses of this sort.

Thirteenth-month bonus

It is the practice in some continental countries to pay a thirteenth-month bonus, and occasionally fourteenth- or fifteenth-month bonuses. In practice this involves the payment of an extra month's salary, or extra two or three months' salary, at Christmas or some other appropriate time. Less frequently, payment of salary may be made by giving a full month's salary (annual salary, divided by twelve) for each four-week period, thus paying for thirteen months in the year.

These practices are rare in the United Kingdom, but where they do exist the total payment over a year is normally quoted as annual remuneration, whereas most other bonus payments are supplementary and are not considered, at least not officially considered, by management as a right.

Summary

A number of specific types of bonus are described above; in actual practice many bonus schemes are combinations of one or more of these basic systems, or one or more special schemes may exist in a single organization.

As a general comment on the value of bonus awards, one factor which many organizations consider relevant is that they appear to have some value in retaining staff, particularly senior staff. Companies which have this philosophy normally make large bonus payments, often as an addition to a fully competitive salary. However, an examination of the timing of staff-employee terminations in organizations adopting these policies shows that there is a peak resignation period in the months immediately following the distribution of bonus awards! The total annual turnover among the people concerned does not appear to be significantly different from the turnover in organizations which pay similar total figures as straight salary, all other things being equal.

A practice more common in the United States than in this country is that where very large bonus figures are payable to top executive staff, they may be handed out in up to four annual instalments. The employee is told of his bonus and how it will be paid. After three or four years he becomes aware that his accumulated bonus expectation over the next few years is so substantial that he is unwilling to forgo it by leaving the company unless he can add very substantially to his basic level of remuneration. In any situation of this sort the real advantage of holding a man who might otherwise prefer to leave the company has to be considered.

Remuneration of sales staff

The payment of Salesmen represents a very special problem in any company. In order to achieve the necessary motivation and incentive, additional remuneration beyond a straight salary is called for almost always. Any plan designed by a company must be simple to operate and easily intelligible to the Salesmen. As with all salary administration techniques it must be flexible to meet the changing needs of the market climate.

Straight salary only may well be paid to sales staff such as those negotiating the sales of large, costly equipment ranging up to millions of pounds in price. In such cases the employee is of executive class and receives a high, competitive salary, calculating a fair commission in such cases would be impossible, anyhow.

Where plans include basic salary plus commission, the salary element can range from a miserable pittance to fully competitive levels, and the commission can equally vary infinitely between a small percentage of salary, say under 5 per cent, to several hundred per cent. Where commission is a part of total pay and is not properly planned and controlled it can well develop into a runaway condition to the point where a salesman can earn more than his chief who is not on commission.

Commission, like any other supplementary payment, should always be significant in the view of the authors, and should not be less than 10 per cent of basic salary. In fact, we consider that somewhere around 20 to 30 per cent of basic salary would be normal for people other than door-to-door salesmen.

In major companies it is preferable for these employees to have a competitive, stable basic salary to prevent the fluctuations in earnings and related insecurity which often result from a heavily commission-orientated system of remuneration.

Many companies additionally give merit bonus to their sales staff for outstanding achievements, and lately in the UK there has been a development in the giving of prizes to Salesmen and their families, including all-paid holidays to glamorous places.

Bonus schemes can become over-elaborate when based on complicated 'points' systems. However, there is something to be said for a bonus plan to persuade Salesmen to concentrate on unpopular or hard-selling products, and to make their full quota of customer calls.

An important further factor of remuneration to the Salesman is his allowances. These should always be generous if he is to perform his job effectively. Clearly, if he is always concerned with penny-pinching when travelling around on the company's behalf he is unlikely to give of his best.

Premium payments

Only a small proportion of staff receive their remuneration entirely in the form of salary. Apart from the various forms of bonus, very many staff are paid for overtime worked, usually receiving premium payments on top of the basic rate per hour they receive for their normal hours.

A premium is an additional payment, over and above the normal rate for a job, to cover some form of unusual working arrangement, condition, or inconvenience. It is paid in accordance with formulae, in strict relationship to the number of hours concerned, and the degree of 'inconvenience' involved. A premium may be paid for a number of reasons other than overtime, for example, night or week-end work may carry an additional premium.

Overtime payment

If an employee is paid by the hour, and he works overtime, he usually receives a level of payment in excess of his normal hourly rate. The supplement to his normal hourly rate is known as an overtime premium.

If a staff employee works overtime, he may also receive payment by the hour for his additional work, and may similarly receive an overtime premium.

There is some considerable variation in methods of overtime payment from company to company. This occurs not only on the determination of actual payment, but also in the wide variation in the level of staff who may be paid for working overtime between one organization and another.

Weekly staff and junior levels of monthly staff, such as supervisors and junior specialists, have been paid for their overtime by many companies for some time. The concept of not paying the executive for overtime has remained unchanged, although difficulty in defining the term 'executive' has led to a variation in cut-off points, from salary levels of around £2000 to points around £5000 a year.

It is no longer unusual for quite senior people to be paid directly for the extra hours they work. It may well be that the long-term trend will be towards all employees receiving overtime payment, other than top executive levels, where extra effort might be expected to be reflected in profit sharing.

It seems clear that where senior staff are required to work long hours, some compensation in the form of direct payment or bonus is appreciated and is becoming expected by those staff who consider themseles in the 'officer' class in industry. The needs of a particular organization and the views most generally expressed by the group of individuals concerned appear to provide the best guide to policy in a specific situation.

For staff employees the requirement of occasional light amounts of overtime is normally covered adequately by overtime payment at 'plain time', the same hourly rate as applies to the employee for his basic work week, weekly salary divided by basic weekly hours.

However, when overtime becomes heavy, the inconvenience factor increases substantially, and some extra compensation is required to encourage ordinary staff to work the hours required. This extra incentive is given in the form of premium payments, which is the payment for, say, one and a half hours for each one hour worked.

This description is, of course, over-simplified, for in practice an individual organization may demand heavy overtime at plain time, possibly providing compensation in some other form, while another makes generous premium payments for occasional insignificant amounts of overtime.

Hourly rated employees demand and obtain generous patterns of premium payments which are gradually extending to staff.

The cost of overtime is not simply either a salary or a benefit cost. The additional work time should result in additional work and output which, at least partially, offsets the cost to the company. However, in practice, output falls off during longer spells of work and premium and similar payments, any payments which raise the hourly cost above the basic rate applying for normal day work, constitute excess costs!

A secondary, but important factor in costing overtime, is the saving resulting from more extensive, and therefore more economic, use of expensive equipment.

To the employee, overtime payment is a benefit, to some a most important benefit representing a regular supplement to income. To the employer, overtime may involve excess costs for relatively unproductive time, or may in some cases result in a form of saving.

Other premiums

Premium payments may also be paid for a variety of other reasons. For example, a standard premium may be paid for all hours worked by employees on a continuous shift rota covering seven days a week with a cycle lasting several weeks. The standard premium has the advantages of smoothing out otherwise irregular weekly payments resulting from the payment of flat salary during spells of daywork and much higher amounts during spells of week-end and night work.

Premium payments are generally given for night and other shift arrangements, mainly for weekly staff category. For more senior staff engaged on the same type of irregular hours, some inclusive allowance calculated on a similar basis may be paid.

To summarize, a premium payment is a supplement designed to recompense the employee as precisely as possible for inconvenience associated with long or irregular hours. As far as possible, the levels of premiums should be established to provide adequate incentive to employees to undertake the special commitments required by the individual organization.

Allowances

The term 'allowance' covers a wide range of special payments which may be given for a variety of reasons. Allowances given when an employee is on an assignment away from home to cover his excess costs of living and travelling hardly rank as additional remuneration.

Allowances which may be considered part of remuneration are those which are made, like premium payments, as part of taxable earnings to compensate for some special or temporary aspect of a post or inconvenience.

In each case, the allowance should be directly related to the inconvenience or special requirement, to provide adequate incentive in the situation.

Part 3

Fringe Matters

Chapter 15

Taxation

Introduction

I propose to examine some of the side-effects of heavy taxation, and the implications of a UK tax bite, which is heavier than in other comparable countries. It is relevant to point to the probable impact on motivation resulting from severely trimmed scope for financial gain. This may not be relevant to all people, the satisfaction of achievement may be enough, but to very many more adequate financial motivation is significant.

Income tax is a misleading term, for this is not a tax levied simply on income. Social factors allow that part of income is not taxed, but where an individual earns above defined minimum figures—presumably related to minimum living standard figures—then that part of his income is taxed.

This philosophy seems reasonable. A single rate of tax would seem logical, but the concession of lighter tax rates for the initial area of taxation is acceptable.

At a higher income level, a further factor comes into play with the introduction of surtax. This is not related to straightforward tax on income above the 'basic-needs' level, but appears to be an equally straightforward charge on that minority of the population which is capable of earning high income—and carrying the executive responsibility of major activities throughout the country. (I am not concerned with unearned income or with inherited wealth, which may justify different tax factors.)

The community at large may be envious of the high earning capacity of the minority and is able to attack their position by this means. The implications of this form of attack need to be understood, for such people are essential to our national well-being. If they are made to feel deprived, their efforts may be directed to activities other than those best suited to the national interest.

Progressively higher taxation rates on high incomes are accepted in many countries. The problem is, how far can we go before the level of tax reaches a point which the individuals affected feel is excessive—to the point of reacting in some way against it? In any day-to-day situation, this reaction is most evi-

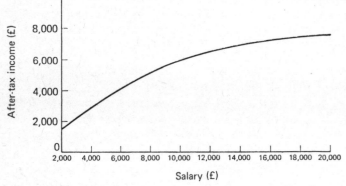

Figure 15.1   Earned income versus after-tax income (UK 1968/9 – married man with two children

dent where a man is asked to consider a promotion, and, after considering all factors, will ask the effect the move will have on his real income. At this stage, his interest is in the rate of tax on his salary adjustment. At this stage, he is extremely aware of that rate.

After-tax income

Income to the individual is the income he receives after the Government has taken its various cuts. Increase in income and differentials are looked at in real money terms rather than in the paper figure of pre-tax.

Figure 15.1 shows, for a 'standard executive' with two children and a mortgage, the 1974/5 figures of basic income and, after deductions, real income at a series of levels. In Fig. 15.2 the figures show the actual size of increments necessary to provide a 10 per cent increase in real money terms (after tax) in the UK.

These figures show severe taxation on high earned income; the detailed figures are not especially important. It is worth commenting that real income for the top slice of the UK working population is generally lower than in other developed countries, and that the differentials within the after-tax earnings hierarchy are less than in these other countries (including Soviet Russia).

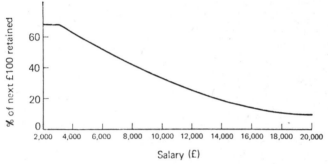

Figure 15.2 Percentage of additional earnings retained after tax

Taxation and market values

It is a curious phenomenon that excessive taxation has not pushed top-level salaries to very high levels in UK. The excessive level of tax has led many managements to a view that there is little point in going beyond certain figures, as the after-tax effect is so slight that no significant change of income is received. (Indeed, for figures much above £15,000 the market is far from clear and big differences in actual salaries indicate differences in attitudes to tax.)

As a result of this phenomenon, the high level of taxation in the UK is linked to executive salary levels below those current in most developed countries throughout the world, so that the whole value structure of higher value jobs is doubly depressed.

Effect of tax on salary increase

How much increase in real income is necessary to encourage a man to take on additional responsibility? There is no straightforward answer to this question for, invariably, the individual, who is initially loath to take on additional burden but subsequently accepts, has been influenced by a variety of factors. For example, he discusses the situation with his wife who thinks how nice it would be—for various reasons. He becomes intrigued by the prospect of greater influence or opportunity; of being able to achieve some of the things he has thought about for years. He thinks about the financial aspect.

It may take a salary adjustment of from 20 to 50 per cent to produce any significant rise in real income, for the 'significant rise' will need to be at least 5 per cent after tax—substantially more if the other factors surrounding the job are not very attractive to him, or if a location move may prove expensive.

If the post is really senior, he might be strongly influenced by an opportunity to acquire a stake in the equity of the business if he is successful. However, he may be put off by the tax implications of an option.

If he is to receive a bonus, he will be aware that tax will absorb a minimum of one third, and generally well over 50 per cent of any bonus payment made to him.

Taxation and managerial standards

With rising managerial standards, obsolescence is a commonly met phenomenon and there is a steady fall-out of executives unable to keep up with the rate of change in their jobs. Faced with having to take unpleasant decisions on such people, a management will look at the personal circumstances of the individual and may feel moral obligation to retain him in some less significant role.

While his future employability may be a factor, awareness that the individual is unlikely to have accumulated any capital reserve during his service as a manager, on which he can now fall back, is likely to influence the decision. Relatively low salaries plus high taxation lead to a situation where we compromise on retention of executives and even on key appointments. 'If he has earned little else, he has earned security!'

Such moves have an important impact on high calibre people lower down the ladder whose promotion may be blocked. They are rarely concerned that they may be similarly 'protected' in twenty years' time. They are very much aware that their abilities will be more narrowly, and less well, used. They seek other avenues of promotion, outside the company.

The cumulative effect of a few decisions of this sort can have a crushing effect on the morale and efficiency of any organization. In the country as a whole, natural dynamism can be slowed as an increasing proportion of senior key positions remain occupied for compassionate reasons by inadequate personnel, and even the high calibre men who break through are quickly tied up in the malignant growth of non-productive administrative procedures. As a nation, our best growth industry appears to be administration, with unfortunate effect on overall productivity.

Tax as disincentive

Tax can become a real disincentive. There comes a point for many people where income is inadequate but where the possible pleasure of additional real income *is more than offset* by knowledge of the additional amount of tax which must be paid. The financial advantage may be significant, but the feeling of frustration at the size of additional tax may be such that a proposal is rejected.

At senior management level, this reaction to salary advancement by one or more of an executive group who have private wealth may establish a level of remuneration somewhat below the market by deliberate choice. Individuals are, of course, free to take such action regarding their own salaries if they wish.

Danger arises if they go on to assume that the depressed level of their own salaries is right and proper, and that normal differentials must exist below. I have seen this compression of salary differentials affect most of the management strata in several organizations. It seems a selfish if not dangerous, act following reaction to a personal tax situation, and invariably leads to all the usual problems of a low payment situation.

If individuals wish to reduce their own tax commitment by opting for a lower salary, they are completely free to do so, but I suggest that their 'official salary' should always be established. Subsequently, they may formally give up their claim to a part, but the basis for proper salary relationships is established.

Tax and differentials

Taxation in the UK has the effect of reducing differentials towards a situation where earnings from different levels of work are not substantially different.

It has been, at different times and places, an ideological objective to give 'to each according to his needs', with particular appeal to the 'have-nots'. By and large, it is a political objective quietly dropped by thriving economics, and it has only really existed briefly in tightly controlled national situations.

If we are to encourage people to accept greater responsibilities, to accept promotion, we need to ensure that their additional earnings seem appropriate to them quite apart from the added satisfaction they will get in time. (We should remember that the added stress on an individual newly in a position at an enhanced level may be considerable, and that the material benefits will be most significant at that stage.)

Some research work has suggested that a differential of one-third to one-half is appropriate between jobs at distinct levels, but these figures are by no means universal and need to be considered in after-tax terms.

At junior levels, it is normal to establish a differential of 15 to 30 per cent between the earnings of operatives and those of the first full level of supervision. Where this is not done, there may be difficulties in attracting good men to become foremen—to take on the additional responsibility and separate themselves from their former colleagues. At this level, the incidence of tax does little to alter the differential in basic earnings.

At comparable levels in office and technical jobs, differentials of around 30 to 40 per cent are normal, and again, the differentials are retained after tax.

At higher levels, basic salary differentials fall into a normal pattern of 30 to 50 per cent, somewhat reduced by tax. At very senior levels, the after-tax situation cuts back differentials very substantially, and we begin to get a similar reaction to that sometimes experienced at foreman level, that the increase is too small to justify acceptance of the increased responsibility.

As we have seen above, the actual salary differential needed to provide a 30 to 50 per cent differential after-tax becomes impossible at the top of a large organization.

Impact of heavy tax

In a free market situation, real dangers arise for the community from the impact of heavy taxation.

First and foremost, the more dynamic entrepreneurs in any society will seek and find opportunity, and will not feel restricted to stay in one place or country. With international opportunity, those with drive may emigrate. Remember the exodus from East Germany where earnings opportunity and standard of living were significant factors; and the boost of interest in emigration to Australia which follows each unpopular Government act.

A further symptom is the multiplicity of small businesses, in which the lesser entrepreneur of any calibre can obtain substantial job satisfaction and, to some extent, achieve a degree of after-tax earning and capital accumulation not possible in an employed situation. At the same time, this takes a degree of drive away from the larger organization which needs his type of flair if it is not to become ossified.

These symptoms must have a national impact, for if one discourages or drives away those who may be motivated to get and to keep an economy in top gear, things begin to slow down. Attitudes to pace change in the direction of fatalistic acceptance, which makes it gradually less possible to alter our situation. As national attitudes change to acceptance of lower standards, and resignation that nothing can be done kills much of the remaining initiative, the task of those who would motivate and drive becomes tougher.

If this seems an extreme view, let us scale down from 'Great

Britain Limited' to any moderate-sized organization and consider its impetus from a point where the pace is slow and the quality of personnel is poor and without drive. Attempts by junior to middle staff with some drive but little influence will achieve very little. Improvement will be most difficult to generate from below due to the inertia above. But place one or more highly motivated people in the upper structure and a reaction occurs. The organization is shaken into different gear and begins, painfully, to 'go'. In a tough situation, substantial personnel changes make way for the major improvements, and movement to successful, re-structured operations.

A nation which is running down will take longer to climb back up. Providing incentives for those who would achieve the change is the surest way of changing gear.

Conclusion

With full acceptance that remuneration is by no means the sole motivator, there should be :

1 Facility to retain a *significant* proportion of all earned income. 'Significant proportion' should be not less than a quarter at the highest level. 'Earned income' may need added definition where an individual has a stake in the equity of the employing organization, to ensure it was properly related to the value of the job rather than concealed unearned income.

2 Greater opportunity for key executives to share in the equity and success of their companies—by tax concessions on stock acquisitions in the employing company.

3 Greater encouragement for saving/capital accumulation generally, by means of tax concession on planned regular saving.

4 Increased discretionary spending money (rather than actual total spending power.)

Chapter 16

Fringe Benefits

While fringe benefits developed originally from reasons of social welfare, much of this original function has been taken over by Governments, or is established as a natural and normal part of company practice. We shall look only briefly at these 'social welfare' benefits.

The new pressure for fringe benefits is more a response to taxation. In looking at the expenditure requirements of employees, to what extent could general demands be met by negotiating bulk purchases of articles or services, and to what extent could these be provided free as an alternative to taxable income? For example, in one company the discussion took the following line :

'We can provide additional life assurance cover for our top fifty people at a cost of £x. If we gave each of these men salary adjustments, sufficient to purchase equivalent cover, after allowing for tax and individual insurance premiums, it would cost us several times £x. Therefore, it is worth providing this, and other similar benefits, as standard arrangements rather than raise salaries—always assuming the benefits are sought by the individual !'

Difficulties arise from the differences in personal expenditure patterns, needs and requirements. As important, difficulties arise from the tendency of many people to accept fringe benefits as a normal service quite unrelated to variations in income levels. Variations from the 'normal pattern of benefits' need to be significant to attract recognition from employees, and the cost may not justify the advantage to the company.

At senior levels where the tax bite is substantial, the possible advantage to an individual may be much greater. However, some benefits have become fairly generally accepted at this level also. Developments in benefits at this level have a tax avoidance aspect. Tax avoidance, as distinct from evasion of tax liability, is considered reasonable as well as legitimate. Without breaking tax legislation, advantage may be given to the heavily taxed individual.

Individual preference

While salary is obviously the primary factor in remuneration, fringe factors do have some importance. As a generalization, fringe benefits used to conform as much to the market pattern as salary itself, and variation below the general standards can have a significant effect on the salary we need to pay.

The provision of benefits beyond the general run may prove ineffective as incentives to attract and retain staff. If additional money is to be spent, it is probably best utilized by straight distribution in salary. If it is to be spent in other ways, these must be commonly acceptable to the group of employees, and offer some advantage (usually tax avoidance) over direct income being privately deployed to comparable purposes.

The difficulty with additional benefits for executives is particularly linked to the problem of identifying commonly required aspects. If we are to improve the widow's benefits within the pension plan at substantial cost to the company, how many bachelors will watch peevishly from the wings? And if bachelors were in the majority and we suggested private flats and subsidized mistresses, how many married men will splutter with frustrated fury in domestic bliss. Really, you cannot please everybody!

So most additional executive benefits tend to cater for the majority in a particular group rather than conform to a standard pattern, with the availability of finance and services as additional factors in benefit selection, e.g. tied capital in Spain may be used for a subsidized holiday base which would not have been considered had the money not been there and otherwise useless.

Fringe benefit costs

When a company engages an employee, it adds substantially more to its costs than the agreed starting salary. In addition to the basic overheads associated with accommodating and equipping the employee to enable him to carry out his function, it provides him with a series of benefits. This fringe component completes the remuneration package, the real total cost to the company of employing the employee.

This package includes a number of diverse items; for example, the company places limits on the employee's normal working day. The employee benefits by working fewer, rather than many hours, but the shorter the defined working day, the higher the cost of each hour's labour. Increased holidays reduce annual hours worked and also increase the cost of actual working time.

A subsidized lunch or life assurance, provided free by the company, also add in different ways to the cost of employing each individual.

The accumulation of these benefits leads to substantial costs over and above basic salaries; in fact these costs usually exceed 20 or even 30 per cent of the basic salary. We shall therefore examine both the generally accepted benefits and the wide range of subsidiary benefits offered by different companies and the part they play in attracting and holding staff.

Fringe benefits and trade unions

Before considering individual benefits it is worth examining some of the attitudes of trade unions to fringe benefits.

For example, it is worth examining the concept which is widely accepted in the United States, but not generally in Britain, of building up a total remuneration package which is subsequently split into the 'pieces' of salary and various individual benefits. In this situation, an increase in the total amount of money allocated to overall remuneration might subsequently be 'spent' on an increase in salaries absorbing part of the total, and on, say, an improvement in sickness benefits. This approach appears to be highly acceptable to United States trade unionists, but is comparatively rare in Britain.

In contrast to this logical approach, the suggestion sometimes put forward by Staff Associations that 'if a company cannot afford a salary increase, it can afford to improve benefits instead' seems quite ludicrous. Perhaps the word 'afford' is misused! Salaries and benefits together make up the total remuneration of an employee; hence the place of benefits in this book.

The major union interest is in shorter working week/more overtime pay; and in longer holidays. It is probably true to suggest that most of the 'welfare' category benefits are looked on as rights which the State will provide, so that the interest in pension and sick pay schemes is no more than marginal.

The cynical view of claims for a shorter working week is that this is invariably compensated for by overtime—which is then paid on a greater proportion of time worked, at a higher base rate. Unfortunately, national statistics have shown the cynics to be justified. The average working week has fallen only marginally over recent years, and there is rarely any drop after agreement on a shorter week. The other side of this argument is that basic wage levels are inadequate and that overtime is the only means of obtaining a basic living wage. Again, unfortunately, this is true at the lower end of the wage scales, but is no justification for similar pressures at higher wage and salary levels. Perhaps there is a need to adjust basic wages and salary scales in some companies or industries to remove this argument.

The trade union view of holidays may have been influenced by Britain joining the Common Market. British holiday standards, and certainly the frequency of public holidays, has been noticeably less generous than our Continental brothers.

In conflict with the union view favouring longer holidays, the average British executive frequently takes less than his holiday entitlement, as he 'cannot spare the time'. And he fails to see why his subordinates should do better !

Let me quote some American thinking on the coming Age of Leisure : The boss will cling to his 50-hour week and his short, irregular holidays, while the unfortunate factory worker will have to make do with a 20-hour, 3-day week, with a couple of months' holiday thrown in. Leisure is one of the fastest growing industries.

Can we imagine a situation in which the union claim is for a longer working week, fewer benefits, and even for less money—for the privilege of keeping members occupied?

Service agreements

A service agreement may not be a 'benefit' within most definitions, but it is certainly a 'benefit' which is now keenly looked for by many senior executives.

These staff are given security of employment in the form or agreement requiring two, three, or five years' notice of termination, sometimes even renewable annually.

If the company wishes to break the arrangement, it usually buys out the balance of the period by use of the 'golden handshake'. But if the employee wishes to be released, this is normally arranged after a short period mutually agreed. There is little advantage in attempting to retain an unwilling employee who is extremely unlikely to contribute his best work.

The cost of service agreements can be negligible where selection of staff given agreements is perfect. Only where agreements are given to staff who are subsequently dismissed, or are redundant, is additional cost incurred.

Hours of work

A salary is usually quoted for a specific period, usually a year, a month or a week. In each period, a set number of days and hours will normally be worked. If this number changes so that a longer or shorter period is worked without change in salary or other payment, then the employer pays less or more for each unit of time.

This relationship of cost to employer and period of time worked is influenced primarily by variation in basic hours and holidays, and to a lesser degree by such factors as volume of overtime premiums, and by payment during absence for sickness, accident or other reasons.

Basic hours cannot be described as a benefit, but some variations in basic hours, particularly where hours are reduced without loss of pay, must come under the benefit classification. Most industries now have clear patterns of standard basic hours, with a long-standing national trend of gradual reduction over the whole field in industry, commerce and public utility.

Within the overall pattern, variations exist both between industries as well as within industries. Many variations are made to conform to local regional practice. For example, one engineering company may operate a working week which is an hour or two shorter than the national standard, and in city centres, particularly in London, office hours may be an hour shorter than elsewhere within the same company as a concession to help with longer or more difficult travelling conditions, or as an incentive in a difficult labour market.

Another form of variation is to be found in starting and finishing times, and in timing and duration of lunch breaks. In this case, the variation hardly justifies the title 'fringe benefit' as no cost to the company in involved, but an 8.45 a.m. start in an area where 9 a.m. is usual for office workers will have an adverse effect on morale and recruitment. Similarly, a sixty-minute lunch break is appreciated where staff go out to shop or home to lunch, but thirty minutes, with the resultant earlier finishing time, may be preferable where employees all use a cafeteria on site.

The basic cost of labour of any category is most easily stated for fringe benefit cost calculations, as a rate per hour. The cost of one hour's work is easily calculated from basic salary and basic hours, and provides a base for all other costs, i.e. costs of holiday and other benefits may be expressed as a percentage of salary.

Consider the cost effect of a reduction in basic hours without a reduction in salaries. If the reduction is from a 40-hour week to one of 38 hours, the cost effect is as follows :

1   Salary of £40 for a 40-hour week
     $= £40/40 = £1$ an hour
2   Salary of £40 for a 38-hour week
     $= £40/38 =$ approximately 105p an hour
3   Ratio of old cost per hour to revised cost per hour :
     $105p/100p \times 100 = 105$

    showing an increase in cost of each hour worked of approximately 5 per cent.

In addition to this increase, if paid overtime is normally

worked, the hourly rate is increased for this also, and may be boosted still further by overtime premium. Where a larger figure of total 'actual' hours worked remains unchanged in these circumstances, the reduction in 'basic' hours may easily add 6 per cent or more to the actual payroll costs !

Overtime payment

Following naturally upon the cost of reducing basic hours comes, in the minds of many employees, the thought of higher pay for hours which are worked beyond the basic minimum. In fact, for some weekly staff as well as hourly-rated employees basic hours means minimum hours before overtime rates begin.

We have seen the effect on costs of reductions in basic hours, particularly where actual hours are little changed, and it is easy to appreciate that such reductions are generally called disguised wage increases.

Chapter 13 contains a full summary of overtime premiums and allowances, and covers the basis for making these additional payments.

Holidays

One of the most important benefits is the granting of paid holidays. In the United Kingdom, there are two distinct parts to this benefit including statutory holidays which are required legally, and discretionary additional amounts granted by most companies in a variety of forms. There is little to be gained by discussing the more of less standard statutory holidays.

At the time of writing, the great majority of staff employees are granted three weeks' paid holidays a year and the steady trend towards longer holidays indicates that the number of staff receiving only two weeks will disappear.

The pressure from unionized hourly paid employees for a fourth week has built up steadily and concessions are likely to increase over the next decade. The inevitability of the universal fourth week is a substantial spur to senior and long-service staff groups to demand some retention of holiday entitlement differential. Managerial staff almost universally expect more than four weeks' holiday, particularly in the Civil Service and Local Government. The steady increase in the number of companies granting a fourth week's holiday is reflected clearly in surveys.

There exists such a clear pattern of behaviour in the award of holidays that organizations which offer some allowance not up to the 'norm' may find severe difficulty when recruiting. For example, a company which offered any of its monthly staff only three weeks would be in trouble when recruiting unless it provided some substantial alternative benefit or an inflated salary. Conformity to common practice is almost certainly the cheapest course.

Weekly staff, made up of clerical and lower levels of technical staff and the first levels of production supervision, etc., do not get four weeks quite so readily. Very few under the age of 21 expect to qualify for a fourth week but, after this age, most staff are granted the extra week once they meet the requirement of some minor reservation or qualification such as completing a few years' adult service with the company.

At the upper end, organizations granting a fifth week to some of their staff tend to limit this to management or executive staff, variously described according to individual company practice by a certain place in the hierarchy, or by a grade or salary level.

Incidentally, informed medical opinion is firm concerning the need for four weeks' holiday for executives to counteract the invitable stress associated with their posts. Two weeks is considered as a minimum period to have any benefit as it takes several days to relax before the holiday can be enjoyed.

An interesting associated trend is the tendency to give additional 'bank holidays' by informally granting a few extra days off each year, although company-sponsored 'bank holidays' are occasionally written off against, or consolidated with the concession of a fourth week.

The minimum holiday entitlement of three weeks plus six statutory days costs the equivalent of over 8 per cent of the payroll over the working year, calculated on the basis that for over 8 per cent of the year, staff are on holiday and not productive.

$$\frac{\text{3 weeks' basic holiday} + \text{1.2 weeks' statutory holidays}}{\text{A total of 52 weeks in the year}} \times 100$$

$$= 8.1 \text{ per cent}$$

Each additional week's holiday adds approximately 2 per cent to costs.

Holiday transport and accommodation

A number of companies run holiday or convalescent homes. However, a few individual organizations go far beyond this stage to provide holiday accommodation for senior executives; for example, to the best salesmen, and so on.

For top management, the award of a holiday trip, the combined business, prestige, sales trip to Europe or America, with leisurely pace and lengthy stays, provides an occasional exceptional reward for a man and his wife.

Payment during sickness absence

The staff employee usually enjoys continuing salary for a specified period if he should fall sick or be involved in an accident, less, perhaps, an amount equivalent to his National Insurance benefit. Thus, most employers continue to pay for non-existent services, which adds significantly to the average price of the productive time of their staff.

Many employers ask for little more than a verbal comment or explanation to cover absence of up to two or three days. They freely grant half-days for dental and similar 'excursions', and may continue to pay full salary for several weeks, or even months, to staff who produce periodic medical certificates.

This benefit is greatly appreciated by employees with substantial family commitments, however fit they may be, but tends to be abused by a small minority group of less-responsible individuals. To these people so many days a year sick-leave is taken as a right, to be used for birthday treats and Christmas shopping expeditions if one's bad health does not genuinely justify time off. Numerous stories have circulated of employees insisting on taking their full annual entitlement although in reasonable health. Perhaps significantly, these stories are often located in local or national government settings, but few organizations do not have at least a few people who come within this category.

Because this benefit is expensive if abused, some Personnel Managers, and line managers have considerable doubts about the merits of continuing full salary payment during extended or frequent short periods of sickness absence. The result of this appears in the current trend away from rigid tables of sickness absence entitlement—whether linked to years of service or calculated on some other basis—and towards more flexible policies.

Analyses of staff sickness absence show that the bulk of staff are absent for less than two weeks in a year. Actually, the average is much less than this. There is little to be gained from trying to control short-term or small-annual-amount absence, and few companies do not pay staff for the first two weeks' absence each year almost automatically.

After the first two weeks, payment can be determined on an individual-case basis, taking into account the existing factors of length of service and amount of recent absence, and also additional factors, such as the probable duration of the absence, the employee's domestic circumstances and commitments, his value to the company as shown by his performance and potential ratings, and any other factors which seem significant in the case under review. These factors can be examined by the line manager, and the personnel department, and a decision reached to pay, say, 80 per cent of salary for the anticipated balance of two months' absence.

A simple published statement explaining the working of the scheme, as a company *ex gratia* payment rather than a right, and quoting anticipated normal payments, helps to overcome suspicion and the suggestion of paternalism which may be raised against this form of policy.

Schemes for hourly-rated employees are not covered to this degree, and are almost always substantially less generous. Some companies give little or no assistance, and contributory sick benefit schemes may pay out the equivalent of one-third to two-thirds of the employee's normal basic wage, excluding overtime earnings, during absence for a limited period only.

In this benefit area, improvements in benefits for hourly-rated employees have too much leeway to make up to have any in-fluence on the staff situation in the near future.

The cost of staff sickness benefit clearly varies substantially with the actual type of scheme and degree of generosity in the particular company. Statistics available from a number of major companies in recent years suggest that sickness absence averages four days a year for each male member of the staff, and almost ten days for women. If we assume this to be typical, and also assume that full salary is paid throughout all sickness absence, the total cost of payment during unproductive sickness absence spread over the whole period of productive time would increase the average cost of productive time by about 3 per cent.

In calculating costs of sickness, the employer's contribution to National Insurance benefit may also be taken into account, but see under 'Pensions', below. In this connexion, the cost of the company Medical Services may also be considered relevant.

Payment during absence for domestic reasons

Some organizations define periods of time permitted for absence with pay for 'domestic reasons'.

This is primarily intended to cover such incidents as the funeral of an immediate relative, birth of a son or daughter, sudden sickness of an immediate dependent relative, or some other personal emergency which necessitates time away from work. In practice most employers give time off for these reasons, but some organizations choose to define it with the result that it becomes a 'right' and as such may be rigidly taken up by some employees.

The cost of five days a year taken by many staff, is 2 per cent of payroll level for a benefit which now is mainly an unapprec-ciated, but accepted privilege. Very many company absentee levels are now far above this level.

Pension

There are few staff employees who do not enjoy the prospect of receiving a pension when they retire. However, the many pension plans which individual companies have developed, or purchased from specialist pension or life assurance companies, vary sub-stantially, both in cost to the company, contributions from the employee, and benefits for the employee.

The simplest type of scheme covers simply a straight pension for the employee at the time he retires. However, many schemes provide for the employee to adjust his pension rights on retire-ment so that he and his wife share a slightly reduced entitlement, which continues to be paid to the survivor, whichever one dies first.

Some pension plans provide for some form of life assurance (see also the note below on this subject). Normally, life assurance cover is provided in cases where the employee dies after fairly long service, or where he dies within, say, five years of retirement and has not drawn a minimum defined sum in pension benefit. An alternative arrangement in more sophisticated and expensive plans is to arrange for the transfer of a high percentage of the benefit to any widow, and/or orphans, resulting from the em-ployee's death, thus providing the widow with a pension for life or until she remarries, and orphans with an entitlement until age 18 years or until they complete full-time studies.

Normal retiring ages are 65 for men, and 60 for women, although an increasing number of plans cater for retirement, without loss of pension rights, up to five years earlier than this. In addition, many plans cater for situations in which the com-pany may wish to retire one of its older staff, perhaps on grounds of failing performance and, in view of a long service, does not wish simply to fire him, but prefers to retire him on a reduced pension. Such plans have incorporated a scale of actuarially calculated reductions in pension entitlement for retirements up to ten years before the normal age, i.e. usually after age 55 for men or 50 for women.

The basis for most pension calculations is an accumulation of a percentage of the average salary for each year of service over a specified number of years' service, or occasionally even final salary. More precisely, a typical example would provide for $1\frac{1}{2}$ per cent for each year's service multiplied by the average salary over the last three, five or ten years' service. There are variations of this formula both in terms of the percentage used for each year of service, and in the period of time on which the average salary is based. Some older plans in use provide for the average salary over the last twenty years' service to be used, while several recent plans base the calculation on the highest year's earnings while in the company's service.

Some pension schemes limit payment to 50 per cent of final salary, although the legal limit is higher at 66⅔ per cent of final salary.

'Top Hat' pension plans for senior executives are becoming more popular; they provide a pension of up to 66⅔ per cent of final salary for certain Directors, and also senior staff who are on salaries of £8000 and above. At present, however, there is considerable variation in the level at which major companies award a 'Top Hat' pension. A Consulting Actuary or Pensions Adviser should be referred to for details of 'Top Hat' pension funding, as the cost of 'Top Hat' pensions for the small number of individuals concerned would normally be substantially higher than the straightforward pension benefits.

A fundamental point in pension plan policy is the question whether or not employees should contribute to the cost of the plan. For some years past it was felt that the most advanced plans were non-contributory, but two pleas, 'cost' and 'tying the employee to the organization', are used to make a case for the contributory plan. The cost of a generous pension plan is very substantial and few companies now feel that they can carry the full cost of a plan of this character alone. It is normal for employees to be asked to contribute something of the order of 5 per cent of their salary, on which there is income tax concession, so as to permit the standard of the scheme to be at a generally higher level than the company alone is prepared or able to afford. Few companies' contributions cost less than 7 to 8 per cent of the company's staff payroll and the funding of a number of the more generous plans has cost over 20 per cent in some years! In addition, following actuarial revaluation, companies may be required to subsidize the plan still further to counteract inflation.

The employee who contributes to a scheme and subsequently leaves the organization will be able to withdraw his contributions, and possibly with interest added. Alternatively, he may be able to arrange a pension payable at normal retirement date by the employer he is leaving or, increasingly in new plans, may be able to transfer his rights to the company he is joining.

Where a contributory scheme exists, this must be run by an

organization quite separate from the company whose staff will benefit, and strict legislation applies to the operation of such plans. A non-contributory scheme may be run within a company and rules on its funding are considerably less tight.

Recent government legislation has resulted in a greatly improved National Pension Plan in which the employer can see clearly the extent of its cost to him. However, this plan has limited benefits for senior staff and few major employers see the National Plan in its present form as any sort of substitute for their staff pension plan. It provides an improvement for hourly-paid employees who were rarely covered by any industrial pension plan.

A rare benefit, mentioned briefly above, now found in some modern plans, is the facility to transfer pension rights at the time an individual moves from employment with one company to another. At the moment, this benefit is dependent on both organizations having compatible plans which allow for the facility but we expect this to become a legal requirement over a further decade.

Life assurance

Some pension plans provide for life assurance cover, or some equivalent benefit in certain circumstances, but special or additional life assurance cover is often provided by larger employers. This usually takes the form of an arrangement through one of the major life assurance companies or the cover of all staff at rates which are substantially below those normally available to an individual on the open market. This cover may be arranged entirely at the company's expense, or more usually is arranged as a benefit, which employees are encouraged to take up on the extremely advantageous terms offered. In the latter case the company's cost is limited to the administrative expense of collecting the premiums, which are normally deducted from salary, and passing them on to the life company. The cost to the company of this benefit can therefore be marginal.

Medical benefits

Many companies arrange for senior members of staff to have regular medical checks to ensure all is well, and may extend this arrangement to other staff to save the time which would be taken by these staff going to private practitioners. Apart from detailed checks of this sort, general X-ray examinations are widely supported, together with the provision of facilities for influenza immunization or similar protection against other epidemics.

Most of these items have a marginal cost which is more than offset by reductions in lost working time. It is also a fact that these facilities are widely appreciated by staff.

A further aspect of medical benefits is the arrangements widely made through BUPA (British United Provident Association) and others, by which individuals insure against the cost of specialist medical treatment. Then they require treatment, a portion of the private treatment fee is covered by the insurance, the proportion depending on the level of insurance premiums selected. At very low cost to a company, group terms can be obtained at advantageous rates which are a distinct attraction to senior staff.

Subsidized meals

Wherever it is difficult for employees to return home for lunch, employers tend to make some arrangement to ensure that their staff are adequately fed at mid-day. On an industrial estate, or in a large factory, this normally takes the form of providing canteen services, while in town or city centres, where the office accommodation is very close to existing canteen or restaurant facilities, some form of luncheon voucher may be issued.

Canteen services are usually subsidized in some form or other. It appears to be standard practice for the employer to supply all the equipment and accommodation necessary, which are absorbed with general plant expenses, plus heat, light, etc., and for the costs to the employees to be limited to the price of food and labour.

Depending on the efficiency of the catering organization the cost of the benefit to the company may be marginal or even nil, but in some cases is equivalent to 3 or 4 per cent of the total pay-roll cost of the employees concerned. In order to control the cost, some employers use one of the many industrial catering organiza-tions who provide a service at a contract price, but these services appear to have a tendency to decline in quality over periods of time.

Provision of luncheon vouchers is also expensive, probably higher than the cost of most canteen services provided. As the value of vouchers is normally 75p a week, the limit permitted tax free, this can equal about 2 per cent of salaries for a large office group, depending on the particular staff 'mix' and on salary levels.

Car subsidy

The award of a company car, with either limited or complete use, is probably the most substantial single benefit given. In general, the larger companies tend to make rather limited use of this expensive benefit and to restrict it to people of director or top management status. Smaller companies often readily make a car available to people who are at middle management levels, and are less strict in controlling the use of the car outside normal business hours. This may help to offset the generally more re-stricted career prospects in the smaller firm.

The cost of providing a medium-sized car, taxed and insured. completely maintained and with a constantly full petrol tank, probably averages around £500 a year or more depending on the type of car. The company may decide to make a charge to the employee of approximately a tenth of this figure for its service outside normal hours and to avoid the tax man's interest in the concession. The effect of this is to provide a benefit which would cost the employee perhaps £500 a year of his after-tax income if he purchased an equivalent vehicle.

The second category of employees who have company cars, such as Sales Representatives and Sales Managers, and others who may be on call to a factory at any time, such as a Medical Officer, often have cars on the condition that they are not used privately. This rule may, however, be ignored by both parties and many people in these categories do make use of the car for leisure purposes. The value of this concession is difficult to determine precisely, because degree and conditions of usage will vary substantially, but it is certainly an appreciable benefit which has little extra cost to the company as the provision of a car is essential in the first place. The additional cost would accrue in the form of faster depreciation resulting from increased mileage.

Some companies prefer not to provide company cars to employees, but pay a generous mileage allowance to people who use their own cars on company business. (See the section on mileage allowances later in this chapter.) In some cases they also pay the additional insurance premium required to cover company use.

Where a mileage allowance is paid rather than a company car provided, a company may arrange for employees to purchase cars at a substantial discount through one particular supplier; a benefit which is appreciable and has a negligible cost to the company. Where schemes of this type operate, employees appear to like the arrangement and the company has a lower capital commitment than one running a fleet of cars.

Housing

There are several forms of housing assistance. On an industrial estate or in a new town, a company may have available a certain number of houses for rental through the housing authority. In these circumstances it can offer, as a recruitment incentive, subsidized rental accommodation which may be of a high standard. A small number of companies have their own housing estates; while they may make a profit on these properties, ownership ties up a great deal of capital and few companies wish to or can afford to arrange such benefits, especially in these days when capital is made to work!

A staff benefit which is greatly appreciated is a company-organized facility for house purchase. Where this is negotiated through a Mortgage Broker or an Assurance Company, the employer may only be required to give some form of guarantee for the people who make use of the service; but in some cases employment by a major company is considered as sufficient guarantee by the mortgaging organization. In these circumstances the cost to the employer is little or nothing.

During periods in which money has been very tight, some employers have entered the loan business and have advanced substantial amounts of their own capital for house purchase at low interest rates. In these circumstances the commitment by the employer may be fairly high and the price can only be evaluated for each particular transaction. Moreover this ties up working capital.

Housing assistance and the payment of removal costs, either at the time of recruitment, or following a company request to transfer from one location to another, is a useful benefit to offer and one which has only a marginal cost to the company except where a major transfer of location is involved, say, of a large number of personnel to a new factory. The extent of help given should be geared to the needs of the company in each case and the amount of incentive required. Payment of full costs involved will be justified for senior staff transferred to a new location and, exceptionally, when recruited.

Subsidized purchase

Virtually all organizations producing or selling any form of consumer product make some concessions to their staff in the form of discount on purchases. The cost of this service to the employer is limited to the administrative cost of the service. This is probably very small and is virtually certain to be more than offset by the profit on the sale, even after discount has been allowed.

Senior staff are usually able to make use of the company's purchasing organization to obtain other goods at reduced prices through various sources with which the company deals. However, an arrangement of this type cannot be made generally available to a large number of employees owing to the volume of buying work likely to be created.

Savings schemes and loans

Savings schemes

A popular benefit is the savings scheme arrangement by which employees can save regularly and painlessly by deductions from their pay which are used to purchase and provide National Savings Certificates. The administrative cost of such a scheme is almost negligible.

A similar scheme is used by some companies in the London area to ease the purchase of season rail tickets. The cost of the cheaper quarterly ticket may be advanced by the company and recovered by weekly or monthly deductions. Such an arrangement probably limits the periods during which junior levels of staff can easily leave the company, as repayment of such a loan would obviously be required.

Free loans

Apart from these small loans for season tickets, some organizations arrange loans at low rates of interest or interest-free to assist employees with house purchase and similar major expenditure.

Free banking

Many companies, about 50 per cent in a recent survey, now arrange for their own bank to provide banking facilities free of normal bank charges for their employees. This is often allied to arrangements for employees to have their salaries paid into the bank accounts rather than in cash.

Children's education

A number of companies provide some assistance in paying for children's education. The usual arrangement consists of assisting with endowment policies to enable an employee to accumulate or save the money required to cover fees and equipment.

Allowances

Part of the Salary Administration function is to advise on all types of allowances. These often run into dozens of different types and combinations, more so if overseas pay and allowances bedevil the situation.

As with any other form of remuneration a study should be

made of all allowances within the company, together with the related regulations and conditions governing their use in order to analyse the validity of the current situation and to establish clear policy and procedures.

Appropriate levels for allowances can be established from a number of sources, but mainly from remuneration surveys carried out with significant competitors.

Transfer

One of the most costly group of allowances is that related to the transfer of an employee from one location to another some considerable distance away which is clearly beyond reasonable commuting distance.

Costs which must often be considered are as follows :

Housing expenses These consist mainly of the cost of agents' and legal fees for the selling of the employee's house and the purchase of another house near the new location. A working limit is usually set for the total cost, often of the order of £500, although for senior executives this figure is inadequate and an 'at cost' basis is to be preferred.

Removal expenses These would cover the packing and transportation of all household effects from the old location to the new one. This is usually paid at cost, but the employee is asked to obtain at least three quotations and to select the most reasonable one. The bills for the move should be presented for payment.

Disturbance allowance This allowance often consists of a fixed one-time payment, such as one month's salary and covers all incidental expenses including the cost of altering curtains and carpets and other household fittings.

This allowance is also widely given by major companies to employees returning permanently to the United Kingdom after lengthy foreign service, to assist them to settle into new accommodation.

Travel expenses Allowances for travel expenditure connected with the transfer should include either the cost of rail tickets for the whole family, or an appropriate mileage allowance for use of a car.

In addition it is customary to allow up to two extra journeys for the wife and the employee for the purpose of house hunting.

Other expenses connected with transfers. These could include such items as losses on school fees already paid in advance and which are not refundable without considerable notice; and the cost of storing furniture owing to sudden transfer overseas.

The above-mentioned items by no means exhaust the possible costs involved when transferring an employee. In addition it is usual to give a salary increase to 'sweeten' the situation, either for promotion or at least as an in-grade promotion. As we have said, it can be an expensive business if many staff are affected.

Travel and living allowances

These allowances usually cover the payments made to employees for fares, hotel and other expenses incurred while travelling on company business. They would normally include the following:

Rail and air travel

The norm is increasingly moving towards second class, tourist or economy class for most levels of staff below top management. Usually tickets or travel warrants are obtained for the employee after the appropriate travel authorization form has been approved by his manager. Alternatively the employee obtains his own tickets and vouchers the cost on his expense account. It must be remembered that companies can obtain discounts if they spend over certain limits for travel, so it pays to centralize the purchase of all travel tickets.

Some organizations set various levels above which first-class travel is permitted. These may be rated to either job, grade or salary level, but there is no obvious breakpoint or common level.

Provision in the policy should also be made to cover employees travelling first class exceptionally when accompanying important customers or contacts in other companies, or other employees who are entitled to travel first class.

M

Living allowances

These allowances cover the cost of accommodation and meals for employees working away from their location. The amounts often vary for different levels of staff, ranging perhaps from around £5 or less for each complete day for lower-level staff to expenses 'at cost' for senior people. There is usually a higher scale of allowances for central London than for the rest of the UK, but it is probably unnecessary to differentiate between other major cities and provincial areas.

Daily allowances are usually reduced for long periods in one place, say visits in excess of two weeks, as it is considered that employees can obtain suitable accommodation on reduced terms for the long-term basis. The daily allowance is designed more for short visits where hotel accommodation is the only choice and a weekly allowance substituted for the longer stay. Incidentally, on long-term assignments away from home it is customary to allow employees the cost of a return journey to their homes at periodic intervals, ranging from weekly to once every two months, possibly depending on the distance and cost.

Where journeys do not involve staying away from home for a night, but involve having to pay for meals, an allowance is given to cover the costs. Unless this is vouchered 'at cost' against receipted bills, there is often a simple scale of allowances ranging up to about £1 for lunch, and from £1 to £2 for the evening meal. The cost of meals on trains is frequently higher and these should be allowed 'at cost'.

The authors consider that the most satisfactory way of dealing with expense of this kind is to pay the actual costs against receipted bills. It is almost impossible to work out a scale of allowances which covers all cases satisfactorily, and employees, being human, tend to claim up to the limit of official allowances whatever the real costs are which they have incurred.

Where an 'at cost' basis is used, however, it is vital to keep the expense under reasonable control. This is basically the responsibility of each line manager, although he will appreciate general guidance from a department or individual responsible for travel and booking arrangements in the company, as well as an audit by the appropriate financial department.

Mileage allowance

A mileage allowance is generally paid only to employees who are officially required to use their own car, or occasionally a company car, on business. There is usually a variable table of allowances to cover cars of different sizes, generally based on cubic capacity of engines, and also varying according to the distance covered during a fixed period such as a month or a year. Mileage allowances of this type have been widely studied by the major motoring

Capacity (c.c)	First 5,000 miles	Second 5,000 miles	Subsequent miles
Under 1,000	4½p	4p	3p
1,001–1,500	6	5	4½
1,501–2,500	7½	6	5
2,501 and above	9	7½	6

Paid for annual mileage from 1st January to 31st December each year.

Figure 16.1   Table of car mileage allowances

organizations, and the data which they publish is useful for establishing a table of allowances along the lines shown in Fig. 16.1.

Some companies allow their employees to use their own cars occasionally on business trips for their own convenience. In such cases it is usual to pay an allowance equivalent to the appropriate class of rail fare only.

Where mileage allowances are on the generous side, they can become extremely costly if unchecked by managers. For example a return journey of 240 miles each way, at an allowance of 7½p a mile, would cost the company £36. A similar journey by rail, if only one person is going, might only cost a half or third of this amount, so it pays to check whether long car journeys are really necessary.

To keep control on the use of cars it is recommended that a careful list is maintained of employees authorized to use them, either officially on all occasions for for occasional convenience. Details of each journey should be recorded on expense vouchers when the claim for mileage allowance is made. This enables the line manager to make a proper check on the expenditure, for statistics to be maintained, and for audits to be carried out by finance departments.

Overseas allowances

It is only possible to cover this subject briefly, as to describe all facets of it would fill more than one fair-sized book.

Many companies will only be concerned with allowances for brief visits to the major towns of foreign countries. Their employees will generally be staying in hotels, rather than renting accommodation, and an all-in daily allowance is usually employed which will cover room, meals, laundry, taxis, tips and other incidental expenses, if the visit is not 'at cost'. At least, with this type of allowance it is easier to issue travellers' cheques for the full amount of the allowance before the employee leaves, and if there is any surplus this can be returned at the end of the visit.

As for many other allowances, a scale is usually developed which varies both according to the employee's status as well as the local costs for the particular country. Allowances may further be varied according to whether the charges in the capital cities are higher than in provincial towns.

Miscellaneous benefits

Social clubs

Company-subsidized social clubs are very much part of the industrial scene, however, they appear to have little attraction to the greater majority of employees, so that over and over again the benefits accruing from the subsidies go to a small group of employees only.

Clearly, the value of social clubs as a benefit or as an attraction to staff has severe limitations, so that in the long term, company-organized clubs may well disappear.

Clothing and safety equipment

Safety goggles and safety boots are supplied at heavily subsidized rates or free by virtually all companies where this equipment is necessary. The overall cost to the company of this essential provision is generally very small in relation to payroll costs.

The provision of other clothing, of attractive overalls for office girls for example, is being more widely used as an aid to attracting and retaining young women employees. Attractive working conditions and the right atmosphere are vital for the retention of female groups which are in short supply, and small additional touches, such as the provision of pretty overalls, have a definite effect on the position.

Certain other groups, such as Chauffeurs, Messengers, Security Staff, Nursing Staff, and others, traditionally have clothing supplied, or clothing allowances to cover the provision of standardized clothes or uniforms required by the company.

Manpower costs

By making use of much of the information given in this book it is possible, without any involved arithmetic, to calculate the total costs incurred by any organization for each and every type of employee.

Manpower cost figures are essential for sound budgeting, and enable employers to make decisions as to where geographically and economically is the best place to locate their operations. For example, after carrying out a manpower costing exercise, as well as taking into account other factors such as local tax and transportation conditions affecting a number of countries, it may be decided that it is more economical to operate in Eire than in London. However, in order to make sound decisions it is first necessary to work out manpower cost calculations.

Basically one decides how one wishes to break down staff into categories for costing. It may be decided to use the categories of Clerical, Secretarial/Typing, Administrative, Salesmen, Technical, Supervisory, Professional and Managerial, plus a combined figure for all types of employees.

The costs are built up in a rather lengthy table which consists of basic average salaries, bonus and allowance payments, statutory and non-statutory payments such as National Insurance, VAT, Holiday and Sickness Pay, Pension Contributions, Canteen and Sports Club subsidies down to items such as free tea and coffee, all of which mount up over an annual period.

Breaking down the figures still further into job families and individual jobs, and then to costing each type of job will help those concerned to make decisions on the most economic use of manpower, when linked with work measurement studies.

Having calculated the current cost of pay and benefits for each category of employee, the cost per hour is easily arrived at and is a useful management ratio.

The next step is to calculate the changing costs of employees due to salary increases, increased holidays, i.e. less working hours, and other fringe benefits, over, say, an annual as well as a five-year period to key in with company short- and long-range profit plans.

These studies can be widened in scope and value by introducing calculations covering employee turnover and projected changes in numbers of each type of employee for the period under review.

When calculating total increased costs per hour for employees, particularly from one year to the next, it is important to build in to the calculation an allowance for payroll attrition.

When calculations of this nature are applied to the forecasting of management costs and future requirements, it will be noticed that fringe benefits often tend to take up an increasing percentage of total remuneration. In fact, if the fringe benefit package for top UK management levels were to be grossed-up for tax, it would be found that the value of the benefits to the executive exceeded 100 per cent of gross salary in some cases.

Flexible working hours

This system of variable working hours was evolved in Germany during recent years. The concept allows employees some freedom in choosing the times during which they will work each day, and in some cases the number of days a week which they will work, that is four or five.

Basically, the working day is divided into two sections. A 'core' period in the middle of the day during which everyone has to be at work, often 10 a.m. until 4 p.m., and flexible periods at the beginning and end of each day during which the employee can, to some extent, select and vary the hours worked.

The company's normal weekly or monthly working hours are offset against the actual number of hours worked and a debit or credit established. No payment is made for accumulated hours but time off is taken instead within a stipulated period.

This system naturally helps to reduce rush hour congestion, and helps employees such as married women with young children to get them to school or take them somewhere to be looked after more easily.

Overtime is usually cut considerably throughout the organizations operating this system, and according to experience to date absenteeism drops dramatically and output increases.

Chapter 17

International and Expatriate Salaries

This chapter sets out some of the ground rules for a subject which is more than complex enough to justify several volumes on its own. There are, I think, two main aspects of international remuneration. The first is concerned with the facets of differences in overall remuneration levels between countries, and with the different patterns of market values country by country; and with the way those patterns and relationships are changing continually. The second is about the problems which arise when individuals are moved by a company into a different 'patch', where not only is the value pattern different, but the difficulties of living and operating in a strange environment alter the financial requirements of the individual and his family.

These problems of international or expatriate remuneration do not only affect the multi-national (although they certainly have the greatest headaches!). Any company tackling an export market with overseas salesmen, and perhaps technical advisory or installation staff, begins to run into problems of pay and allowances very quickly indeed.

We have examined how the salary market works, earlier in this book, and that working is normal in most countries. However, the working is generally specific to each individual country, as are the 'country' patterns which emerge. For example, a relative shortage and high demand for marketing skills in Spain may lead to marketing managers in that country being highly paid compared with other functional groups; but in France, there may be an abundance of marketing talent in relation to demand, so that the relative level of marketing salaries is much lower. A key factor in these two independent sets of relationships is that the ability of an oversupply in one country to flow in to meet an undersupply situation elsewhere remains very limited—largely by language and cultural difficulties. There is mobility between English language companies—including multi-nationals at top levels—but the total movement of this sort still represents a small part of the market for almost all categories.

Separate from the differences in individual country patterns, is the difference to overall levels of structures. For example, it is clearly understood that a comparison of UK executive salaries with salaries of comparable jobs in France and Germany will show the UK level to be substantially lower. The basis for the comparison is the official currency exchange rates. It follows that substantial increases in UK wage and salary levels would not automatically bring UK levels up to those of France or Germany, for the controlling factor is the exchange rate, and currency is likely to devalue if there is a high level of wage and salary increase relative to equivalent measures of productivity. In fact, the only way in which UK wages and salaries can come reasonably into line with those for comparable jobs in some other country would be through strengthening of sterling in relation to the currency of the other country. The details of how this may be achieved I shall leave to the economists and politicians.

The starting point in international remuneration practice has to be acceptance of the present set of values and relationships, and the inevitability of future change. The further factors arise only from the individuals concerned.

An employee transferred to another territory raises many questions, many of which relate to his expected expenditure pattern. For example, the period of time he will be in the new country will influence whether he expects to stay in a hotel, rent a flat or buy a house; whether he will expect to go alone, take his wife, or uproot his entire domestic establishment and emigrate. The country he goes to may limit his options, for an undeveloped country may not have services of the sort he had been used to, and our employee will begin to think in terms of compensation for the hardships he is about to endure 'for the good of the company'.

Once established in his new area, our employee and his wife—duly compensated for differences in costs of living—quickly find that the allowances are inadequate. For example, the local delicacies they enjoyed in their north of England town are only available at an enormous premium in Milan and Madrid, and ability to go to the local markets to purchase many items at discount rates disappears until you locate equivalent services in the new territory. The costs of that initial finding one's way around become another hazard for the Salary Administrator seeking fair but not excessively generous policies.

Transfer of employees at a company's request from one country to another break down into four main categories, and each must be covered by a basic remuneration and allowance policy. (This policy would not apply to staff who transfer for personal reasons unconnected with the company's staffing plans.) The four main types of transfer are as follows :

1 *Casual visits*   These consist of short assignments for odd days or periods of a week or two.
2 *Short-term transfer*   This heading would cover staff assigned for a specific job for a period of up to six months, or exceptionally, up to nine months, e.g. as member of a start-up sales team.
3 *Long-term transfer*   This category would cover employees posted on a more permanent basis, for periods of from one to five years, depending on the territory and the assignments.
4 *Permanent transfer*   Permanent transfers are rare and involve an employee emigrating to another country with no intention of returning. He would be likely to take up local nationality, e.g. emigration to New Zealand.

The factors which must be considered in each of these four categories vary between other developed countries and underdeveloped territories.

For remuneration purposes, developed countries can be identified as those which adopt Western standards of living and may be expected to have normally developed salary administration policies. These consist of Europe and North American countries together with Australia, New Zealand and South Africa. The 'underdeveloped' bloc might be defined in economic terms, or as those countries not under Western influence, including the African continent except South Africa and virtually all of the Near, Middle and Far East.

It should be the company's intention that employees transferred from one country to another should suffer no financial loss. Also, it should be intended that an employee's standard of living in the new country should be not less than that he enjoyed in his home country.

The remuneration of an expatriate employee consists of several parts. The first part is basic (or pensionable) salary. The basic salary of an employee is the salary which applies in his home country and should remain in existence throughout temporary assignments anywhere else in the world. Only where an employee transfers permanently to a different country should his basic salary be re-established in the local currency of the country concerned. It is likely that his pension arrangements will be continued at his home base.

In addition to his basic salary, an employee will probably receive two other allowances associated with salary:

Expatriate allowance The first allowance is paid for the inconvenience of working in an overseas country and takes into account all the various disadvantages of such an assignment. It may vary from 5 per cent in some European countries to 30 per cent or more in some African and Far Eastern countries.

Cost of living allowance The other allowance is associated with the difference in costs of living. This may be nil where the cost of maintaining comparable living standards is lower than in the home country. In the underdeveloped countries in the Near, Middle and Far East the national standard of living is generally lower and very different from European concepts, but it may be extremely difficult and expensive for a European national to maintain his home standard of living, so that the cost of living allowance required may be extremely high.

Casual visits

Remuneration of employees on casual visits is likely to be made up of two components: salary and expense allowance. The former will be the same as in the home country. As regards the latter, a basis of 'at cost' coverage of expenses incurred plus an allowance to cover other incidental costs is usual in the case of an individual seconded on a very short assignment. The generosity of these allowances would be related to those normal in the company for his status.

Short-term transfers

Employees' remuneration on short-term transfers of less than one year should include two components : basic salary and cost of living allowance. His basic salary should be the same as that in the home base country. The cost of living allowance should be determined from the cost of living in the country concerned and is intended to cover the following expenses :

1   Living accommodation, either at an hotel or in a furnished flat (unless this is provided separately by the company).
2   Food.
3   Light entertainment.
4   Essential services.
5   A premium for inexperience in local buying (for 3–6 months only).

Where an employee's wife accompanies him on a short-term transfer, the allowance should allow for her additional expenditure.

Where there are any regular transfers, local companies may be requested to supply recommended scales of living costs in their own country, indicating use of hotels or furnished flats, and differentiating between capital cities and other cities. The Head Office should then co-ordinate appropriate scales of allowances for these countries and also determine appropriate scales of allowances elsewhere in the world.

Long-term transfer

Remuneration of an employee on long-term transfer will vary according to the type of country to which he is transferred. In general, remuneration should be made up of a basic salary and one or two allowance components.

Basic salary should normally be that of his home base country converted at the normal rate of exchange. However, for some of the underdeveloped countries a special arrangement may be necessary to ease the impact of exceptionally high taxation of salary.

In the case of a transfer to a developed country, a cost of living allowance should be paid where the overall cost of living in the new country is greater than in the home base country. A higher level of allowance may be given during the first 3–6 months, during which the employee (and his wife) are finding their way around and may be expected to incur higher than normal expenses.

Where the transfer is to an underdeveloped country, the allowance should be based on ensuring an appropriate standard of living taking into account the facilities available. (I know of a small team of senior engineers who spent nearly two years in a remote part of Greenland. There was no cost of living allowance as everything had to be provided. However, they did enjoy the accumulation of salary plus an exceptional 'expatriate allowance'.)

An expatriate allowance is paid to compensate employees for the inconvenience of working in another country. This may be from 5 to 30 per cent or higher according to location and to other circumstances of the transfer. For example, risks of war or internal revolution may require a high premium.

The allowance should be established for one country at a time. Where an employee is subsequently transferred to a third country, his expatriate allowance should be revised.

Permanent transfers

Remuneration of an employee on permanent transfer should reflect the fact that eventual phasing-in with local salary levels must be the prime object.

The basic salary for an expatriate employee on permanent transfer to another country should be determined by a comparison of salary levels in the two countries. The new base salary should be in line with standards in the new country as far as possible. Where job grades and salary ranges are established in each country, the local base salary will be arrived at by assessing the employee's worth within the relevant salary range—unless the values in the new country are substantially lower than in the old, in which case a special salary may be agreed.

Expatriate allowances would not be paid to staff transferring permanently to another country.

Any individual establishing himself in a new area incurs a level of expenditure in excess of that which is likely to be normal when he knows where best to buy, to eat, to live, to be entertained. An allowance to ease the first three to six months of a permanent transfer is usual practice.

Transport, transfer allowances and accommodation

Transport costs

For all types of transfer, the employer should decide the most appropriate method of transport for employees (and their families where applicable) and pay the full fare of each person travelling. Where possible, any scheme of subsidized passage should be used.

Accommodation

Permanent and long-term transfer help should be given to an employee to find local accommodation in accordance with his status. The company should pay all legal and associated expenses that an employee incurs when having to sell his home in one country and buy another in a new country. Survey fees of new property should be paid. In addition, where the employee is required to sell his house quickly and thereby make a loss, the company should agree to pay the difference in price up to a fair market price. In these cases, at least two valuations of the current market value of the property should be obtained. The amount the company should pay is the difference between the average of these valuations and the actual price obtained.

The company may provide loans to enable employees to purchase houses in their new local country, but assistance with obtaining a normal building society mortgage is preferable in most cases.

As an initial measure, the company may agree to pay the cost of temporary accommodation up to a maximum of three months to allow staff time to find satisfactory permanent accommodation. The cost of this temporary accommodation should include rent, rates and essential services, but should not include food and other living expenses.

In the case of a long-term transfer to an underdeveloped country, it is normal practice for the company to supply accommodation and in these cases a house will not normally be purchased by the employee. A typical arrangement would be for the company to obtain an unfurnished residence in accordance with the status of the employee and rent this to him at a rent of 10 per cent of his basic salary.

For short-term transfer and casual visits, the company will normally book accommodation for an employee in a hotel or rent a furnished flat where necessary.

Removal expenses

For permanent and long-term transfers, the company should reimburse employees for the full cost of moving his personal effects and furniture from one country to another. The company should approve the proposed method of transport, and should obtain at least two quotations. In addition, a disturbance allowance of 10 per cent of basic salary may be paid as a one-time payment to cover costs of changes to carpets and curtains, etc., and the company will reimburse employees for reasonable out-of-pocket expenses incurred on the journey.

Social benefits

The company should pay the appropriate scale of charges of BUPA or a local medical insurance scheme for employees and their families posted to countries where there is no adequate State Medical Scheme and where no reciprocal agreement is in practice for a subsidized medical service.

In the event of a long-term transfer to an underdeveloped country, the company should make a contribution to the school fees of children educated at boarding schools in the home country. This should be at a realistic level in relation to the expenditure incurred.

Consideration may be given to the payment of school fees in other cases where this is considered essential.

Return fares of children at school in the home base country may be paid by the company in accordance with a scale such as :

Continent of Europe   Three return fares each year for—

    either   (*a*) the mother to visit the children

    or   (*b*) each child to visit the parents.

Other countries   Three return fares in a tour of two years for—

    either   (*a*) the mother to be reunited with the children.

    or   (*b*) each child to be reunited with the parents.

Arrangements are usually made so that employees on permanent and long-term transfer receive continued coverage in pension and insurance schemes.

Families accompanying employees on transfer

Employees do not normally take their wives with them on a transfer of less than three months' duration except in the case of senior management.

Where employees are transferred for a period of over three months, but less than a year, the company may decide that the employee's wife should be allowed to accompany him at the company's expense. In most cases where the transfer is over six months, you should consider allowing a wife to accompany her husband anywhere in the world.

On practically all long-term transfers the employee will be allowed to take his family with him at the company's expense.

Taxation

Where income tax in a country is at a penal level above minimal earnings, you should investigate and ensure that the employee does not suffer a financial loss.

Also, where countries do not have reciprocal tax arrangements and an employee has to pay two separate tax bills, the company should endeavour to ensure that the employee does not suffer any financial loss.

Chapter 18

Staffing of the Salary Administration Function

Salary administration, as a continuing process in every organization, requires staff to carry it out. However, the variation in systems of salary administration, in size of organization, in types of employees, and many other factors mean substantially different salary administration staffing requirements. In this chapter, we look at some typical salary administration posts and at the numbers of staff required in different situations.

The large organization

In a very large organization, the number and range of salary administration posts is likely to be substantial. On the basis of current organization in a number of large companies, one would normally expect to find :

In a central personnel department, a Salary Administration Manager with a small team consisting of Advisers and Officers. Occasionally, the organization might be so large that a centrally controlled points system of job evaluation is used. In the latter case supervisory level Officers and Analysts covering various specialist aspects might be included.

In line organization, a staff man with specific salary administration responsibilities, under the local Personnel or Staff Manager. This Officer might be a salary administration specialist and might, on a large site, even have specialist assistance. Where this is not justified, or authorized, the salary administration function might be combined with other responsibilities such as career planning, or general personnel work for senior staff or staff as a whole. However, in our view, operational responsibility for salary administration in a line organization will always be a management duty, guided and assisted only as much as they require by personnel specialists.

Detailed descriptions of typical jobs and responsibilities will be found elsewhere in this book, but first let us complete a preliminary run through the typical salary administration staffing of organizations of varied sizes.

The medium-sized organization

This heading covers the wide range of organizations not so large as the giants, but larger than the companies which get by with little more than 'one-man-band' personnel departments. The smaller ones in this category have a Personnel Officer who includes salary administration as a significant, but part-time responsibility.

Rather bigger organizations, possibly multi-locational, often have a Salary Administrator who may be aided by an Officer or two, and perhaps a Job Analyst. Use of points evaluation inevitably swells the strength requirement of any salary administration team.

A useful ratio for use as a starting-point, but subject to variation for all the factors discussed in this chapter, might be one full-time Salary Administration Officer or Analyst to every 2000 staff.

The smaller organization

Personnel staff become progressively less specialized in direct relationship with decreasing size of organization. In the smaller organizations, the number of staff in the personnel function is also very small and they must cover the full range of personnel work, including salary administration.

The part-time Salary Administrator has less need for formal job and pay structures and complex procedures, but still has a clear responsibility which is basically identical with, although less deep than, that of the specialist in a larger organization.

Descriptions of salary administration posts

This series of descriptions is not intended to be exhaustive, but does cover a selection of typical posts and responsibilities found in this field in a variety of organizations.

Salary Administration Manager or Adviser

In a major organization, he normally reports to a Group Personnel Manager or Personnel Director. He is responsible for the full range of staff remuneration and benefits policies. To achieve this, his responsibilities can be listed as follows :

He is responsible for initiating, developing and advising on all aspects of salary policy and procedures.

He develops and co-ordinates a Job Classification Plan.

He plans and conducts salary and benefit surveys with organizations with which the company competes for staff.

He establishes Salary Structures to fit the Classification Structures at all levels, and makes recommendations which ensure that they are maintained at competitive levels.

He defines and produces a statement of the company's Salary Plan, and ensures that all managers are fully acquainted with it.

He plans and co-ordinates Salary Reviews and advises management at all stages of the Reviews.

He may participate in trade union negotiation covering job evaluation, grading, salary ranges, etc.

He plans and co-ordinates an audit of all salary movements to ensure that these are within the company's overall Salary Plan.

He undertakes studies of allowances and benefits, and any aspect of staff remuneration, and makes appropriate recommendations to management.

He initiates and develops new salary administration procedures as is necessary from time to time.

He trains and advises managers throughout the company in the arts of salary planning and in the company's basic salary administration philosophy.

Salary Administration Officer

In a large organization, the Salary Administration Officer is one of the aides helping the top Adviser. Basically, his or her duties might be :

He assists generally in the administration of a Central Salary Administration Department in a major organization.

He is usually responsible to a Senior Officer or Head of the specialized unit.

He undertakes job analyses and evaluation; negotiation of non-major issues with middle management, and with trade unions; audit of salary and classification changes to highlight exceptions to policy for the attention of his supervisor; straightforward surveys of junior salary levels or benefits, and so on.

He may advise middle management and supervisors of policies and procedures, within defined limits.

Job Analyst

He undertakes, as a member of a team, studies of staff jobs as a basis for salary administration, or for organization studies, etc. He interviews job holders to obtain detailed standard information on their jobs; prepares standard job descriptions and organization charts based on the information he has obtained; and checks these with job holders, supervisors and managers. He may also evaluate jobs in relation to the company's policy and may obtain agreement to the grading of individual posts.

Line Personnel Officer

As a member of a line personnel team, he has a variety of duties and responsibilities, including that of assisting and advising local supervisors and managers on salary administration matters. In this connexion he assists in obtaining job information and in grading all new posts, up to a defined level, within the area he covers. He assists on determining local recruiting rates for all vacant posts, in line with job grading and his knowledge of local market rates. He also assists and advises supervisors and managers in respect of proposed salary adjustments, including those likely to result from local negotiations.

In a large company, he may be advised in turn by a central Salary Administration Adviser and would inform the central authority of all anomalous situations regarding grading and market salary levels.

Salary Administrator

The top man on Salary Administration in a medium-sized organization would be substantially occupied with the development of policy and with the creation and maintenance of job and salary structures.

He may also have to deal with all the small increases for juniors from an audit viewpoint, assist and advise people of all levels in respect of their own peculiar problems, and generally handle every salary problem which may be raised within his organization.

Personnel Manager (small organization)

The salary administration responsibility of a Personnel Manager in a small company who has only two or three—or even no—supporting staff takes basically the same form. However, with smaller numbers of staff, the necessity for the more complex types of job and salary structures is reduced.

Line Manager

Any manager with responsibility for staff employees has a fundamental responsibility for the planning of their salaries. To do this, he must acquire a full understanding of his company's salary procedures and philosophies, and give proper and careful thought to planning his organization, its staffing, the associated career development of his people and the related planning of their salaries.

Establishment of Salary Administrators

'How many Salary Administrators do we require?'

If you are asked this question, there is no straightforward formula of, say, 1 for every 429 staff, to give an answer. The establishment will vary with a number of factors such as:

    The type and mix of staff.

    The type of job evaluation used.

    The type of salary reviews applied.

    And so on.

The more important factors are discussed here briefly, but no clear guides to establishment are possible due to the wide variation in individual company outlook. While the basic factors can give a guide to the requirement in 'average conditions', a heavy interest by top management may boost the establishment, while a tight personnel budget could limit staff availability. Management attitude, then, is a significant but indefinable factor.

The staffing during start-up and overhaul stages is inevitably heavier than is required to run established systems. To some extent, long-term cycles can be planned for. Groups of staff can be trained up to meet peak requirements, although subsequent run-down is difficult to achieve unless other personnel activities are programmed to absorb these staff.

Returning to the basic factors, the type of evaluation selected has a major effect on staffing. It has been estimated that upkeep of a points evaluation scheme requires a Job Analyst for each 500 staff, while a basic ranking scheme can be kept up to date with management support by one Administrator for each 2000 staff. The use of committees, particularly with points evaluation, would worsen these ratios. Individual company operating experience, which can take into account the idiosyncrasies of management and the shortcomings or inexperience of Analysts and Administrators, should be evaluated wherever possible as the most realistic guide to the individual requirement.

The methods used for the administration of individual salaries, the frequency and control of reviews and adjustments, the degree of central control or delegation of responsibility— these factors all affect the amount of time absorbed by day-to-day administration and by major reviews. Analysis of the procedural requirements of a company is necessary in order to assess appropriate staffing levels and, once again, individual competence will heavily affect the result. For example, a requirement for the audit of salary adjustment recommendations may be tackled by two people at six or sixty an hour although the basic knowledge of policy and procedure is, on the surface at least, at the same level. Personality, and flexibility of thinking, depth of appreciation, and so on, all affect the variation in output.

The third major factor is the type and 'mix' of staff being administered. A heavy bias towards clerical and lower technical staff covered by a rigid salary structure would lead to a low level of demand for a Specialist Officer's services. A high proportion of senior people with complex career and salary planning requirements, perhaps complicated by shift, sales incentive and overseas allowance problems would tend to require higher-calibre Administrators and a higher ratio of Administrators to staff.

Beyond this, individual organizations demand their own special procedural requirements, and staff are necessary to carry these out.

Finally, it is probably unwise to divorce the salary administration establishment from that for the personnel department as a whole, as the requirements of the Salary Administrator or other specialists, and vice versa, imply an integrated whole rather than a series of separate units.

Training of Salary Administrators

Any training plan should cater for periods of specialization. The Administrator should work as a Job Analyst in order to acquire operational job analysis experience. Similarly, he should undertake salary survey work, be concerned with establishing job and salary structures, take part in day-to-day salary administration and be involved in negotiation with line management on all the various aspects of the function. This is a comprehensive programme, but provides an aiming point for any potential Salary Administrator.

Looking at this schedule in more detail, an essential part, and often a starting phase in a career, is job analysis. The Job Analyst acquires a knowledge of job make-up, and a roving commission on job analysis provides the young man with a very wide understanding of the operation of all functions throughout an organization. Of course, job analysis itself also requires certain basic training. This is best provided in practical form by a period of work directly under the wing of an experienced Analyst, following on from an initial induction period to enable the new recruit to acquire a basic knowledge of the organization and the traditions of the company.

As a natural follow-on from job analysis, evaluation experience provides the basic understanding of job structures, families, groupings and market value patterns. Experience of all forms of analysis is unnecessary, but the most educative is points evaluation. While this system is not normally recommended for operational use, for schooling purposes it shows more clearly than any other system how each job consists of a series of related and partially definable factors. It also shows that these factors do not apply to all jobs.

The Analyst comes to understand the complexities and limitations of a process that no amount of reading or theory can possibly impart.

The trainee Salary Administrator can learn a great deal from participation in salary survey work. While he is obviously unready for the 'front' position of negotiating for information, he is able, under guidance, to prepare internal analyses and subsequently study and analyse the information obtained. From this he can learn something of the variety of structures, systems and policies which operate, to counteract the insularity he might otherwise acquire. He also learns to challenge systems and procedures and consider the relative advantages of other possible methods.

The analysis which follows a salary survey generally requires a basic statistical knowledge. If a trainee does not possess this knowledge, he can read it up to the level required in any standard textbook on statistics. The formulae and their meaning, together with the calculation procedure, can be recognized and understood by most intelligent people.

The normal processes of developing a salary structure should be followed through in a current example or by reference back to a previous study. Similarly, the process of establishing various special rates should be carried out, and the circumstances in which these rates are established for a particular area of location should be understood.

This training in the build-up of the various structures should, wherever possible, precede any contact with their application to day-to-day administration. The operational policy and philosophy of salary administration in a particular organization will have been evolved and written by staff experienced in policy development and should be fully absorbed as quickly as possible, and all queries and doubts discussed and clarified.

The next stage involves little more than sitting on the sidelines, examining authorized salary changes, correlating these with policy understanding, and continually asking questions until the finer points of operational practice become clear.

There are many other aspects of salary administration. The budding Salary Administrator needs experience of each of these aspects before he is competent to deal with them—needs experience of expatriate remuneration, sales bonus schemes, and administration of salaries of young graduates.

To summarize the training requirement, breadth of experience is the target. Full appreciation of salary administration philosophy, applied by advising and encouraging managers, can be an absorbing and rewarding contribution to personnel and general management.

Index